Bradford born and bred, award-winning presenter Anita Rani is one of the most recognisable faces on British TV. She is a lead presenter on *Countryfile*, hosts Woman's Hour on Radio 4 every week and regularly presents on Radio 2. Anita is well-known for her work on Channel 4, Channel 5, the BBC and most recently with Netflix. She is also a Goodwill Ambassador for the UNHCR. You can find her on Twitter and Instagram @itsanitarani.

Praise for

The Right Sort of Girl

'So beautiful, so brilliant'
CAITLIN MORAN

'Brilliant'
LEMN SISSAY

'Extraordinary . . . Beautifully written'
DAILY MAIL

'Warm, honest and funny, filled with hope and inspiration . . .
A must-read for every young person with big dreams'
NIKESH SHUKLA

'As engaging and entertaining as she is . . . a joy'
SARAH BROWN

The Right Sort of Girl

Anita Rani

BLINK
bringing you closer

First published in the UK by Blink Publishing
An imprint of Bonnier Books UK
4th Floor, Victoria House, Bloomsbury Square,
London, WC1B 4DA
Owned by Bonnier Books
Sveavägen 56, Stockholm, Sweden

facebook.com/blinkpublishing
twitter.com/blinkpublishing

Hardback – 978–1–788–704–23–6
eBook – 978–1–788–704–25–0
Audiobook – 978–1–788–704–26–7
Paperback – 978–1–788–704–24–3

A CIP catalogue of this book is available from the British Library.

Typeset by IDSUK (Data Connection) Ltd
Printed and bound in Great Britain by Clays Ltd, Elcograf S.p.A.

1 3 5 7 9 10 8 6 4 2

Blink Publishing is an imprint of Bonnier Books UK
www.bonnierbooks.co.uk

For daughters with secrets.
And for my mum, who now knows (some of) mine.

Contents

Dear Anita   1

Introduction: The Right Sort of Girl   3

A Rough Guide to Being Punjabi   7

Go Back to Where You Came From   19

Families Are Never Simple   33

Food Will Always Be Life   41

Mum and Dad Aren't Perfect, But They Are
   Superhuman   51

Be Your Own Superhero When You Can   71

Own Your Womanhood   83

Love Your Skin Colour and Your Nose   105

Yorkshire Will Always Take Your Breath Away   117

Half-Arsing a Job is Not in Your DNA   131

Every Woman Deserves a Room of Their Own   145

Give Yourself a Break   159

You Don't Need to Compromise on Your Own
   Happiness   173

You Will Party, Whether You're Allowed To or Not   187

Embrace Your Inner Drama Queen   195

You Can Love Home But Also Desperately
   Need to Leave   203

Work Harder Than Everyone Else and You Might
   Have a Shot   215

Freedom is Complicated   225

Find Your Sound   235

If You Don't Do It, Someone Else Will   245

You'll Never Feel 'English'   261

Travel Like Your Life Depends on It   269

You Will Fall in Love and Be Loved   283

You Will Be Accepted   305

Your Anger is Legitimate   315

Conclusion: The Right Sort of Woman   329

Bonus chapter: Your Voice Will Be Heard   337

Rani's Dhal   340

Acknowledgements   342

Dear Anita,

At 40, you will be a TV presenter, and you will have a share of the spotlight. You will be seen as a success. You will have your voice heard across the nation on the radio, across the world on programmes and documentaries. You will push forward with boundless energy, enthusiasm and optimism, you will have a ton of fun and will get swept up in it all, in the belief that if you work hard, you will climb the heights of success — and you will, to a point.

Only, it will be at a slow, steady pace. Sometimes it will feel like you are trudging through sludge to get there, sometimes it will feel so slow you wonder if you are moving at all. Life and its struggles will get to the point where you begin to doubt yourself and who you are. It will wear you down, but you will continue to smile because that's what TV presenters do.

Sometimes, quite often really, you will feel like a fuck-up, a failure, a shell. You will get to 40 and realise you don't really know who you are anymore. Once you realise this, it will become the most important thought you ever had. You will realise it's time for a reset. To rethink, recreate and remember who you are.

We're going to figure out if there really is a right sort of girl, together. It's a question we've been haunted by. How is a woman built? What sort of building blocks in girlhood are needed to create the right sort of woman? A woman who nails everything in life, who hurdles over any boundaries in her way, who never stops, never fails, and really does have it all. Can such a girl or woman even exist?

So, young Anita, we're going to delve into lessons I wish you had known. Things like the fact that 'Food Will Always Be Life' and 'Families Are Never Simple'. There will be ups and downs, laughter and tears. But there will also be the essence of you, a portrait of a girl and the woman she grew into.

Now is your time. The pressure cooker has started to whistle. It's speak or explode.

So speak.

Love,
Anita

Introduction:
The Right Sort of Girl

I've spent no time on self-reflection at any point in my life. Seriously, I've been too busy. I've been occupied from the minute I was born. Learning how to speak two languages, navigating two cultures, figuring out how to express who I am and planning my escape. An escape to freedom. Working, playing, thinking about boys, listening to music, going on Instagram. All the while trying to be the right sort of girl, and then the right sort of woman. I've been far too busy working life out to think about my life thus far. It seems right that in my forties, in midlife (ish), I take stock. I could have gone on a retreat, taken a holiday or just gone down the pub to do this. But I thought I'd share my tale with you, instead.

As one of the few brown women in TV, you might recognise me or my name. You might have mistaken me for someone else at some point – 'You're the one off the news.' Try again! 'Kids' TV?' Nope! My parents gave me an international name, one that doesn't really give much away. For a long time, I kept my family background to myself. I didn't want to be branded or seen as belonging to any gang. I'm whatever you think I am! It's the way I've liked it. But the last 40 years have been spent exploring my identity in one way or another, and the world around me has helped it take shape. The world around me has made me question where I belong.

How do I fit in? Where is my place in the world? I've spent so long morphing and shapeshifting into what's expected of me in every situation I'm in, I think I've lost who I really am along the way. Am I the daughter, the wife, the TV presenter? Indian, British, Northern, Punjabi, a Londoner? These are the questions I needed to find the answer to, they are my motivation to write this book. To remind me of who I am. To tell my younger self not to lose her sense of self in her quest to fit in, trying to be the right sort of girl.

How on earth did I get to where I am today? This is no overnight success story, this is not a fairy-tale, not in the traditional sense, but there is plenty of magic. No one is going to save me, spoiler alert! This is a story about grit, determination and tenacity. I may have carved a niche in a landscape that wasn't designed for me but, in the process, I may also have forgotten the most important thing. Me. I've spent so long trying to fit in, learning what's required of me and adapting to any given situation, I may just have lost the point of who I am.

This is a book about time and place and escape.

It's about food and family and friends.

It's about years of trauma, shame, fear and anger.

Introduction

It's about power. Reclaiming power for myself, sending some back to teenage me and channelling some through to you, too.

I'm the first-born daughter of Punjabi immigrants to this land, and I have to share my story. We have to tell our stories. We need to explain who we are, whether we want to or not. For us, art is political. Our existence is political. I'm a broadcaster and presenter, so my job is to tell important tales that tell us about the world and reflect something back about who we are. Now, I'm going to tell you my story. The story of a determined and frustrated lass from Yorkshire who wanted to find a place where she could become something more than what was expected of her, and a place where she's accepted for who she is.

I believe it's an important tale to tell. It's a tale of a life of confusion, fear, shame, joy, love and laughter. It may not be what you're expecting, but God knows I wish I'd read a book like this when I was a kid. Maybe then the world might not have felt half as lonely as it did. At times, this is a lonely tale. It's the tale of an outsider, a misfit, an oddball on the periphery, a loose cannon, a nonconformist who was made to conform. I might make you sad at times, but I hope to hell I make you smile too. It's just growing up, after all.

I've experienced life as an Asian woman, so my book is naturally written from that perspective, but there are themes which are universal to the human experience, that I hope will resonate with every sort of reader. I've exposed my secrets, aired my dirty laundry – including my actual pants – and dealt with issues I've kept buried for many years. Even now

I'm nervous about what I say. How much I tell you. How much I share. Telling my story seemed important to me, for me to discover who I was again, what I stood for, the very essence of myself. But it's not just for me. It's for you, too. For anyone who has never felt enough, who has ever been left out, othered, made fun of just for being slightly different to the norm.

This is my opportunity to let it out. To tell you, I am you. That I come from nothing, that every day sometimes feels like a fight, that I still don't feel seen, that I have a voice but sometimes feel mute, that I can still feel like an outsider in a system not designed for me, that I've made mistakes. But I also feel like a warrior who has a job to do that is bigger than me, as the voices of all the women around me, before and after, make their presence felt.

Externally, I have achieved great things and broken boundaries and barriers. But this, writing this, is my greatest challenge yet. To be this raw and this exposing – first of all to myself, and then to others, is the biggest leap of faith I have ever taken. But then I'm from a long line of badasses who have stepped into the unknown.

Before we get into it, I need to introduce you to my Punjabi side. I'm a girl *and* northern *and* brown, didn't you know? A triple threat!

A Rough Guide to
Being Punjabi

I'm from Yorkshire and I'm Punjabi and I'm fiercely proud of both. I used to think I could only be one of these, that I needed to be strictly defined – not fitting in was so confusing, but mainly for other people. I felt shame for my differences. Society made me feel shame about my ethnicity, my colour, the very essence of me. I knew I was from a proud and rich heritage and I have loved visiting India and understanding its ancient culture. But I have also spent a lot of time dialling down my 'Indianness' when it was required, trying to blend in. Which is ridiculous, because the one thing I could never do was blend in.

Bit of geography: Punjab is right up in the north of India, a landlocked state that was divided between India and Pakistan in 1947. Punjab is my tribal heartland. The state your family are from in India is important, it reveals something about your identity. Each state varies culturally: the food is slightly different, the language, the embroidery, the clothes, the folk traditions, the landscape, the history, the religions. Pre-Partition, Sikhs, Muslims, Hindus, Christians, Buddhists and Jains lived side by side in Punjab. Sufism, a mystical Islamic belief, was a major part of Punjabi culture, and is a culture and heritage we share across religions. Punjabis are Punjabis, regardless of faith.

Punjabis are an extreme bunch; we don't do things by halves. We have the best and the worst of Indian culture. We are basically the Irish of India. We are people of the land, a hard-working agrarian community. Brought up on hearty earthy carbs and dairy-heavy diets, we are gregarious, bois-terous, open-hearted, loyal, salt-of-the-earth types, a proper laugh. You'll find potatoes and Punjabis pretty much any-where in the world. We're also people of a divided land, divided by the British. Punjabis are rowdy and proud. We love a drink and we love a fight. We are brilliant at cussing as it's hands down the best South Asian language to swear in. It's the community that gave the world tandoori chicken and bhangra. We like to party and we are generous. You'll never leave a Punjabi party hungry or sober, or in any doubt about how much money we have. If we have it, we'll flaunt it. Punjabis can be right flash bastards. You get the idea.

I'm bilingual since birth and love speaking Punjabi (well, I'm actually trilingual now, but I don't want to show off). This might be surprising, as some second-generationers have very sketchy language skills. We either understand Punjabi perfectly but haven't quite mastered speaking it, or are too embarrassed to speak because we do so with an English accent and family just laugh at us when we try. This was the case for my little brother. When asked to speak Punjabi as a child, he'd just wobble his head and in an Indian accent say, 'My name is Kuldeep.' This changed after he got married to my brilliant sister-in-law, who is fluent not only in Punjabi but Hindi too, and now they have my niece, they are desperate to make sure she too can communicate in Punjabi, so her understanding and connection with her culture isn't just through clothes and Bollywood. Bollywood is not Indian culture! We all want my niece to be able to speak her mother tongue. Even Rafi, my puppy, is bilingual.

Being bilingual from birth is a gift I treasure. To speak a language is to understand a culture. How a culture thinks and laughs and expresses itself gives you an insight into its people, and the nuances of that culture. I've loved being able to sit with elders and hear their stories, to approach strangers, particularly elderly Asians in Britain, and offer them help. It makes me feel humble and connected to my roots. I love to hear elderly strangers call me 'beta', a beautiful word that means 'child', a term of endearment and affection that makes you feel you are theirs, a kind word offered after a kind gesture. I love to make elderly Asians feel proud that 'one of theirs', born and brought up in a foreign land, can speak the mother tongue and understands the culture enough to respect an elderly stranger because their lives in Britain were tough. I love blowing minds in India, when elders fully expect us 'Britishers' to come with airs and graces and noses turned up. Even amongst certain upwardly mobile wealthy middle classes in India, English is the only language they'll converse in. (I've also blown a few white and British minds when I've spoken with a Yorkshire accent, too.)

Maybe my generation, the second generation, the last generation to grow up with people directly from the source, will be the last ones to speak the language fluently. I sincerely hope not. My beautiful little niece will be spoon-fed it, whether she likes it or not. She will be forced to say things in Punjabi, just like I was. Let's hope she doesn't do what her dad did and just wobble her head and put on an Indian accent! Maybe holding onto aspects of our culture is more important to the diaspora. Maybe speaking the language and learning the folk songs and celebrating all the ancient rituals and festivals in the old-fashioned way is really only being upheld by those who left the land, as a way of staying connected. India, or at least the middle and upper classes, have moved on – for them, modernising and moving away from the old-fashioned traditions is important.

There are some amazing aspects to Punjabi culture and a load of tribal shit we really should have left in the pind. The diaspora can be accused of being trapped in a time warp from 60 years ago. My family included. So, it's important to me to explain what it means to be Punjabi. I claim all my identities and I have many, to think that we only have one label is reductive and dangerous. You can also be proud of something that is flawed. Being Punjabi isn't straightforward (being British isn't straightforward) and, as a generalisation, us Punjabis are quite messed-up. But then which culture isn't? You've just got to be able to acknowledge the good and the bad.

So, what does it mean to be Punjabi? How will you know if you don't meet the people?

Punjabi mothers

She likes to feed, any time of day, all day long. She can whip something up as quickly as the doorbell rings. Just as a guest's car is pulling up in front of your house, the Punjabi mother won't even be detected sprinting into the kitchen, like some culinary ninja. In five minutes, she can produce a plate of 5,000 pakora – you can never be short, to not have enough food would be a huge disgrace. In and out of the kitchen, an entire feast prepared, done, five minutes, bosh! The faster they are, the prouder they are. I'd love to watch a speed cook-off show between Punjabi mums called *Fatafat*. I'm calling Netflix with the idea now.

They are mechanical in their domain: make chapatti, stir pots, shout for kids, cut salad, water in jug, shout for kids, glasses ready, plates out, SCREAM FOR KIDS, pickles decanted. 'KIIIIIIIIIDDDDDS, roti khalo! Jaldi jaldi!'

Do not interrupt when they are in this robot mode, this is when they are at their most impatient and can really lose it if you get in their way. If they have a rolling pin in hand, they are armed and dangerous. Beware, they have excellent knife skills. Punjabi mums do not use chopping boards, they cut everything in their hands. Angry, impatient, cursing the day you were born. Still, there's nothing like being fed from the hands of a Punjabi mother, whether she does it patiently and kindly, or whether she's taking the day's frustrations out on you. Nothing beats those beautiful hands that made the chapatti, feeding you, one burki at a time.

The Punjabi mother can wear two faces at once, just like the dude from *Batman*. The smiling, gracious, obsequious

'We have guests' face. Then the angry, questioning, impatient 'Where the hell have you been, we've got guests, it doesn't matter that they turned up unannounced, get in that living room, be nice and don't embarrass me, we'll talk about where the hell you've been later' face.

The Punjabi mother likes to cuss. She'll cuss her husband and her children, but mainly she'll cuss her own fate, her own kismet. She'll spend a lot of time asking God, 'What did I do in a previous life to deserve this one?'

Punjabi mothers are hassled. Punjabi mothers do everything. Punjabi mothers also know everything, all your secrets, whether you know them yourself or not, and they'll sometimes use them to blackmail you.

Punjabi mothers love their own children fiercely but have various weapons of control at their disposal:

1. Religion
'God sees everything. All the things you do behind my back, God knows.' Not a Heaven or Hell thing – if you're Hindu or Sikh, there's no threat of Hell. Just plain old guilt and karma. If you do bad, you mess up your own karma and you may come back in the next life as an amoeba, or worse, someone with a sticky-out belly button.

2. Fear of the father
'Wait till your father gets home.' It always worked, as Punjabis fly the flag for patriarchal bullshit. Well, Punjabi men demand the flag and Punjabi women design it, sew it and then tie it to the mast.

3. Humiliation
Sending your child to school with coconut oil on their heads. I'm still working through the trauma of that incident.

4. Superstition
My all-time favourite mad method of control! This one is complicated as there are so many superstitions, it's hard to keep track. All of them are mainly to keep the evil eye away. I'm not sure who has this evil eye and why it's going to particularly affect me. I have spent a lifetime wondering how people who are not Punjabi and don't do anything to ward off the evil eye manage to live fulfilling and happy lives. But these are not questions the Punjabi mother is interested in. Not when there are evil eyes to destroy.

Here is a selection of superstitions I have been asked to adhere to at some point in my life: don't cut toenails after dark, don't wash hair on Tuesday, water the plants on Wednesday. If a cat crosses your path, turn around and use a different route. If someone sneezes just as you are about to leave, take your shoes off, sit down, have a sip of water and then go. Hang lemon and chilli above your door, or carry lemon and chilli in your handbag. (This one is useful if you find yourself eating a particularly bland meal.) Wash all your dishes before bed otherwise the pots and pans cry overnight and your home will not prosper. Don't sweep up after sunset. Don't leap over small children or they won't grow. Never leave the house at a quarter to the hour.

It's a wonder I've been able to leave my front door and live a relatively sane life. There's also a confusing combination of religion and superstition. When pandits, gurus and soothsayers get involved, Punjabi mothers get serious. There are various moonstones and crystals and rings and trinkets to place around your house or carry on your person. I have a drawer full of things my mum has given me over the years. Each one of them is meant to be placed in a certain part of my house and to be looked at during certain times of the day. I've now revealed where they really live and I predict a concerned phone call asking me to place them where they belong. The minute Mum reads this sentence. We will argue and Mum will say, 'Other people's daughters just do what their mothers tell them to.' Deploying another method of control: guilt.

Punjabi aunties

The aunty network, or illuminaunty. Be warned. The illuminaunty have ways of downloading and storing personal information about thousands of people. They have unknown secret methods, sinister tactics, they use strategy and subterfuge to glean this information. The CIA, MI5, KGB and the illuminaunty: the most powerful secret services on earth. They have always known that data is the only weapon of control and power you need.

Their business is your business. If you don't want them to know your information, I can try and help with my technique. Deploy operation 'goody two shoes'. Greet Aunty with a namaste, satsriakal or assalamualaikum, then simply smile and nod. The smile and nod can go into overdrive when Aunty starts telling you about her son and how well he's doing. To tap out of the aunty death grip of boredom, ask her if you can bring her another cup of tea and always, always compliment Aunty on her outfit. The illuminaunty can get through gallons of tea. They are never hungry but will always manage to demolish a plate of barfi. Aunties will turn up to your house unannounced and no matter how much they say, 'We've already eaten,' they are always hungry.

When aunties get past a certain age, they love nothing more than getting together and discussing their ailments. It's a sickness battle. One of their favourite pastimes is comparing notes about how high their 'BP' (blood pressure) is. They also love discussing their 'sugar'. 'Sugar' is a euphemism for diabetes. Pretty much every South Asian knows someone with Type 2 diabetes.

The illuminaunty never gossip. Not according to them. They are spiritual and God-fearing and never gossip. 'It's all in God's hands. Who are we?' But they can't resist telling other people's news to other people. They see this as their 'community duty'.

Punjabi uncles

Punjabi uncles come in two volumes, quiet and loud. Punjabi uncles drink whisky. They get together and gather in sitting rooms, saying very little. The loud ones hold court and tell Punjabi jokes in booming voices yet also say very little, while the quieter ones smile and nod. They are adept at this technique, being married to a member of the illuminaunty. In the eighties, they loved a grey silk shirt, a gold medallion and a gold Rolex. They enjoy eating salty snacks, including raw onions covered in salt and vinegar, while listening to old classic Bollywood tunes. At every occasion, only once suitably inebriated, Punjabi uncles get the urge to move their bellies onto the dancefloor and sing.

Punjabi sons
Spoilt. Sometimes aloof and living their own life. If married, torn between wife and mother.

Punjabi daughters
Highly educated, switched on, independent and can't wait to get the life they want. The bridge between two worlds. Permanently guilt-ridden, constantly conflicted between wanting to live the life they want and keeping their families, mainly their mothers, happy. They are cool as fuck.

Punjabi dogs
Classic Punjabi dog names: Rocky, Prince, Rambo, Julie, Motthi or Gandhi. Maybe it was just my grandmother who named their dog Gandhi. Punjabi dogs also eat chapattis. Well, Gandhi did.

Punjabi food
Bloody delicious! You all agree. The food you mainly get through your local curry house is some kind of bastardised version of Punjabi food. Real Punjabi food is hearty, full of ginger and garam masala. It's meat, wheat and dairy, food to sustain big, hard-working farming types. Nothing is done in small measure. Anything tandoori is from Punjab. I've eaten in enough farmhouse kitchens in the UK to know that hearty food full of love is not just the preserve of Punjabis, but farming communities around the world.

Punjabi music

Punjabis dance. Punjabis gave the world bhangra. Music is a core part of the culture. Just like everything else, the music and the dancing is big, bold, sweaty and started life in a field. Most festivals and celebrations in the region are connected to the harvest, including the dancing. The big dhol drum gets hung around a neck and sits on the belly, it's whacked rhythmically with two sticks to create a beat that somehow gets your body moving involuntarily. You really have no choice, it's either hypnosis or witchcraft. There's no worrying whether you've got the steps right or how you might look, this is arms-in-the-air and shake-it-like-you-just-don't-care dancing.

Punjabis and money

Punjabis are not shy about money. We love to celebrate success and each other's success. Once we've made a bit of brass, the first thing a Punjabi will invest in is a car. I know cars aren't for everyone, but Indians, specifically Punjabis, love a prestige automobile. To have a nice car is a sign of success and shows that you are doing well. When you start from zero and work your way up, doing good is celebrated. Every single one of us has known hardship to achieve success. So, the next time you pass a semi-detached house in a suburban neighbourhood with the garden concreted over and a Mercedes parked up outside it, chances are it's a Punjabi family indoors.

Now you've met a few of the archetypes of my tale, let's go back to the very beginning.

Go Back to Where You Came From

My paternal grandad, Kebal Ram, an only child, was the first person from my family to land in the UK in 1953. He left his small town in Punjab and set sail for Blighty.

'Go back to where you came from.' 'No one wants you here.' 'No one invited you.'

Actually, they did. The British government did 'want us here'. They absolutely 'invited us'. The doors to Britain were wide open to any citizens of the former colonies. The 1948 British Nationality Act gave my grandad and anyone else from the Commonwealth a free pass to enter Great Britain as a British national. How wonderfully generous of the British government, I hear you cry! Great Britain was suffering a bit post World War II and had a labour shortage that needed filling, and what better way to recruit people to do the jobs locals didn't want to do than invite people from your former colonies. Tried and tested grafters. The first wave travelled on the *Windrush* from the Caribbean, excited by the prospect of coming to work in the land they'd always believed to be the mother country.

Grandad took up the offer too. Like most of the men who arrived, he first came over alone in his early twenties. To establish himself a bit, get some work, find a home, and then he would bring his family over. How on earth did he end up in Bradford? Most men would go where the work was – London, Birmingham, Manchester – cities that had big industry, foundries and mills, usually a city where someone from their family, village or community may already have been working. The network was set up by the pioneers who arrived soon after 1948. Often the men would rent a cheap house (from people who were willing to rent to 'darkies') between a few of them and share rooms and single beds. They would take shifts sleeping in the beds depending on work rotas.

A giant vat of dhal would be made in the kitchen, they'd share responsibilities to make chapattis and would share the food they cooked. Food for South Asians is always a communal affair. This is how they started out, how they survived, the old boys, the old uncles who, before arriving in this country, may never have set foot in a kitchen in their lives. Here, it was survival, and they ate the food they knew and loved, the only food they understood and recognised. Food with flavour, food with spice, food with a kick, food of the gods: curry. Maybe someone had brought over a jar of homemade pickle, if they were lucky! Homemade pickle is an essential in every Asian household. The warmth, flavour and satisfaction a piece of pickled carrot or ginger can bring to the soul would have eased away, for that moment at least, any stresses or worries of the day, of their new life in their new alien world, I imagine. But until their wives arrived, they would have to make the one jar brought over on the ship last as long as possible, scraping out every last drop of satisfaction, of home.

They came here for a better life but also brought their rural, tribal, feudal, patriarchal, peasant mentality with them. Step forward my grandad. Who finally set himself up enough to bring over his wife and two kids – twins, my dad and his sister. My grandma gave birth to four more children in the UK, in Birmingham, then all eight of them moved to Bradford, where Grandad got a job in a mill. (I think there were too many extended family members in Birmingham for Grandad.) Grandma and Grandad were always Grandma and Grandad. They were never Dadi and Dada, the Indian names. Maybe it was part of being British? Always British – somehow being English was never on offer. Bradford in the sixties was rows and rows of terraced, back-to-back houses along cobbled streets with gaslit streetlamps, housing hard-working white families. My family were one of only two Indian families on their street and we remain friends with the other family to this day.

Although Dad remembers the Asian kids mainly playing together, all the kids, regardless of background, would congregate for a game of cricket. This continued to my generation, with street cricket bringing everyone together, using milk crates as wickets. Dad doesn't remember any racism towards him as a kid, although he had Enoch Powell banging on in the background of his youth. I've never heard my dad talk about any racism towards him generally, but then Dad doesn't really ever talk about his childhood, says he can't remember. I asked him a few questions but, in my bones, I can feel there's just too much buried away for it to be picked at by me. Maybe he'll share his tale with his granddaughter in years to come – sometimes it takes a generation.

I always thought that my paternal grandparents were illiterate, but Grandad could read and write Urdu – not Hindi or Punjabi. Prior to Partition, Urdu was the language of administration, journalism and artistic expression in Punjab. Neither of my grandparents could read, write or speak English, however. This meant Dad had his work cut out as their official translator, and as the eldest and the son, the responsibility fell to him. As a kid, he'd have to go everywhere with them, to any official appointments, open official letters, deal with anyone coming to the door. Basically, he had to take charge and grow up pretty fast. He hated the responsibility. A responsibility he has had his entire life.

So, what the heck do you do if you're my grandparents? You've landed in Britain, it's the 1960s, you can't speak any English, you've got six kids and you've got to make a life. Grandad worked in a mill and Grandma was a seamstress. Sewing was a life skill for that generation of women. Most South Asian clothes are bought as loose material and then stitched to fit you to perfection and in any style you choose – and there are so many styles. My gran would make all her own clothes and would make do with the material she bought at the few Asian clothes stores that popped up, for herself and her three daughters. This is why my aunts were often dressed identically and in the same lurid fabric as the sofa covers. Granny was a very smart dresser – she was also very houseproud. She was immaculate in a perfectly fitting handmade suit, always in some kind of pastel colour. I never saw her in anything bright, always a Marks & Spencer cardigan, and in the depths of winter a fabulous faux fur coat over the top. She always wore thick jam-jar glasses, but the black frames were a little bit fashion, pointy at the end. Gran had a great hairline, a sharp widow's peak, that would form a perfect V on her forehead. And her gold: gold hoop earrings, a gold necklace and always gold bangles.

Gold was the only wealth a woman would have when getting married, her bit of security, that turns into treasured family heirlooms. A bride steps into her new married home blinged to the max, dripping in gold and seen as the goddess Laxmi, bringing prosperity to her new family. In theory. Often, though, the yellow metal is valued and treated with more respect than the woman wearing it. But we'll get to that.

She was striking, quick-witted and to the point, my gran. She never seemed to age, to me she was always old. She was only 45 by the time I was born in that vintage year, 1977, but she looked the same in her seventies. She wasn't getting her hair changed at the hairdresser's or following fashion fads, and she really didn't wrinkle that much. Her beauty regime was Astral cream and surma or kajal (kohl) for the eyes. Surma is a powder that comes in a little ornate metal bottle with a stick in the top. You run the stick swiftly between your eyelids, swoosh, and you have beautiful, mysterious eyes. The traditional powder used to contain lead, however – this may explain Grandma's jam-jar specs. Indian women have been wearing eyeliner expertly for centuries. It's a rite of passage for any brown lass the first time she puts it on. Make sure you have a steady hand because you put it on your waterline and so one false move and you have your eye out, which just makes you cry and ruins the entire effect. Unless it's the Alice Cooper look you're after.

When Grandad wasn't working in the mill, he was usually down the pub, playing cards, an Indian game called Seep, with all the other old Indian lads, getting tanked up. It was here, getting to know the other men and through talking over pints of bitter and glasses of cheap whisky, they'd hatch their plans. Pubs and Punjabi men were a perfect fit. In pubs like this up and down the land in the 1960s, the first wave of Indian immigrants were coming up with business ideas that would set their progeny up for the future (and some were just getting pissed). It was in these pubs that they laughed together, reminisced about 'back home' and drank their worries away. At the pub, they didn't feel undermined or belittled, here they didn't feel like outsiders, here they understood the language, they could communicate. Here they felt worthy and equal. From here, they stumbled home. Remembering the harsh, hard reality of their difficult lives with every precarious step, until they got to the front door and brought home the fear, the only place they could wield any power and release their frustrations.

I don't know about the other men in that pub, but when Grandad got home, he was always angry. He barked orders at everyone. Never spoke to his family with any respect or love. He didn't stay working at the mill for long. He too wanted to work for himself, so he acquired a few market stalls and Grandma sewed some of the coats they sold. The markets did well for them and, for a while, it was the family business. It was Dad and my aunts who had to help set up and run the stalls. They had no choice. My grandparents came here to work and make a better life for themselves, but letting their children fulfil their dreams, or have any kind of dreams, was not on the agenda. I'm not sure my grandad particularly liked his kids or his wife. I'm not sure what Grandad did like, apart from drinking and his allotment. He loved his allotment and, even in his eighties, officially registered blind, he grew coriander, spinach and fenugreek.

I always say my dad's childhood was like the film *East is East*, but worse. Back-to-back houses, cobbled streets, outdoor toilet and a tin bath. A tin bloody bath that they'd put in the living room in front of the fire and take it in turns to wash in. Not sure I'd want to be the last one in the water! And if you didn't fancy the tin variety, there was always the public bath. The kids basically did what their parents said and that was it. And if they didn't, all hell would break loose. It was a hard life in Yorkshire in the sixties if you were working class, but life was harder in rural Punjab, so my grandparents' generation just got on with what they came here to do and put up with all the racism and feeling second class. At least the outside toilets here were not an open field. Don't be too shocked by this – I know outdoor dumping is not alien to this land, I saw someone taking a shit in central London in broad daylight just the other week!

Dad had to grow up fast. I think the worst thing for him was that Grandad took him out of school at 15 to get him to work. My very smart dad has never really forgiven him for this. What little foresight, regard and understanding of education my grandfather had. He didn't care at all about his children bettering themselves and learning. The joy in Dad's life was when he joined the ATC, the Air Training Corps, a youth organisation sponsored by the RAF. Dad's dream was to join the RAF, he even tried to sign up at 15 but he was too young. All the things he could have been, all that potential, but he was never given the chance. At least Dad had Captain Kirk and Mr Spock as his besties: *Star Trek* was Dad's escape. So ahead of its time, with its multicultural cast and first mixed-race kiss, and predictions of plasma screens and mobile phones, and wonderful stories of adventure and exploration, not afraid to tackle topical issues. Dad has been a loyal Trekkie his entire life. (Which means we are *all* devoted.)

My memories of visiting my grandma and grandad at their home are defined by food, music and TV. There was always a kind of comfort staying at Grandma's, not because she was particularly loving – she wasn't not loving, but she just didn't show her affection in an over-the-top way, there was no smothering with love in this household. I'd stay the night sometimes when I was very young. She'd hand me a hot water bottle and I'd roll over in the bed and stare at her false teeth sitting in a glass of water on the bedside table and imagine them talking to me. My aunts loved us both when we were little, at least I think they did. They particularly loved Kul, but then everyone loved my brother – my aunts and my uncles, total strangers, anyone who met him, and you couldn't blame them. Kul came along two years after me in 1979 and was so unbelievably cute, absolutely adorable, the kind of kid you'd stop to coo over in the pram (people did), the kind of kid people would look at and he'd make their heart smile – he was Hollywood cute and had an amazingly sweet temperament to go with it. He didn't say much, I guess he had me to do all the talking for both of us. I was very aware that Kul was the cute one. He was a wide-eyed, floppy-haired, cherub of a child and I was a cheeky-faced, often frowning, loud-mouthed, questioning kid.

When I visited, I loved watching *The Cosby Show* and listening to my aunts gossip into the night, usually about girls who had run away from home. My youngest uncle was my favourite and the one me and my brother had the closest relationship with. He went to art college in the eighties and managed to pursue his dream (as he was the youngest and a boy), smashing all Asian stereotypes early doors! He'd drive back from Lincoln in his imported left-hand drive VW Beetle and swoosh into my gran's in his big Dr. Marten 18-hole boots, massive green parka and black eyeliner. Gran's nickname for him was 'Gandu', basically calling him gay. There's Granny's unique sense of humour for you . . . He'd disappear into his bedroom in the attic. It was a wonderful world of mystery and fantasy, when we were allowed in it, that always smelt of patchouli, with art and polaroids all over the walls, an easel set up and a pair of bongos on a stand. He once had a pet rat called Bastard in there, who did a runner. It was sitting outside his bedroom door where I first heard the music that embedded itself somewhere in my brain.

In the darkness on the top step in the attic of my grandparents' house, a musical agenda was being set without me even realising. The Cure, The The, Frankie Goes To Hollywood. My uncle Gov, or Gindha Chacha, or Govinder Nazran, was unique. He was an Asian man who didn't fit my own generalisation about 'Punjabi uncles'. He was tender, vulnerable and thoughtful, funny and beyond cool. He was brilliant. He was, for me and my brother, an absolute hero and role model. He somehow broke free from his own upbringing to live the life he wanted as a very successful artist. Until the trauma of his youth caught up with him.

My dad was also a frowning, questioning kid, like me. Once he was put to work by his dad, he turned into what you might call a bit of a bad lad. Or maybe he was just a frustrated and angry teenager. My grandparents panicked and did the only thing they knew to do: arrange his marriage to a young woman from India so he was no longer their problem. At 19, he was 'married off'. The worst thing my grandparents did was to take Dad out of school even though he loved it, closely followed by arranging his marriage at 19. I do appreciate if my dad hadn't married my mum I wouldn't have been born, but I wouldn't know any better and maybe my parents would have had a life less stressful. They met for the first time at Heathrow airport, having only seen a photograph of each other before that point: 'There is the person you will spend the rest of your life with.' The TV show, *Married at First Sight*, if remade for the Indian market, would be called *Marriage*.

'Surprise. I'm yours for life!'

What if one of them had had a sticky-out belly button?!

* * *

I spent a lot of my childhood trying to figure out the adults around me. They were an extreme and capricious bunch: extremely busy, extremely energetic, extremely angry, extremely fun and extremely sad, but I didn't recognise the sadness until much later. I listened in on their conversations like a nosey little blighter, I watched their moves, I was highly attuned to the energy in a room as, at the drop of a hat, it could go from laughing to screaming. I was constantly walking on eggshells, waiting for the situation to turn. Wishing I could be transported somewhere else with a 'Beam me up, Scotty'.

There is a shift in perception at some point in all our lives, where you start seeing your parents as humans rather than just the people trying to ruin your life. They had lives before you. Childhoods that defined who they would become, or not become. I've spent a lot of time piecing together my parents' stories, who they were, what lives they lived, their relationship with their own parents. Putting them, as individuals, into some kind of context.

In doing so, I learnt to ease up on their flaws, because I understood they too had it tough when they were little and they were just babies when they had me. Plus, my parents' lives were so completely different to mine – they grew up in another universe. Within one generation so much changed within our family and, on the other hand, some things stuck around for centuries. I'm trying to dismantle it all, really. I'm trying to understand how my parents and their parents have shaped who I am, the qualities I possess, the good and the bad. Which are the cyclical habits that have clung on, like the reek of fenugreek in your armpits, that I don't want to take forward? When you're in a land where you are constantly made to question where you belong, it's vital to understand where you came from and not be made to feel shame about your story, but to be empowered by your epic tale of survival. Whatever the circumstances, you take what you're given and somehow figure out what to make of yourself.

Who your parents are defines who you become, and my parents were not straightforward. Neither were my grand-parents. They took a huge leap of faith in coming to the UK. Setting sail for a land on the other side of the planet, with no idea who or what was waiting for them when they arrived. Their objective was simple: make a better life for themselves. Some of those who came to the UK maybe thought they'd work hard for a few years and then return home, but once children arrived, this was no longer a viable or sensible option. Their kids were British and this was their land. My grandparents went back to India pretty much every year, checking up on the home they kept in Punjab their entire lives, the home that was supposed to be for all their children, who never set foot in the place. Since my grandparents died, we have no physical connection to the place, no land, no home. Britain is home, whether people like it or not. Britain looks like me.

They worked hard, my grandparents, and their lives were tough. I wonder what went through their minds when, 50 years after they set foot in Great Britain, they saw their granddaughter on television. They might have thought the entire operation, on some level, was worthwhile after all. Progress had been made in leaps and bounds since they arrived. It took resilience to build a life in Britain, which was a skill I had to pick up very early too.

Families Are Never Simple

On the day my mum gets married, in August 1976, Mum is 23 and Dad is 19. She steps into a three-storey terraced house, her new home, where she is to live with all her in-laws. An extended family set up. She's in the attic, surrounded by the wide-eyed girls of her new family, who look at their beautiful new Bhabhi (sister-in-law), all shiny and new and speaking English (able to quote Wordsworth – not sure my British aunts had ever heard of Wordsworth!). They compare their forearms to hers, wondering how she is fairer than them, even though she is from India. Her sisters-in-law, still children. She can hear raised voices, deep guttural shouting, charging up the staircase. It's hard to tell the difference between Punjabi men arguing and having a good time, but the girls' faces give it away. The little girls' wide eyes become even wider, their breathing stops for a second, their faces switch to terror, a fear that these girls know well. All hell has broken loose and there's a blazing row going on downstairs between my grandfather and someone else. Drink is involved. Drink is always involved.

My firecracker of a mother, in her innocence, goes downstairs to break up the fight. She stands in the living room, in her full wedding regalia, with her hands held in prayer position, asking my grandad to stop the fighting. It's a scene straight out of a Bollywood movie. It might have worked, but she was 20 years too late.

This was the welcome my mum got on her first day in her new home, a massive family bust-up. Not quite the 'cream teas and ballroom dancing' England she's dreamed of.

Welcome to Bradford, luv.

* * *

There was always fighting. Grandad was always angry and whenever he was at home, everyone would scarper out of the living room, his domain. There was always tension. Grandma and my aunts hid in the kitchen and if my uncles were in, there was never any conversation with their father. Just a lot of grunting. Both my grandparents spoke no English and their kids hardly spoke any Punjabi (well, my aunts did, but their three sons didn't. An excellently dysfunctional set up).

As well as excelling in dysfunction, my dad's family were all rather remarkable in their own way, too. Remarkably clever and creative and beautiful and Bradford. One uncle was a tattoo- covered motorbike-riding martial arts obsessed deep-sea diver, who introduced us to kung fu movies and David Lynch. I had two drop-dead gorgeous aunts, often found in Wham T-shirts. I never got to know my Dad's twin as she was married three years before my dad, at 16, but my favourite relative of all was his youngest brother, who went off to art college. They were all very cool. They were all proper Bradford.

Working-class Asians fit in quite well up north because pretty much everyone was working class. Men worked hard, women worked harder, and you brought up your kids as best you could. Life was tough but you just 'ged on w'it'. My gran had no time to be cooing and cuddling. We weren't really a huggy kind of family. Between working, cooking, bringing up six kids and dealing with my grandad, you'd forgive her if she was a bit emotionally exhausted with no space for extra love. She probably gave all her attention to my dad, seeing as he was the first-born son. Indian mothers love a son, especially the first-born. I know that his twin sister was not given the same love or attention and it didn't help that my dad was fairer-skinned.

Life for everyone soon got worse when Grandma and Grandad started trying to marry everyone else off. My dad's middle brother (the tat-covered, motor-bike loving, deep sea diver) had a massive fight with Grandad when he discovered they were trying to arrange a surprise marriage for him. Arranged to the point of the girl's family arriving at my grandparents' house to 'seal the deal'. Only, they'd failed to mention any of it to my uncle. More drama followed this time, not so much Bollywood but kitchen sink:

The guests in the living room with my grandad, drinking tea and exchanging sweets to celebrate the union.

My gran in the kitchen, breaking the news to my uncle, trying to convince him to just say yes to save face and then turn down the marriage later. Great plan, Gran!

My mother trying to tell Gran that you can't play with young girls lives like that.

The women in the kitchen panicking and trying desperately to keep the peace, knowing full well that a serious hoo-ha was about to go down.

We are exceptionally talented when it comes to fighting in my family. Another Punjabi skill. Why talk when you can just have a good old ruck? It was all sorted by my uncle going into the living room and stating he had no desire to get married by shouting this in my grandad's face. Did I mention we have major communication issues in the family? Cue the punch-up. This resulted in Grandad kicking my uncle out and changing the locks. There was so much drama. Sounds traumatic, doesn't it? And I guess it was, only when I talk about it with my dad, we find the entire thing hilarious. Maybe that's the Yorkshire sense of humour. Maybe that's a good way of dealing with it. In hindsight, you see how farcical it all was.

Both my uncles left home to live the life they wanted, but I never found the fate of my aunts very funny.

'I know no one. I've just married a man I don't know. I'm on a rooftop of an old house in a village in Punjab. My head's down, thankfully protected by the heavily embroidered wedding veil I'm wearing that I didn't choose. This is called mu dikhai. My face show. For the first time, my in-laws will see my face. I'm scared and don't bloody belong here. I want to be home in Bradford. I should smile. I need to lift the veil.'

She's my aunt and she shouldn't be there. Like so many other women, her life is traded like a commodity, one that isn't worth a great deal. This is what I imagine went through her mind. I'm pretty certain neither of my aunts wanted to get married, but, essentially, they had no choice. They didn't have the same option as my uncles – of just leaving home and doing what they pleased. My aunts both married men from India and all I remember is how stunningly beautiful they were (solid tens) and how the men were nowhere close to their league, ugly to my eyes. They were all forced to do what my grandad wanted and it definitely didn't seem like happiness. He consulted no one about anything, just made decisions and expected everyone to go along with them. Do as I say, not as I do.

They were all over the shop as a family before my mum came into the equation. But when she did, it gave my dad the perfect excuse to get out. There was an almighty row about something – surprise, surprise – and my dad decided it was time for him and his little family, which at this point consisted of baby me and Mum, to leave. In 1978 we walked[1] out of the door and we never returned. This is quite a major event in traditional Indian households, where everyone lives in a giant shoe together and somehow makes it work. Sons stay in the house, their wives join them, everyone works and brings money into the family, grandparents are there to help bring up the grandkids. In theory the system is good, but you need to like each other for it to work. Not realistic for

---

[1] Even me – I was one when I first started to walk!

my family. I think this rather aptly sums up the complexities of it all: 'They fuck you up, your mum and dad'.

* * *

My dad's upbringing was tough, but you never really know how it's going to affect you until later in life, when you have to go off and figure out your own path with the tools at your disposal, the tools your parents gave you. Or didn't. You really have to stare your issues in the face to overcome them. At some point the legacy of all the anger, all the fear, all the fighting, all the silences and pent-up feelings will blow like a volcano and take you out when you're least expecting it. You'll continue to make choices based on a self that you don't fully understand. Childhood trauma can manifest itself in many ways in adults: anxiety, depression, self-harm, addiction, violence, suicide, memoirs. We've had it all. It can mess up your future relationships, impact your sense of self, your self-worth. The sad legacy of my father's family is that we are now estranged from them. I haven't spoken to any of my dad's side in years.

I absorbed it all, growing up. Watched quietly, often while holding my breath. I didn't know what the hell was going on most of the time but, without me even realising, I was slowly filling up with rage. My inner Kali was awakening. My family and the world around me was teaching me how little value there is placed on a woman's life and that every aspect of her life is dictated to her. And I hated the injustice. I hated how infantilised women were and are. I hated the dialogue of control. When I was very young, I was used as a pawn in the battleground between my granny and Mum. Grandma would declare, 'Your daughter will run away from home, too.' I was only three when she said this. This is the same granny who also said, 'We don't celebrate girls', the day I was born. Thanks, Gran.

Why did she say it? Probably because she was so bitter about her own lot in life. Or because she had a sharp tongue, which could also be very funny, and would cut anyone down, including her own grandchild. Did I mention Punjabis are dramatic? She was a straight-talking woman, my gran. She was basically telling my mum that I would bring her great shame and there is nothing worse for a Punjabi family than a daughter bringing great shame. Running away from home, which seemed to happen a lot back then, was a major act of shame. Surely anyone who had run had made a very difficult decision to go and live their own life? Just that – made a choice for themselves. SHOCK HORROR!

Already, at three, it absolutely terrified me. I was my mum's protector. I didn't want to bring her any pain or shame, but then I also quite fancied living my own life when I was older. The actions of all the adults around me were already making 'running away' seem like a very good option. My inner turmoil had begun! If I could, I would have put all of my thoughts, when that inner turmoil first started churning, away in a box. I'd have used industrial strength brown tape to make sure it stayed in there. I could already see I wanted to get far enough away to make sure no one could tell me what to do, as well as spend a lifetime trying to make everyone happy. It's only now, looking back, going through the scenes of my life, that who I am makes so much sense. Why I feel so much inside, but can't always express what I want. Why I get twisting knots in my stomach, why I'm so afraid of conflict, why I feel so angry. I'm still constantly battling with doing what I want and doing what I'm told. I clearly understood, even as a toddler, that I was balancing a big invisible glass box of shame on my head – one false move and it would smash for everyone to see. I was also carrying my mum's shame, too. If I messed up, it was my mum who would be exposed in some way. It's a bloody heavy box. I was made to feel as though everyone was watching and waiting for me to trip up, so they could turn around and shout in Mum's face: 'Told you so', 'Shame, shame'. And at three, I was terrified. I didn't want to mess up. The seeds of control were well and truly sown. One . . . false . . . move . . .

I do also have fond memories of my dysfunctional childhood, even amongst the fighting and arguing. There were moments when we would all shut up and come together. The one thing that was always there to comfort us: food.

Food Will Always Be Life

Thankfully, there is more than one way to show affection. My family were definitely not a 'touchy feely' family, thank God, (I'm not sure people generally are up north) so we show our affection through food. This is what my gran did, too. Her kitchen, like the rest of the house, was always tidy, with blue lino, a sofa bed, fold-down wooden dining table, one of those multicoloured strip blinds in front of the door leading out, and a blue wall-hung cabinet with glass doors that housed all Gran's crockery, including her prized Charles and Diana wedding mugs, and Gandhi, our beautiful Rhodesian Ridgeback, in the corner.

I can smell it now. Her delicious chicken curry. Her hypnotic halwa made with semolina, sugar and entire blocks of Anchor butter. Fridays were always a treat – homemade fish and chips (although Yorkshire has the best chippies in the world. Why do you leave the skin on the fish down south? It's just wrong!). Nothing beats homecooked chips, drenched in vinegar and brown sauce and a sprinkling of garam masala. Granny's sausage butties were always delicious: Wall's skinless sausages made in the frying pan, sliced in half, then laid between two slices of margarined Sunblest white bread, so the fat soaked straight through the bread, and always with brown sauce. Then there was my granny's party trick: if you want a dish to demonstrate how we truly had become a working-class British Indian family it's ... SPAM CURRY. I'm not messing with you, she didn't make it often, maybe she only did it once, but my God, it was good! It has now become the stuff of myth and legend.

I used to love Spam. Spam fritters, mashed potato and peas was one of my favourite school dinners. Greasy, salty, fatty goodness, the spam fritter is iconic. I say used to, because naturally my tastes have developed, now I'm a la-di-da, solid middle-class, east London type, and I've not tried Spam for years. I do have a tin of it in my cupboard and a tin of corned beef. Those were the gifts my husband and I gave to each other on our tenth wedding anniversary. Maybe I should use the little metal key and get into that tin? Maybe a spam curry recipe needs to be resurrected? Or maybe I should leave it consigned to my memory banks ...

While Granny used to do the Asian shopping, I loved going to Morrisons with my two young aunts to get the basics and essentials: Mellow Bird's instant coffee, Sunblest bread, Birds Eye fish fingers, marg, bottles of Dandelion and Burdock, Nice biscuits, digestives, Spam. Morrisons was only a short walk away but a bit too far to have to carry all the bags of shopping, so my aunts wouldn't think twice about using the trolley to wheel the shopping all the way home. We may be the reason the pound slots were added ... Sorry! The discarded trolley would then get recycled as a go kart for the local kids.

During the week, all of six years old, I was at a prep school, wearing a school hat, pinafore and gabardine, having sleepovers in the poshest parts of West Yorkshire, learning to eat roast dinners with homemade Yorkshire puds and make polite conversation sitting at dining tables. At the weekends at Gran's, I was nicking shopping trolleys. Already effortlessly moving between worlds, you might say.

Gran was no-nonsense about food. When Mum first arrived from India, she'd make dainty little round chapattis. 'You'll be here all day feeding them with those little things,' she told Mum, talking about her husband and sons. 'Double up the dough and feed them a big roti so you won't have to make as many.' And just like that, Mum's chapattis doubled in size.

Even now, two generations later, food remains a constant. I cook and eat cuisine from all over the world, but at least twice a week, I have to eat curry – authentic, rustic, flippin' fabulous Punjabi food. I'm not just bragging because I'm a proud, biased Punjabi, I know for a fact you agree with me. The food available in most curry houses, even though they are Bangladeshi-run, is a bastardised version of Punjabi food. For years, through the seventies, eighties and nineties, you were not really eating curry that resembled the curries we ate at home. Homecooked curries never glow in the dark, each has a distinct flavour (not generic onion and tomato mush) and they allow you to taste the vegetables – but the main ingredient missing is the love.

Britain's palate has now matured and opened up and most people know a damn good curry when it hits their taste buds. Which is a godsend when I'm filming *Countryfile* up and down the land – if all else fails, head to the local curry house for dinner and everyone leaves smiling, overly stuffed but delighted. There's always someone on the team who still thinks everyone should order their own individual curry. Let me explain: that's not the way it works. You order a variety and everyone shares.

The easiest and most nourishing dish for the body and soul is dhal. A simple, delicious, yellow dhal. (My recipe is at the back, if this chapter is making you hungry.) Dhal has bubbled away in pots for generations on the Indian sub-continent and was brought to these shores by the men who first got here, who needed its nourishment and familiarity so far away from home. You might think it was the East India Company who first brought curry to these shores and, yes, Queen Victoria apparently loved it so much she ate it twice a week. But kedgeree is not kitcheree and sultanas have no place, none whatsoever, ever, in a curry, so I will stick to my statement: that curry, real curry, was brought to these shores by the first wave of South Asians to arrive in the UK.

While we're talking food, there's something else you need to understand. When the old Punjabi boys first arrived on these shores, they would always eat chapatti, never rice. If you think of Indian cuisine, you might automatically think of rice. Not in Punjab, not if you want a proper meal. For Punjabis, no meal is complete without roti. Unleavened wholemeal bread, dripping in butter. Landlocked Punjab is the bread basket of India and nearly 40 per cent of India's wheat is grown there. It's incredibly fertile land and agriculture is big business. If you went to work in the fields, as a lot of Punjabis did and still do, then you needed a diet that was going to sustain you. The Punjabi diet is not shy when it comes to carbs – there's nothing we like more than carb on carb with a bit of carb on the side, and an extra dollop of carb just in case. Roti sustains Punjabis.

Chicken . . . Oh, how we love to devour a chicken! I've seen people at weddings leap at a plate of tandoori chicken like a pack of wild dogs, demolishing it in seconds, slathering at the jowls. Naturally, my gran made the best chicken curry. The old-fashioned way, before supermarkets started packing chicken into polystyrene. Vegetarians look away now! I heard stories of Dad having to get the bus out to a local farm and bring a still lively and breathing chicken, loving life, back home in a sack to be put in a pot. Consequently, my dad doesn't eat chicken curry. He's a Punjabi anomaly. He doesn't do chicken, tea, garlic or ketchup – all fundamental pillars of Punjabi cuisine.

As Asians arrived and settled, Asian grocery shops and butchers, usually two in one, began to spring up on street corners in Asian areas. These shops were and still are an essential part of life in any Asian household. We always did our English shop at the supermarket and the Indian shop at the local Asian shop, the mini supermarket. They all have a distinct smell of spices and incense and sell all the stuff that you could never get in a Morrisons or Asda that is essential for an Asian kitchen. Everything from Asian veg: bindi, karela, mooli, tinda, big bunches of coriander, sacks of onions and potatoes, ginger, chillies, garlic, corn on the cob still in its husk (not individually packed, but open boxes so you can buy as much as you need). And all the best fruit: mangoes, lychees, pomegranate and guavas also bought by the box load.

Of course, they would have all the spices. As much spice as you need. Haldi, jeera, elachi, ajwain, saunf, turmeric, cumin, cardamom, caraway, fennel, black cardamom, cinnamon, garam masala. This aisle always had the headiest aroma. They were also the place to get giant sacks of rice and chapatti flour, to be dispensed at home into the chapatti flour bin, an actual bin. They also stocked jars of pickle, poppadoms, incense, kids' toys, sweets, crisps, tins of everything that you could buy in bulk (tomato tins are never bought in small quantities), giant packets of lentils and pulses, yellow dhal, green dhal, black dhal, orange dhal, pots and pans and disposable plates. Asians always need disposable plates. You could get all of this plus a cuddly toy at the Asian shop. This was before the Asian Cash n Carry opened up. Now South Asians just do a trip to Costco to buy in bulk!

As a kid, it was such a chore going to these shops with Mum. She'd spend what seemed like an eternity in them, inspecting aubergines and ladies fingers, before she decided which to buy, getting into lengthy conversations with the shopkeeper. A packet of Space Invader crisps for 10p would usually shut my moaning mouth up for five minutes. Now, I can spend days in the aisles of these shops. I love visiting Ilford High Street or Tooting Broadway to stock up on everything I need – authentic Asian produce, with less packaging and always cheaper than at a large supermarket. I can get lost in the spice aisle (even when I really don't need any more cumin because my mum bought me a kilo of the stuff last time she was there) and you can never have enough pickles.

Some of these shops would also have butcher's in the back. This is where Asian women would always buy their meat. I'm not sure what the health and safety standards were back then, I'm not really sure I want to know. We all survived, anyway. Now, the only way to cook a proper traditional chicken curry is to curry the entire chicken. You'd ask the butcher to chop up the whole bird and once it was cooked, fight to get the bits you wanted the most. The neck. Always the weird little neck – give it a go. Gran would start with an entire block of Anchor butter in her big metal pan, in her pathila. To this she would add her spices and onions, ginger and chilli, then the tomatoes, chicken, then water and simmer. I can taste it. I wish I could taste it now, I really do. Maybe some of you haven't got past the 'entire block of Anchor butter'. Butter is a staple. Not only butter, but all dairy products. It is a fundamental necessity in a Punjabi diet. I'm lucky enough to have experienced fresh buffalo milk being delivered in a churn to the doorstep of my family home in a village in Punjab. The fatty, creamy goodness would then be turned into a variety of dietary essentials, churned into white butter/makhan, boiled and turned into yoghurt, then boiled and turned into cheese/paneer. Yoghurt and cheese were always made at home, even in my lifetime in the UK.

It's the blocks of butter melting in a pan that I remember best. Maybe it's due to my huge weakness for butter, or maybe it's what caused my huge weakness for it? I love it dripping through toasted bread and the only reason I can't resist biscuits (shortbread, digestive, jammie dodger) is because of the butter. My ingrained love of all things dairy keeps me away from becoming a vegan. I could easily give up meat and I did, for a very long time, but give up dairy? My hefty Punjabi bones would take you down for that last spoonful of yoghurt.

We've not even got to the small matter of sugar. Naturally, Punjabis, like the rest of India, have a massive sweet tooth. And Indian sweets are probably some of the sweetest in the world. Barfi, jalebi, gulab jamun and, my favourite, rasmalai. Even the plain sugar I ate in India as a kid on holiday was a treat in itself. Either chini, granulated sugar made from sugar cane that gives it a delicious flavour, or jaggery, unrefined sugar cane, that has a fudgy taste and texture. Which I now use all the time at home. I've even reinterpreted my banana bread recipe to use jaggery instead of caster sugar and my jaggery mojitos are THE ONE!

The Punjabi diet maketh the Punjabi.

* * *

I need you to know that, after finishing writing this, I was overcome by the urge to cook a chicken curry, just the way Granny did. I've currently got two large onions and a load of whole spices sautéing away in half a block of Anchor butter (only half). In a big metal pathila. I'm cocooned by a comforting smell and a warmth in my heart and I'm opening my kitchen door to share the love with anyone walking past my house. Do I have a recipe? No. Did I bring out the pot and just cook with my instinct, a little bit of this, a sprinkling of that and a bit more of the other? Yes, and it worked. The lessons in cookery, passed down from grandmothers to mothers to daughters, have worked. Now, we should start to include the sons.

I'm not sure how many generations this recipe has been passed down, how many centuries old it is, what my ancestors may have been thinking when they were making it, but I am almost certain of the comfort and feeling of home the smell and taste would have made them feel. The same as I'm feeling now. Maybe they too were thinking about their granny while cooking it.

Food really will sustain you. Food is a hugely important tradition that has been passed down to me. My food heritage is my family's love story. It's what binds us. It's still the most important daily ritual for me. I live for food, not just to sustain me but for pure pleasure and pure greed. And when we are together for family events, a wonderfully communal affair, that's when I get to learn the secrets and observe the magic up close. Traditions and recipes are passed down from one generation to the next. We always reminisce about Grandma and Naniji when eating their recipes; happy memories are triggered and I'm back watching the butter melt, swiftly followed by the dull heartache of missing them. All we have left of them are the memories and the food. Cooking is a life skill but, in my kitchen, it's so much more. Cooking is conjuring up the past. It's a nod to my loved ones. Food is love, food really is life, and it's a part of my family legacy I'm keeping with me, always.

Mum and Dad Aren't Perfect, But They Are Superhuman

'Are you well-orf?'

Who the hell asks a question like that? Apart from nosey Indian aunties? Nine-year-old Kate at her roller disco birthday party in 1986, that's who.

'What? Erm, I don't know. Yes?'

We hardly knew each other, to be fair. She was obviously doing her research. I'd just joined Lady Royd, part of Bradford Girls' Grammar School, after acing the 9+. I had left my first ever school, which was a beautiful little private school in a very posh residential area of Bradford, where I was taught French, that 'ginormous' isn't a word, and also how to maypole dance. It's where I discovered that some girls wore knickers over their tights to keep them up. Its main job, however, was to prepare me for the ideal mapped-out school route: take the 9+ to get into Lady Royd, which would prepare me to become a proper little lady (didn't work) and then for the 11+ exam for the senior part of

Bradford Girls' Grammar School, where I'd stay on for the sixth form and then head to uni. There was never a question about it. This was the plan.

My school buildings were breathtaking old Victorian mansions. I was learning in luxury, old-fashioned luxury. And I loved being in those magnificent grand buildings, feeling inspired simply by the architecture. It was easy for me to imagine the beautiful grand homes in the Victorian children's novels I was reading because I was sitting in one every day. Lady Royd had a grand entrance hall with a spectacular ceiling, painted midnight blue with little gold stars all over. I wore a school hat, carried a hockey stick and even had a school regulation basket. No wonder the kids from the comp down the road would spit on us from the bus. What did we look like?! This was the best education money could buy in West Yorkshire, which meant a lot of girls I went to school with, the vast majority, were loaded, and the vast majority were white.

I loved school, I loved learning, I loved answering questions, but this one had me flummoxed. I'd never encountered a question like it. She wanted to know if my parents were rich, and for some reason this was important to nine-year-old Kate.

I remember this birthday party really well for two reasons. First, for the strange question she'd asked and second, because back at school after the party, Kate announced in front of a group of girls that 'My mummy thinks you're a loon and you can't come to my house again.' Which I suppose I shrugged off . . . I was a confident kid and loved a party, I may have been excited. I still love a party and my friends will confirm, I get very excited and may even act like a 'loon', if your definition of loon is keeping the drinks flowing, making sure everyone is having a right good time, letting people stay however long they want (someone stayed for two weeks once) and regularly end up dancing on my kitchen worktop.

I've racked my brain to think what I could have possibly done to make Kate's mum decide that little old me was not allowed to come round and therefore not allowed to be friends with her daughter. Kate's house was huge, beautiful, and I wished my parents had a house like it too. A classic big Victorian Yorkshire stone number, with a sweeping staircase and a smooth and shiny oak banister. And rooms for every occasion: piano room, dining room, lounge, playroom, snug, utility room, dog's room.

I happened to be the only non-white person invited to the party. What do I now as an adult read into this? Kate and I had got on well, we loved talking about *Top of the Pops*. She loved that I knew so much about the latest releases, like all the words to George Harrison's classic 'I Got My Mind Set On You', even at nine. There is no way of knowing if Kate's mum was a little bit racist, but what we do know is that she thought I was a 'loon' and put a full stop to our friendship. I'm not sure how long our friendship would have lasted anyway, with her child being so fixated on finance.

Back to her line of enquiry: were we well-off? I asked Dad.

'We are comfortable.' And back then, when I was nine, we were.

My parents, Balvinder and Lakhbir, or Bal and Lucky, (or, as Dad used to be called back then, Bill) worked hard. Seriously hard. They had a successful manufacturing business and a factory in the centre of town. Most Indians in the seventies, eighties and nineties had their Indian name and an English name they'd use at work, to make life easier for the white people around them. Sukhjit became Pauline, Avinash became Richard and Gurbax became Dave. At least Dad's English name made sense. Punjabis love a nickname – Pinky, Rinki, Shwinky, Babbloo, Tinku, Nani, Nane, Nikki . . . I'm not just writing down strange noises, these are actual Punjabi nicknames. Dad's nickname at home was Billa, which was shortened to Bill.

They were a self-made Asian family in the 'rag trade', like a lot of Asian families in the eighties up north. You didn't need qualifications to set up businesses and Indians are an enterprising bunch. Most of my mum and dad's mates were doing the same thing, setting up small businesses which then went on to grow into very successful ones. They have a crew of upwardly mobile friends up in Bradford who are closer than family. They are all phenomenal people who have built huge companies in electrics, printing, wholesale, import and export. They are there for each other through the ups and downs, and in good times and bad they stand shoulder to shoulder. All of them over time went on to grow their once small businesses exponentially. My parents' story, however, is a little different.

My folks manufactured jackets and coats for wholesale and they also retailed too. They had a shop on the street next to the factory, in the heart of the city centre, and were busy market traders on Saturdays, with various stalls dotted around Yorkshire, in places like Shipley, Doncaster, Ripon, Castleford and Morley. All of this was built from scratch by the two of them, with no help from anybody else. They are what you'd call proper grafters, my folks. Life's doers. Good people. Full of energy. They worked tirelessly and without complaint. I don't suppose they had a choice. Which to me is the most amazing quality. I don't ever remember a day my parents moaned. I mean, they argued, daily, but moan, never.

What you must know about my parents is that they are not human. I can't remember them ever saying 'I'm tired', or that something hurts, or to even cry for that matter, at least never in front of us kids. Not human, see? They were and still are the most dynamic couple I know. Completely different, but at least their energy levels matched. It would be quite an imbalance if they didn't. They shared a common goal and motivation: to give me and my little brother Kul the best chance, to make sure we got to experience things they never did, to give us the best start in life they possibly could and to build a life for us. They wanted us to have every opportunity and, most importantly, the best educa- tion. For Mum, uniform was key. Schools in India have very strict uniform guidelines and kids are always immaculately turned out. She was shocked to see the schools in Bradford. Dad explained though that the best schools with the kind of old English uniform my mum was thinking of were schools you had to pay for. For Mum this didn't seem strange, as her parents had paid for six children to go to school. They wanted us to have the best start in life and if that meant paying, then so what? They'd find a way. They were also very aware that it would help shunt us up through the ranks of the British class system if they sent us to private schools. We'd learn to speak the lingo of middle-class white folk.

They first ran the business in a small rented industrial unit, which was huge to us kids, down the road from the first home we lived in. This was a small rented two up two down terrace house. When the shutters of the factory were open, I'd ride my tricycle through the factory and out around the car park. This was our playground and where we'd spend most of our time while our parents worked away. This is when things really began to take off. I was put into a private day nursery, the only day care that would let me stay late. I was often the last toddler to be collected, well after 6pm. Already getting used to being on my own, learning not to be too needy or reliant on anyone. The local newspaper, *The Telegraph & Argus* no less, ran a story about my folks and described them as 'myth breakers', a young couple in their twenties with two young kids working hard and smashing it. I wish we still had the article but, as you'll learn, my parents aren't really the hoarding (or even just holding onto things for nostalgia) types.

Mum has only a few things from our childhoods: my baby blanket and school scarf, Kul's school cap and first ever cuddly rabbit (which she won when pregnant with him at a fair, she knew the moment she won it he would be a boy), plus our first ever passports. Passports are important. Apart from giving us the ability to travel – and we did a lot of that, particularly to India – our passports prove our much sought after British nationality. Our passports were our passports to a freer and better life. The objective of operation migrate for anyone who decides to leave their own land: make a better life for their kids. In my story, that'll be my bro and me.

My dad is incredibly bright, a natural entrepreneur, a born hustler, very creative with an incredible eye for detail. When it came to stitching the jacket samples to show clients, often he would do them himself as he was so good and neat on the machine. Plus, he can look at an item of clothing and cut material without a pattern. Anyone who knows about sewing knows this is a very difficult skill. Dad should have been the Indian/Yorkshire Paul Smith. If he had been born in London and was white, I imagine he would have been an eighties ad man. I imagine if he had been born white, he could have been anything.

The business boomed, enough for them to buy the next factory. These guys were going places. They were going into Bradford city centre! The factory was a three-storey building in town, painted sky blue. A proper old warehouse with Crittall windows and big double doors. Exactly the kind of space a property developer would drool over to convert, so that property addicts could then drool over it, so that some banker from the city could purchase it. Although this is Bradford and I'm not sure anyone really wants to live in the city centre, handsome as it is – not opposite one of the shadiest pubs in town. I know it was shady because the police once used the factory, mine and Kul's room in the factory to be precise, for a stake-out spot. We'd regularly see people stumble out of the pub arguing or bleeding, or both. Not quite the friendly Yorkshire pub you'd want to pop into for a pint of mild. Definitely the wrong end of town.

What are your guilty pleasure websites you disappear into when procrastinating? Puppies are a pretty good source for vanishing away the hours but, for me, the ultimate hit, the purest rush I get, is from property porn . . . All property, but mainly warehouse conversions. I just love industrial spaces. The more exposed brick, metal beams, concrete staircases, the better. I even have a soft spot for breeze block walls. This is all because of a childhood spent in factories.

I'm going to give you a personal guided tour of the factory – in we go. Keep up! Through the big double doors just to the right of you is the huge concrete staircase running up all three storeys – there was no lift. So, we'll pelt up the stairs to the top floor, to the cutting room, where a giant long table sat in the middle of the room ready for layers of material to be laid out across it and stacked up against one wall were rolls and rolls of material, of all different colours and textures. The best were the giant thick quilted rolls, these made a great soft play area for me and Kul to clamber about on and hide in between. The next floor down was the sewing room, where around 25 women, most of them Indian and Pakistani, were sat at machines. Dad had set it up so that the machines were facing each other, the chatter was constant as was the sound of the machines, 'RUUUUU RUUUUU RUUUUU', and the chugchugchugchug of the overlocking machine, a vital piece of industrial equipment that finishes the edge of a seam, that reverberated through the wooden floorboards. In the far corner of this vast room was a separate area for trimming and packing. Down on the ground floor was the kitchen – a little canteen area with a kettle and microwave, all mod cons. There was always coffee, tea, coffee mate and a big old bag of sugar. This was before the days of Asians knowing anything about diabetes, two/three/four/seven teaspoons were standard for most people in the factory.

Also on the ground floor was Dad's office, with his own filter coffee machine, a filing cabinet and a huge wooden desk. He also had two comfy armchairs and a little coffee table, his break-out space for meetings. I loved this room, it was clean and organised and quiet, and is where the business really happened. When Mr Wright, a big customer for Mum and Dad, would come over from Harrogate (a swanky bit of Yorkshire) for meetings, at the end I'd come in and join them. Mr Wright sat me on his knee and taught me Irish sea shanties. I was 17. Just kidding, I was a kid. Mr Wright was lovely and always smartly dressed, and he carried a leather suitcase just like my dad. Sometimes at lunch, Dad would give himself a little break, take the sack of small change out of one of his drawers and head up to the arcades at the top of the street. Yes, that's right, a legit businessman, with his own factory and all the responsibility that came with it, would head up to play the slot machines at lunchtime. He was barely out of his twenties though, remember, and this was the time before computer games.

In front of Dad's office was a room three times its size – the stockroom, full of big metal shelving units, like the ones in B&Q that are bolted together. I remember Dad building them himself. In one of my rented flats in London, in a warehouse conversion, I bought and built myself a similar unit. This flat had exposed brickwork that Mum couldn't stand or understand. 'Poor people live like this in India! Put some wallpaper on it,' she advised. The room next to my dad's office was the cloth overspill room and in this room at the far end by the window were two little sofas and a small white TV, plus a little table, all for Kul and me. This was our space. Our den, our universe.

It was the factory, as well as our ethnicity, that set us apart from everyone else at school and that made our home life so unconventional. Every day after school, or after roller disco birthday parties, rather than go home, Kul and I were brought straight to the factory. Straight to our little den where we were left to our own devices, while Mum and Dad worked. We made our own choices. We'd have a snack, something picked up in town. Our favourite was always a classic cheese and onion pasty from Thurstons (now known as Greggs), or a Pot Noodle. I loved Pot Noodles, especially drinking the brown slurry left in the bottom of the pot. We ate delicious healthy home-cooked Indian food every day but, when it came to Western food, we ate junk, delicious junk.

If my parents had to work late, then we'd stay with them. There was no other option. Bags down, blazers off, homework done (sometimes), pasty in hand, TV ON! We watched a lot of TV in that room, we watched a lot of TV full stop. TV was our pacifier, our babysitter. This was the heyday of kids' TV and we were indiscriminate about what we'd watch and had no channel loyalty. Cartoons like *Dungeons & Dragons*, *Thundercats* and *Gummy Bears*, shows like *Fun House* and *Grotbags* and TV kids' dramas *Grange Hill* and *Round The Twist*. Of course, we watched *Blue Peter* and *John Craven's Newsround* (I still can't believe he's now my colleague and mate!). But our religion was *Neighbours* and *Fresh Prince of Bel-Air*.

It's where our imaginations flourished. We'd invent games. And we'd play. And we'd fight and play fight. We'd dance, we'd dance fight. Dance fighting was my favourite game. You dance for a while and then switch to a karate spar and then switch back, without telling your opponent when you were going to switch. Dance, fight, now dance ... fight ... dance. You want to play, don't you? We were probably inspired by our hero, Bruce Lee. He was, in fact, a trained ballroom dancer as well as a major Kung Fu badass. What a dream boat! Kul spent a lot of time drawing. He always had a sketch pad and would disappear into his world of creativity.

This was our happy space, our safe space, where my little brother and I looked out for each other. We were each other's best friends because we had to be. Only me and Kul were going through our particular life together. A lot of the time we'd help out in the factory too. Now, you could say this was child labour and you'd be right. But Asian families would say, this is just having kids. Working is part of the unwritten contract of being born to brown folk and no, you don't get paid and you NEVER moan. Moaning about it gets a very stern look. Not a death stare, not a screw face, but a look so terrifying it would get you out of your seat in a shot. Our jobs would be in the packing area. Threading the jackets with tiny little scissors, trimming off any dangly excess cotton thread, tagging the jacket with the label, using the cool tagging gun, then folding neatly and uniformly, sliding into a polythene bag and sealing the bag with Sellotape. Ready for collection or for Dad, if he was to take the delivery. If an order needed to be ready and we were up against a deadline, the four of us would stay at the factory until it was done. Even if it got late and we had school the next day, we couldn't go home until the job was complete.

The last thing to do at the end of the day was the rounds, dropping off big sacks of unstitched jackets to the seamstresses who worked from home. They were scattered around Bradford, mainly in the inner-city areas. Dad would drive the van, Mum, Kul and me squeezed onto the other two seats next to him. The laws were different back then . . . We Asians always managed to squeeze another one (or seven) more bodies than were legally allowed into any vehicle. These were the women who were unable to come to the factory so had industrial sewing machines at home, usually in their kitchens. Their reasons for working from home varied, but it was usually because they had young families to bring up. Kamala Aunty had two young sons the same age as me and Kul but was also helping run a small electrical shop with her husband. She sewed to supplement their income. Some of the women sewed at home because they were not allowed to leave to go to work.

We'd drive down streets of back-to-back houses, with kids running around everywhere. Beautiful little children, screaming and playing, covered in dirt. They'd chase the van down the street as we'd arrive and leave. Speaking a combination of Urdu and Mirpuri and English with a Yorkshire accent. A sack would be dropped off and a previous one collected. We could identify which house the sack came from by the smell of the tarka that had permeated the cloth. Most women sewed in their kitchens, stirring giant pots of gosht or chooza, wiping snotty noses, feeding crying babies. I adored the women who sewed for my parents and they all adored us. They were more than simply employees, they were our family, and they became each other's families, too.

The factory was a daily soap opera. The women who worked there would laugh and argue, and they'd share their stories. Azra Aunty and Darsho Aunty both worked in the factory. They were proper besties, both Punjabi, but one was from Lahore in Pakistan and the other from Jalandhar in India. There may have been historic divides and modern-day divisions in Bradford between the two communities but, in the factory, no one really cared. There were more Pakistani than Indian women, but there were also Bangladeshi and English too. The majority were Punjabi, whether Pakistani or Indian, so they all spoke the same language and shared similar values and culture and, crucially, all these women understood something about each other without having to explain. They understood and held each other's pain. They worked hard, these women were warriors. A few had alcoholic husbands, one had a son who had started committing crime, there was a son in prison, a husband behind bars, a runaway daughter, there were mental health issues and forced marriage, miscarriages, abortions and so much domestic abuse, but in this space, on that sewing room floor in my parents' factory, they had each other. My parents knew the home situations of each of the women and became their confidantes.

The seamstresses loved my young parents. They referred to them as brother and sister, they were either Paaji and Penji or Bhaijan and Bhaji, depending on which side of the border you were from. We were invited to lots of weddings, because of this! Hindu, Sikh and Muslim, and my folks would always have an Eid party, Diwali party and Christmas party for them, sometimes in our home. All the women would cook and make a dish, including Mum. Indian women would cover the veg dishes and the Pakistanis would bring the meat, playing to their strengths. If you want to eat a delicious tandoori lamb chop, head to a Pakistani restaurant. If you want to eat amazing vegetarian food, always hit up an Indian and if prawns are more your bag, then you could do far worse than head for a Bengali. Mum and Dad were so young and hard-working, but they were also generous and kind-hearted. Everyone would get a present for Christmas. Usually a Marks & Spencer cardigan, which for an Asian woman of a certain age is a piece of 'kwalti'.

Every so often, Dad's adventurous spirit would extend to his workforce and they'd organise factory outings to the seaside. The summer of '86, Dad hired a big old coach to take all the women who sewed in the factory AND even a couple of the women who sewed from home on a day trip to . . . RHYL! Women who really were not allowed to leave their front door without a male family member – the furthest they'd ever been was a trip to Manningham Park, not even into the town centre – yet somehow their families had enough trust and respect for my young parents to let them join us on the adventure to the Welsh seaside. My mum is incredibly persuasive. All the women were invited, plus they were told they could bring other family members too, mothers, cousins, aunts, sisters-in-law and of course their young children. The only rule my mum had set was that no men were allowed. The only two men on the trip, apart from the bus driver, were my dad and my younger brother. Watch out, Wales!

They all piled onto the bus. Jageero Aunty, Ram Payari Aunty, Azra Aunty, Parveen Aunty, Satto Aunty, Shameem Aunty, Shakeela Aunty, Sarbjit Aunty. Mum had bought boxes of food for everyone to share on the coach. Samosas, bananas, plums, packets of crisps. Buying in boxes is not strange – there are certain things that can only be bought in big boxes in large quantities. Lychees, cherries, onions (they come in giant sacks) and mangoes. One mango wouldn't even touch the sides. And samosas, if you're going on a coach trip! It was a sweltering day in June and the air on the coach was fizzing with excitement and a mild aroma of puke. It didn't take long for the heady mix of freedom, a bumpy coach and the samosa-banana combination to take its first victim. Sarbjit Aunty vommed into a Morrisons plastic bag. Asian women are always able to produce a Morrisons carrier bag at any moment. Producing carrier bags and singing

65

folk songs are their fortés. The soundtrack of voices, of varying standards and pitches, singing Punjabi boliyan as loud as they could accompanied us all the way to Wales.

When we arrived, the only instruction was to be back at the coach by 5pm. Other than that, Dad said they should go and enjoy themselves. On that glorious sunny day in June on the beach in Rhyl, amongst the children building sandcastles and the women sunbathing in bikinis, a group of women, never before seen in this part of the world, approached the sea for the very first time. Daring each other to touch it, the sea beckoning them towards it, so they approached. Teasing each other, giggling like girls, playing like children. Their worries left in a house in Bradford. They rolled up their shalwaars, aware that they were revealing the bottom half of their calves and ankles, enjoying the feeling of danger and freedom and safety in numbers. Like a symbolic ritual, they stepped into the Irish Sea, looking out to the horizon for the first time in their lives, feeling peace and joy, letting the waves wash away the sadness, letting the breeze carry away their pain.

And then Shameem Aunty slipped. Now, there was a full-on wet shalwaar kameez situation. But with no husbands, brothers, uncles or cousins around, the women just howled with laughter. They thanked Mum and Dad and said, 'Today, you've shown us a new country.' I have such deep respect for these women. The lynchpins of their families, struggling in a land that's not their own, sometimes with husbands who have no respect for them. Some of them quiet, some of them vocal, but all of them warriors, selfless warriors and the most powerful forces I know. Time and time again, they take a battering from life and, every time, they rise. They should be treated with the respect and admiration they deserve. We, their children and grandchildren, should recognise their greatness and daughters and granddaughters and great granddaughters should see that we are born of these warriors, and we owe it to them to own our narrative.

*　*　*

I'm connected to these women. I feel them. It's their courage and strength I admire the most. This generation of women, the first who landed in Britain, had to straddle so many worlds and leave their own behind. Nothing in their lives was easy and they worked so hard to ensure a better life for their children. They are the hardest workers I know. Looking after everyone, but I'm not sure anyone ever looked after them. Maybe they didn't need looking after. But they were certainly never understood. These were not pampered women, they were not treated like princesses, not even with any respect, by anyone, not inside their homes or outside.

I never felt close to my gran, she wasn't easy to get close to, and she'd had a sticky relationship with my mum, so I would feel disloyal if I was too close. Even when she died, I didn't know how to feel. But it's Gran that keeps coming back to me while writing this, my grandma, Dhan Kaur. Her life was hard. It was hard before she married my violent grandad, it was much harder afterwards. Her life was always a struggle. Today, I really miss my gran. I wish I'd understood her. Today, I'd give her a hug, whether she'd want to or not, I'd squeeze her and nuzzle into her and smell her oiled hair and take pictures of her tattoos and ask her what they mean. I'd stare at her elongated earlobes, weighed down by a lifetime, I'd touch her soft skin once again and I'd ask her for one of her M&S cardies. But most importantly, I'd ask her to tell me about her life. The girl she was, the woman she had to become.

None of these women had easy lives, none of them had any choice in their lives. They all had to be the right sort of girl, wife, mother, sister. On some level, being like them is what I've been fighting against my entire life. I don't want to be answerable to anyone, I want complete power to make my own choices, I don't want to have that weary look of complete helplessness which is often what I saw when I looked at them. Struggle and exhaustion and loneliness. But these women were anything but weak, these women are my heroes. These women struggled so that I could have a voice. I honour all these women, I see their struggle and the system that bound them, strangled them. But each one has a story and her secrets. Each one had desire and dreams. To them, I bear silent witness. It's easy to look to the loudest voice and believe that they have the power, because they make most of the noise. In my family it was the men. The men may have had the power, but it's the women, the incredible Asian mothers, I have learnt, that have the strength, and their strength was, and is, love. I learnt all this from secretly listening to their conversations, from walking around the sewing room floor in the factory, from observing their faces and reactions and from feeling their love towards me.

The factory defined us. It was our world. We all revolved around the business. There was no work/life balance, a luxury not afforded to my folks or anyone of their generation. Or Kul and me. A template was being set for my own work ethic and what I wanted and didn't want for my own life.

Be Your Own Superhero
When You Can

'Bloody Pakis.'

They shouted at the kids playing on the cobbled street outside their home. The kids had put bricks on top of her bright red mini metro, her pride and joy, and she wasn't happy about it. The kids just laughed and flicked the vs. These two teenage girls were beautiful, one with back-combed hair pinned into a messy bun on top of her head, the other with long silky hair, cut neatly just below her shoulders. They were both in high-waisted stonewashed denim trousers, cinched in at the waist with a belt and Choose Life Wham! T-shirt tucked into the jeans.

I observed their sass, ballsiness and casual racism towards the kids with admiration and confusion. They are my aunts. My buas, my dad's little sisters. We were all Pakis to the outside world, but within the Asian community in the eighties, there were *Pakis* and then there were *Pakis*.

By now Mum, Dad, me and Kul had moved to the suburbs, but my grandparents still lived in inner-city Bradford which, by the late eighties and early nineties, was full of

Asian families, mainly from Pakistan. Even though Asian communities lived side by side, we are communities within communities within communities. Indians, Pakistanis and Bangladeshis. And there were strong divisions and some animosity between them. Crazy, considering we were all one country not two generations earlier. How quickly we all bought into our borders.

Snobbery within the Asian community is hugely connected to the five Cs: Country, Class, Caste, individual family Culture and the dreaded Community. Indians have a tendency to be both snooty and judgey, and there's so much prejudice. The Punjabi word pind means village and a pindu is a villager. If you're called a pindu, you are basically being cussed as a villager – the term is used jovially but also in a derogatory way, suggesting you are backwards, straight from a field, not worldly wise, not educated, uncouth. Indians, especially Punjabis, are a tribe of pindus who aspire to be more sophisticated town folk and we are upwardly mobile. Sadly, this doesn't always mean more educated, it just means making money. Class and caste and cultural snobbery are alive and bhangraing in Asian communities.

Mum is from a middle-class family in India. My maternal grandfather was educated and in the Indian army, and they lived all over India depending on where Nanaji was posted. Mum and her sisters went to army schools and were friends with children from every state of that vast subcontinent. My mum, because she's bright, clever, openhearted and the most social person I know, can consequently speak around seven Indian languages. Dad's family are classic Punjabi economic migrants. There is a difference between the Punjabi my parents speak: 'Your dad's family still speak village Punjabi, rough Punjabi, whereas ours is more refined,' Mum has explained to me my entire life. 'They don't use the polite form of the language.' To not use the polite form when speaking to other people is rough and ready and shocked the shit out of my mum when she landed in Blighty. She'd left a lovely life in India to move to the more 'advanced' UK, but had travelled backwards to rural Punjab, a life she hadn't even witnessed in India. Britain, for Mum, seemed full of Pindus.[2]

We Indians are a right bunch of snobs. Everyone is looking down on someone. We delight in patronisingly letting other Indians know that 'we don't really speak any language other than English' and we love nothing more than people thinking we are any race other than Indian. But then we don't know our history. How can we feel pride when we have been sold the myopic Western narrative of Empire? How can we feel pride when we've been made to feel ashamed? How were we ever meant to feel pride when we believed we had nothing to be proud of?

On the other hand, I was accused of being a coconut all the time as a child because of my perceived proximity to whiteness, the way I spoke, my taste, my white mates. To

---

[2] My dad's Punjabi was pretty atrocious when Mum married him. In the 45 years they've been married it's much improved but, sometimes, even I have to correct Dad's words. (Dad's been correcting Mum's English for over 40 years and she's tried to correct his Punjabi for the same length of time.)

some, I'd ditched my Indianness, which was far from the truth. It's tragic. If we as a community cannot be proud of our heritage and identity it leaves us in a sorry, lost state.

Those kids shouted back to my aunts: 'Paki slags,' I hate the word Paki. I hate it. I hate the way it makes me feel, the memories it conjures up, the divisive nature of it. I hate that Asians have used it themselves sometimes as a joke, sometimes with spite. WE ARE ALL BROWN. It's never funny. It's humiliating and demeaning. In Bradford, in the eighties, racist slurs were chucked around like tennis balls at Wimbledon. All with the same motive, to smack the other person in the face. And if they were slung your way, you just batted them back. Usually with 'I'm Indian', like that made a difference, or by just ignoring them. Someone might feel the urge to bellow it across the street at you. A boy in a club might shout it in your face if you din't want to dance. Your eight-year-old mates, who you play with you every day, might sometimes let it slip out.

'Sticks and stones may break my bones but words will never hurt me.' Bollocks. Words can wind you. They can cripple you, knock the air right out of you. Render you gasping and confused. They can make you seethe, they can destroy your sense of self, your confidence.

Somehow, as a kid, the word didn't have the same impact. It was heard with such frequency that it was more of a constant hard punch in the arm, reminding you of what you were. That word was so common when I was young, sometimes random strangers would feel the urge and the need to shout it out at you across the street. And you'd just carry on walking. So as a kid, it didn't really hurt that much, it just reminded me that I was different and that people are racist. I might have been tough because my parents shielded me, or because I didn't fully understand the implications of the word. The implication being that my country had a problem with my existence, that my country doesn't want me here, that it is 'tolerating' me as best it can.

One method to try and avoid the name calling was to not draw too much attention to my Indianness. As a kid, my relationship with Indian clothes was complicated. I loved wearing them but only in Indian situations. I never, ever wore them at any other time. The only person who wore Indian clothes all the time was my granny. I mainly wore them on a Sunday, for trips to the Gurdwara, and always when going to a wedding. As soon as I was home, I'd get changed. I was very aware that my Indian clothes didn't fit the rest of my world. One particular Sunday when I was 11, an ice cream van pulled up the minute we got home from the Gurdwara. I was in a dilemma. I couldn't resist a screwball on a Sunday, with the red sauce and two bubblies, but I was still in my little Indian suit. I refused to go out, but Mum and Dad convinced me I looked lovely and to just go.

It was a warm day and the queue was long. All the kids on the street were in it, the kids I played with regularly. I lined up with my pound coin in hand, feeling a little self-conscious but the excitement of the ice cream overriding it. One of the girls looked me up and down and in front of everyone said:

'We didn't know you were one of those.'

I was mortified, humiliated and ashamed. The veil had slipped and she saw something I didn't want her to see. She thought I was 'one of those'. What did she mean? I knew exactly what she meant. I was ashamed because my identity was intricately curated. I made sure that who I was and how I was seen was kept compartmentalised based on the situation I was in, just so something like this wouldn't happen. Indian situation equals Indian clothes, anything else equalled my 'normal' clothes. I had many guises and disguises and, in this situation, I got it mixed up. This lot were never meant to see me like this because I'd already predicted the reaction. People may deny that Britain is racist but a lot of us have a very different lived experience.

I was ashamed but also confused. The clothes I was wearing were me, they were a part of me, and this small thing, my outfit, made her put me into a different category to before. I love my Indian clothes. I like the way they make me feel, I adore the freedom and femininity, I love feeling Indian. It's a simple way for me to connect with my heritage, when I'm already one step removed by being born in Britain. Asian clothes are elegant and graceful and women in shalwar kameez and sarees look beautiful. But this lass who humiliated me would never know that. To her, Asians probably come in two varieties: those who wore Western clothes and the lot who didn't. The idea that you might do both would never have crossed her mind. She exposed her ignorance and thinly veiled prejudice. If you dress like me, you're alright with me . . . just about. The rules of engagement for battling through life in Britain were already being laid down.

This lass was lucky, because if I'd wanted to, I could have taken her down. I was a kickass karate kid! While all my friends at school had pink tutus and learnt to plié and point, I was learning to jab, block, roundhouse and sweep. It kept Kul and I focused, fit and agile, and there was a great deal of discipline involved. We loved being karate kids. I was pretty tough and they'd have me train with the adult men, the little boys in my age group couldn't handle me. I'd won trophies and competitions and I was pretty handy with my arms and legs . . . It also taught us discipline and self-control, and fundamentally teaches you that you should never have to start an actual fight. So, I walked home and ate my screwball, and I'd like to tell you I never thought about the incident again, but that's just not true.

Being made to feel other happened at school, too. My classmate, Sarah, decided she wanted to tell a joke in the fifth form common room to a small group of 15-year-olds. It was a racist joke and to add insult to injury, it wasn't funny. They're never funny. She looked at me and said matter of factly, 'But you're different.' Ha! I heard that a few times. Like that made it OK. Like I was getting a free pass, some kind of badge of honour. All you want is to be accepted. But the 'you're different' line never washed. It's not true. It's a tactic, and it is divisive, setting you apart from others like you. It means you're a palatable brown, it means, 'I'm a racist, just not towards you'. Which, by the way, still makes you a racist. It was complicated, though. My parents were paying for me to fit in. But it was made very clear that I was to keep my ethnicity at home. I was 'different' because I didn't make Sarah feel uncomfortable with my Asian-ness. My ethnicity was not in her face, I had dialled it down to zero, but I couldn't do anything about my skin colour. That giveaway. My classmates only saw what I knew would be acceptable to see. But walking down the street with my family, in Indian clothes, I became 'one of those'. Sarah was right, I was different. I prided myself on being different. Only not how she perceived it. Turns out, Sarah was the racist joke!

Once, I popped into my neighbours' house, as I did all the time – my neighbours who I loved, who I grew up with. The entire family was in the sitting room watching a VHS of their favourite comedian, Roy Chubby Brown. He's a working-class hero up north and my neighbour's kid insisted I sat and watched the genius at work. I was too young to get it properly but when his racist jokes started flying, it sure as hell made me feel awkward. I felt like an outsider on every level. Where the hell did I fit in?

Back in the eighties and nineties, the buzzword was ASSIMILATION. No one really thought about integration. And my parents did everything right. They were textbook immigrants:

Immigrant (definition): Immigrants to this land come to work hard for a better life for their children and then their children, who are now British and pay a fuckload of taxes into the system.

My parents worked their asses off, bought into the system, believed this land was fair and full of opportunity. They didn't moan or complain even when they encountered racism, they had the heartbreaking capacity to shrug it off. They moved to the suburbs, didn't wear 'ethnic' clothes unless it was a special occasion, sent their children to private school to make sure we spoke 'proper English' (or, as Mum proudly says, 'the Queen's English'), to make sure we moved in white circles and had English references. They thought this was what was required to make sure their kids had all the opportunities they didn't. It worked, to an extent. That is, until you get into the workplace and realise the glass ceiling is real and it's triple-glazed. And no matter whether you've done everything they expected you to do, whatever they told you was the right way to go about keeping your brownness to yourself and assimilating, ultimately you are still going to stand out as other, as different. They can't see beyond that. My parents thought they'd armed me with everything I'd need to succeed in Britain. A perfect balance between my Britishness and my Indianness. But they had missed out the most important lesson: how to deal with the harsh reality that, for me, merit alone will never be enough. Hard work, even working three times as hard, will never be enough. That I'll spend a lot of time justifying why I'm capable of doing anything because people won't see me how I see me.

All of us are trying to figure out where and how we fit. What values do we want to live by? How do we define ourselves? How do we make sure the next generation don't lose their identity? How do you adjust to your new environment, yet keep rooted to the old one?

* * *

The last time I heard the word 'Paki', it completely knocked me for six. It was only a few years ago. I was in a work situation, having a light-hearted social drink with colleagues, so-called educated, well-travelled, liberal TV types, until someone decided to drop the P bomb. Right to my face. It could have played out in so many different ways, but what followed was the worst-case scenario. I'd not heard anyone say this word out loud for years, not since I was a kid, or maybe since watching a rerun of *Only Fools and Horses* – the episode where they casually talk about going to the 'Paki shop.' I was caught off guard, I was transported back to the school yard, but this time it was worse. In the school yard I would have been humiliated but, more than likely, said something back to defend myself. In this present-day work situation, as a full-grown adult in my forties, all I did was laugh it off awkwardly. Why did I do that? I remember feeling pathetic, crushed. Where was my voice when I needed it? I hated myself. I should have chucked a drink in the person's stupid face, kicked him in the balls, or simply told him that there is no context, none whatsoever, where it's OK to say that to me. But all I did was shrink into a mouse. Me, gobshite Rani, tell em straight and tell em good, defender of the meek. I always stand up for other people whenever I hear anything vaguely racist going down. I've turned into an anti-racist superhero and jumped in with a furrowed brow and a loud northern NOOOOOO on many an occasion!

Where was my superhero self when I needed her? It exposed the true power dynamic of my work situation. Those around me felt they could say it to me and get away with it and, for whatever reason, I did not stand up for myself. I felt humiliated and wanted to get away as fast as possible. There were other people there, who were white, and they said nothing. No one else stood up for me. If ever you want to know what it feels like to be made to feel like an outsider, try imagining that. I believed that in my world, where people knew me and were close to me, they saw me for who I am – the same as them. I believed this, I naïvely lived in my blinkered little world. I might as well have believed in unicorns and magic fairies. My world was a cocoon and I was safe, but this was one almighty bubble-bursting moment. No, you are not and never will be one of us. It messed with my mind so much it was the spark I needed to start figuring out what the hell had happened to me.

I've been in a tailspin for a couple of years, wondering who on earth I am. Why, as a woman in my forties, I'm affected by things so much, so emotionally, and feel as though I'm losing my power as the years go on. It's as though far from becoming more confident as I grow, I'm becoming more fragile. Is this what happens in middle age? Because if it does, I wish I'd been warned. I'm choosing to see it as a blessing, an opening of my eyes and my soul to my inner world and the world around me. It makes me ask myself, how do I want to live? How does the right sort of girl react, in any kind of situation, good or bad?

I certainly don't want to feel crushed by things that are out of my control. I want to finally relax and enjoy my life to the fullest and believe that I have earned my right to be at the table and take charge of myself, the only thing I really have any charge over. I so welcome the open discussion around race and identity that is finally happening more publicly, and privately. People of colour are finding the courage to speak their truth, but sadly there is always a backlash and it's exhausting. Recently (in January 2021 – that recent), I filmed a piece about a Black girl's hiking group for *Countryfile* and the BBC received complaints about it.

What was offensive? Why did people take it so personally that two women of colour were having a chat about their experience of walking in the countryside? The outraged reaction says so much and it's so disappointing and disheartening to say the least. I feel let down by my country when this happens, and it is happening more and more. But acknowledging the truth about my home, in a strange sort of way, is making me whole. I've ditched the blinkers and taken my fingers out of my ears, and it's made me more powerful. The right sort of girl isn't crushed, she grows and rises and bosses it! There's work to be done. There's work to be done by all of us. I don't want any child to feel shame or any less valued because of who they are – why would we want to live in a society that does that to a child? That's not the Britain I want. I can say this to you and mean it in this moment. However, it does make me wonder, do I ever truly see myself as an equal? Or am I always just a little bit grateful to be here?

How do I decolonise my mind? By remembering who the hell I am.[3]

---

[3] I've still never worn a saree to any Western event. It's a secret dream to rock up to the Baftas one day floating along the red carpet in Sabyasachi couture.

Own Your Womanhood

The first rule about puberty as an Asian girl is, you do not talk about puberty. The second rule of puberty as an Asian girl is, you DO NOT talk about puberty!

It's a secret code of conduct. How you come to know this is also a secret. It's never explicitly expressed because, well, that would involve speaking about puberty. So how do you know you're to stay schtum and not talk about it? It's hints, behaviours and reactions you notice throughout your life. It's widened eyes if you happen to be wearing something a little too revealing. It's being told you can't play with the boys. It's judgemental comments you overhear about other young women. It's never being treated the same as the boys. It's the burden, trepidation and fear you sense around you, the vibe you get from everyone so you innately understand: to be a little girl is a shame, but manageable.

But to be a woman, well, no one wants to deal with that. So keep it to yourself.

Aaah, fuck it. I've never particularly liked rules and it's high time someone spoke about it, if only to save the next generation from more unnecessary shame, shaving off their teenage moustaches (a terrible idea) and a drawer full of ruined, blood-stained knickers. Blood is a bitch to get out, no matter how much Imperial Leather soap you scrub into them secretly in the bathroom . . . Trust me. Being a teenager is hard enough to navigate but having to do it alone, feeling isolated and full of shame and fear – I don't want any of you to have to suffer that.

By the time I was 12, I had already been indoctrinated enough by an endemically misogynistic culture that I was fully aware that anything to do with becoming a woman is a disaster and going through any kind of change was not to be celebrated or spoken about, ever. You deal with it all on your own, fumble and feel your way through getting your terrifying period: SHUSH, getting your first crush: NOT ALLOWED, growing boobs: NEVER draw attention to them. Filling out around your hips (for some reason, fatness is good), growing hair (growing hair every bloody where, but not any old hair, thick black stubborn hair, all over your face kind of hair and everyone can see your moustache hair), secreting new odours (mmm, that made it sound delicious) and, of course, teenage zits.

However, beauty is a must. Girls should always be pretty and clear-skinned. Beauty is the one topic Indian women can discuss openly and freely without fear of being shamed. We can look pretty but must stay quiet. Not just Asian women either, every culture in the world celebrates the beauty of women – young women, to be more precise. There's a global multi-billion dollar industry built around it, around the belief that to remain young or at least to look young on the outside is all that matters and must be achieved at all costs.

And cost it does. Especially when your look doesn't match what the culture around you has decided is beautiful. I was never going to look like Michelle Pfeiffer or Julia Roberts, or Barbie, so believing I was beautiful was always going to be complex. But we'll get to that. Let's start with the bloody mess of getting my period.

My mum didn't have the talk with me, she didn't even take me to buy sanitary towels. She just acknowledged that it had started and that was it. Nothing more was ever really said. I hid a pair of blood-stained knickers in a drawer once, because the sneaky monthly visit can catch you unawares and, when you're a kid trying to come up with an idea of how to deal with a bloody leak, sometimes hiding them in a drawer seems like a good plan. Mum found them and got really cross with me and told me if I did it again, she'd tell my dad. What would Dad have done about it? What a weird thing to think about. My dad is a very good problem solver and could definitely figure out how to remove a stain if he wanted to, but I'm not sure this is a situation he would have wanted to be part of. So, why did Mum say it? Dad was scary when I was a kid and Mum often used him as a threat to keep Kul and me in line. This was a different scenario, however, this wasn't about him telling me off. This was the double whammy: a shovel of shame and a shovel of humiliation mixed together and shoved into my teenage face. Could it have been handled differently? Possibly. It makes me so sad to think about that day. I was scared, filled with guilt and shame, and totally confused.

But you know, it's not Mum's fault, I don't blame her – well, I don't blame her entirely. It's just history repeating itself!

No one had had the chat with my mum either, or her three sisters, nor did the sisters ever talk to each other about it. They didn't use disposable sanitary towels growing up, they used reusable homemade pads, much better for the environment (and now they are alternatives to plastic sanitary products, but back then, I imagine it all being a faff and not very practical as you've got a massive thick towel wedged between your legs). When Mum started her period, she thought she'd hurt herself and had no idea what was happening. Naniji told Mum off, got cross with her for eating too much tamarind (apparently tamarind brings on your period) and said now her period had started, she wouldn't grow any more.[4] Mum went to bed for a few days and cried and cried because she thought her growth spurt had ended.

I think back to that day, pant-gate, and I can still see the anger on my mum's face and I thought, she's angry because I'm a girl, she's angry because she has to deal with this, she's angry because shame and guilt is all she has been made to feel about being a woman and that's all she knows to pass on to me. She's angry because she has a daughter. She was possibly also angry because I'd destroyed a perfectly good pair of pants and she realised that her daughter is the sort of idiot who thinks hiding a bloodied pair of kecks in the clean underwear drawer is a good plan.

---

[4] Girls are told not to eat eggs, meat or rich food too, as it will speed up the onset of their period.

Puberty for my school friends, it seemed, was an entirely different experience to mine. From where I was standing, as a 12-year-old, they were having the one off the TV adverts, running and laughing and jumping and playing basketball and singing 'Wwwaaaa, BODYFORM, Bodyform for yooouuuuuu'. For them, entering womanhood was a badge of honour. A celebration. Girls at school were huddled around in little groups discussing the changes their bodies were going through. Most had had some kind of talk with their mothers and now they were exchanging notes – imagine that. I was already so laden with shame and disgust I couldn't even join their conversations. How is a child of 12 so aware of shame and guilt? They were far too risqué for me. I'd float around on the edge of the group catching bits of their chat. Training bras, tampons, boys they fancied, boys their mums fancied. This was all too much for my sheltered ears. I didn't want to grow up, it was already too difficult to navigate. It was hard enough being a little girl, the last thing on earth I wanted was to become a woman.

In the Asian community, everything is relative. My experience may seem Victorian to some of you but at least I didn't have God shoved in my face as well. At the Gurdwara one Sunday, where I hung out with other Punjabi kids, my friend whispered in my ear in a secret, conspiratorial way that she'd heard that if we were on our period we weren't allowed to do any Sewa. Sewa is selfless service, a fundamental tenet of the Sikh faith. It can be performed in a number of ways to help the community at large but in the Gurdwara, it's helping out in any way you can: cooking langar, the food that will feed the congregation, washing up, serving food, clearing away the tables and chairs. It was the bit I loved the best, apart from playing table tennis in the kids' room, as it made me feel useful and I loved to help out. Being a Little Miss Fidget and a kid, I hadn't quite got my head around the meditation and prayer aspect of temple yet, which involved sitting cross-legged in the prayer hall for at least two hours. Not when I could be playing with my mates downstairs and exchanging notes on period laws.

'WHAT? Not allowed to do sewa?' I'd never heard this before.

'Because we are dirty,' she continued to whisper in my ear. WHAT?

'We can sour the food.'

WHAAAAAT?

I may have been too shame-filled and shy to talk about boobies and bras with my brazen, white school friends but in the temple context, in my Indian world, where my parents were relatively liberal, this was some next level control. I could sniff out a swindle and this one stunk to the gods. 'Well, I think it's utter bakwaas.'

'I'm not going to help today, God sees everything.' My friend was worried by my rejection of the idea.

'Yeah, well, if God sees everything, She knows you're on your period and She put your period there in the first place. I don't think God's really that bothered. I'll test it out, I'm off to serve the yoghurt, that's sour anyway.'

I'd always helped out in the temple and nothing was going to stop me, plus my mum hadn't told me this piece of lore so I had a free pass. (I probably wasn't told because that would mean having to talk about puberty.)

There are so many socio-cultural taboos and myths around menstruation in the Asian community and all it achieves is an additional problem for us to have to worry about. It adds to the state of our mental health and sadly means we are not equipped with the clear knowledge about menstruation and our bodies' wonderful reproductive system as we enter womanhood. Another form of control by people who don't even have periods, so what do they feckin know about it anyway? It's bad enough that women and young girls around the world lose working hours and education through period poverty, including here in the UK, without being made to feel we are dirty and that it's some kind of curse. The female body is amazing and girls should be told this. We should feel no shame around talking about our periods just because some people find it awkward.

I had no idea about cycles or dates or period pains or changes in mood or, crucially, to always carry sanitary products with me just in case. Which meant I was often caught out and it never ended well.

Case in point. I was invited to go on a week-long camping trip in a proper caravan park in the Yorkshire Dales with Katie and her family. Finally, I was going to experience an actual family holiday. Indian families don't do holidays, or at least mine didn't. Holidays involved taking time off and spending quality time together, neither of which was high on my parents' list of priorities.

Asian family holidays involved staying with other family, usually to attend a wedding, that would last the length of an average British holiday. There is no Punjabi translation for 'overstaying your welcome'. Being a relative, or vaguely acquainted, means you can turn up and stay for as long as you like. That's right, just knock on the door and expect to be welcomed in at a minute's notice. We'd schlep off to India or America, London or Birmingham (the benefit of having a global family network) for weeks at a time. Immerse ourselves in and properly soak up another world and culture, laugh, argue, cry, cook, cook, cook, eat and come home. Now, I can see the beauty and benefits of these epic trips abroad but, back when I was 12, all I wanted to do was go on a proper (white) family camping trip to the South of France to snog Dutch boys like my mates, or at least look at Dutch boys (I was not yet thinking about snogging). My family holidays always involved tons of relatives, making it a collective experience. There was no way I was ever going to have the chance to explore on my own or experience what it was like to hang out with boys, maybe even have a holiday crush. Not with masis and masers and mammas and mamis all cramping my style.

That's why I loved staying over with my school friends. There were no relatives! It felt like going on a mini break and experiencing something completely different. I loved the normality of their lives. I loved eating their meat and two veg dinners at a table and making conversation that didn't end up in fighting. My parents loved my middle-class school friends and their lovely families and, unlike my Indian friends, I was allowed to have sleepovers. It would have been heartless to send me to a predominantly white private school and not allow me to socialise with any of my friends. But I knew loads of Asian girls whose lives were just that. School and home and nothing else. The only friends they had out of school were family. My childhood was filled with sleeping in playrooms and taking dogs called Marmaduke for walks.

Katie's caravan was pretty posh. A lot of girls at my school were quite well-to-do, you had to be to afford the school fees, so most of their stuff seemed posh to me. The caravan seemed really flashy and came with an extra attachment, an awning which became the bedroom for Katie and me, with a fold-out camp bed each, sleeping bags, tons of boiled sweets: pear drops, pineapple squares and my all-time number one chewie confectionery – my dentist's nemesis – Black Jacks. We'd also packed the all-important cassette player, so we could practise our dance routines to New Kids on the Block.

My brief but utterly devoted boyband crush was NKOTB. My Swatch watch was even set to EST, GMT-5 so me and the lads were always in the same time zone: Boston, Massachusetts. Katie and I could spend hours in our little imaginations dreaming of our future lives with them. Katie was getting married to Joey and I was joining the band in some capacity, to go on tour with them, to travel the world, sometimes get called on to join a routine. Even though Jordan Knight had many adult girlfriends, I was his favourite girl, his best friend. And yes, I loved him more than any of the other girls, but there was the slight problem that I was only 12. At 12,

I really didn't want any kind of relationship, not even in my head. I was a proud and happy late developer. I liked my life simple. I did not want boys to mess up the equation.

Talk of boyfriends and relationships was also such a taboo in my house. Even as a joke, boys were no laughing matter. But my parents didn't need to worry about me, not yet anyway. I didn't want to grow up. I liked being a kid. I had no desire to wear Mum's high heels or lipsticks, I didn't want to look older than I was, not until later, when my motivation was solely to buy alcohol from the offy without getting ID-ed! I didn't want to draw attention to myself, I didn't want male attention. I found being a little girl so difficult and unfair at times that I often wished I was a boy.

Katie and I made friends with other kids on that holiday, and I experienced my first camping shower: put 50p into the slot for hot water and you'd better wash quick before the money runs out. Obviously with hair down to my bum, 50p's worth of water ain't going to suffice. I had head full of shampoo and had to scream for Katie to put more money in. I popped my head out to show her and we both found this very funny. I liked making Katie laugh, I liked making people laugh, usually by doing something silly.[5]

_____

[5] Once, at a ninth birthday party, we were all given half rubber balls that you turn inside out, place on a flat surface and they then slowly unfold until they ping into the air. I decided to sucker the rubber thing to the middle of my forehead, which everyone found hilarious, so I left it there, like a proper wally. Half an hour later, I prised it off and had an oval-shaped bruise left in the middle of my forehead that didn't go for a week. Idiot.

The best part of the campsite was the outdoor swimming pool and we couldn't wait to get in there. I'd packed my swimming costume and I was ready for my classic British holiday. But my body had other plans, period plans – big bloody, you're 12 years old on holiday with a friend and you are going to have your second ever period, plans. I hadn't even talked about periods with Katie – she hadn't started hers yet and here I was, totally not prepared and too shy to tell anyone.

What the hell was I going to do? First, deal with my dignity and the soggy issue in my pants. I needed to improvise and fast, so toilet roll it was, wrapped around my hand a few thousand times – that was my solution for the rest of the week. Rolls and rolls of campsite toilet roll, the cheapest, scratchiest bog roll you can get. All the kids were in the pool, splashing and laughing and having fun. I feigned illness. Katie's mum kept asking what the matter was but I just said I wasn't feeling well and was happy to sit on the sun lounger, fully clothed, watching the other kids play. Katie's mum was lovely and God knows what she thought, maybe that it was against my religion to swim! It probably is against it if you're on your period . . . The strange little Indian girl who won't wear a swimsuit! I still couldn't bring myself to just say I was having my period. I was cripplingly embarrassed, so the secret has stayed with me until now. I went home with a terrible case of cystitis and a tan. Both of which were a problem. Thank God I didn't have to worry about shaving my legs as well. That fun was just around the corner.

* * *

My period was just the beginning of my bodily changes, but at least no one could see it happening. The other nightmare I had to deal with was hair. More specifically, hair removal.

There's no way I can have a chapter about puberty (still feels awkward saying it) without talking about hair. For most girls on the planet, becoming a teenager means having to deal with periods, growing boobs, the odd zit or possibly the hell of acne. Asian girls also have to contend with getting a full-grown moustache. A black-hair line of soft fuzz on your upper lip. Like Clark Gable, Freddie Mercury, Tom Selleck, Borat. Not a good look on a 14-year-old girl. Come on, you all remember the Asian girl at school with her hair scraped back into a long plait and the moustache. You might have even taken the piss out of her, or secretly fancied her?

Light brown skin and jet-black hair, all over your body. And so much of the sodding stuff. It's always been there, but before it was just a cute downy dusting of fluff all over your soft baby body. Now you've become a teenager, your hormones are raging and the hair has mutated into a coarse, thick, stubborn mat. It's your worst enemy, living on your body. And it all coincides at the same point you begin to notice boys and all they can see is your moustache. Maybe this is why some Punjabi parents don't let their daughters remove the hair from their bodies for years – they see it as a natural male repulsion method. It's the ultimate cruelty! Give your daughters a break. It's tough enough being the brown kid who doesn't fit in, without also being the yeti in the corner of the room.

This is where my mum flourished as the liberal, progressive, open-minded mum she prides herself on being, because hair is Mum's specialist subject and she has a lifetime's worth of wisdom to impart and impose on her beast of a daughter. This is Beauty. And NOTHING matters more than beauty, remember? Beauty is a must, it's what you will be judged on forever. This is Beauty with an Indian mumma twist – the first thing I was handed was a box of Jolen face bleach. Yes, you read that right, bleach. This stuff lightens the hair on your face so it's no longer black but, depending on how long you leave it on your face, it develops into red, light brown or blonde and, in theory, blends in to match your skin tone. The night before weddings, it's a ritual for all girls to mix up a giant batch and cover their faces in the thick white cream, eyes streaming from the hydrogen peroxide. Before I learned to do it myself, my mum would slather on tons of the stuff so my hairline would also go light brown.

Face bleach is the most straightforward method of disappearing unwanted dark hair. There are so many other ways of hair removal and I've tried them all. Bleach, wax, shave, pluck, tweeze, singe, sugar, thread, electric shocks to the core of each facial hair follicle, rolling metal cups up and down my arms. Every technique painfully attempted with varying degrees of success. And it takes years. Years of pain, misery and humiliation before you get on top of it, before we become masters of depilatory and disguise and, by that point, in your forties, your hair has started to fade away naturally, all apart from the odd stubborn one on your chin. In my case, the invention of laser technology and spending a small fortune changed my life and the smoothness of my legs forever. But that came later, much later, when I was living my best life in London.

I'm currently still a clueless, hairy mess in Bradford, now studying for her A-levels and about to go on a week-long cottage break in North Yorkshire with a load of friends. My crew of misfits from school and an equally oddball bunch of boys from the boys' school. It took me and my closest girl mates longer than the rest of our year, but we found a gang of lads, equally nerdy, (they'd never admit to the nerdy bit) to hang out with. My parents knew them, liked them and, most importantly, trusted them, so they didn't have an issue with us all heading off for a break together. I was well aware that my social life was completely different from a lot of my Asian girl mates – I had one, for starters. This was partly to do with my parents being more liberal and open-minded than other, more strict, Asian parents and partly because I was allowed to do what my white friends did . . . to a point. Plus, they trusted me.

I loved my little collection of girl friends at school. We called ourselves 'the freaks': Jo, Rob, Al and Rach. A self-excluding, creative bunch of independent thinkers who enjoyed being on the outside looking in. None of us fancied conforming at school, we didn't know how. Our fashion sense was free and wild and definitely not the uniform clothes everyone else seemed to wear, or what one might be described as 'fashion-able'. This lot, my lot, were one-offs. We bonded over our love of music and Keanu Reeves and watching *Bottom*. We could spend hours trying to do Ade Edmondson impressions and quoting lines from *My Own Private Idaho*. My friends were The Good Girls. Kind and thoughtful, productive, whip-smart and clever, proud to be clever. They didn't judge me or make me feel different.

Mum booked me in for a leg wax a week before the trip, at Aunty Bubbly's Beauty Parlour. Aunty Bubbly had a beautician's shop but I'm not sure she had the required beauty qualification. She loved nothing more than invit-ing Mum over on a Friday afternoon to sit in the back room of her little shop and crack open a bottle of red. Dad had been called in, on a couple of occasions, to collect my slightly worse-for-wear mother. Mum never drank as a young 'un, she started later in life, just on the odd occa-sion, but she's not equipped with the 'handling of drink' gene, nor the 'remember it's not fruit juice' gene. Her style is: back it, giggle, puke, sleep. The puke has been in plant pots at garden parties, at a fancy dinner in Dublin and once in the back of Dad's car. We all find this very funny and kinda sweet. I've got no room to judge. Like mother like daughter, I've been there a few times.

Picture this, please, my leg wax has begun: wax pasted on, try to rip, gets stuck halfway. Several attempts later, skin is getting tugged harder and harder. Not all the hair is removed so the process must be repeated, skin is red raw. This. Is. Torture. Just when I think it can't get any worse, Bubbly Aunty suggests I should get my bikini line done while I'm there. Mum thinks this is a great idea. I'm still trying not to focus on the stinging sensation on my legs and before I can throw myself off the torture bed to escape, Bubbly Aunty is coming at me with a wooden spatula dripping in hot wax.

On it goes. I'm nervous as hell. I've never had a bikini wax before, I'm not sure Bubbly Aunty has ever done a bikini wax before and to make matters worse, I think she'd already begun her afternoon wine party. Next comes the strip of material, smoothed down over the wax, which should be swiftly ripped off, taking the hair away from the follicle and leaving smooth skin behind. Only Bubbly Aunty tugs the wax strip hard and not fast so nothing happens, apart from the most excruciating pain I've ever experienced. The wax strip is stuck to my pubic hair. A few more failed tugs, now I'm screaming. Mum and Bubbly Aunty take a break to think of what to do. Maybe another sip of red while they're there. They come back with scissors. It's a nightmare. They manage to cut off the strip and leave a ton of wax behind. 'Should I even it out and try the other side?' NOOOOOOO. At least my legs are smooth and ready for my holiday. Even if I'm walking with a limp.

The cottage was in the middle of nowhere in stunning North Yorkshire and properly rustic, a mile away from the nearest pub (Tan Yarn, also the highest pub in the country). Behind us was a valley and across the road in front of us was a very inviting hill. We cooked a giant Indian feast, chicken curry, aloo gobi for the veggies. All my girl mates and I had been veggie for years after discovering Meat Is Murder by The Smiths. We were a resourceful bunch at 17. We'd bought all the ingredients we needed to cook and together we made pilau rice with cumin and peas and we even made chapattis. The Fugees' classic album, *The Score*, was on repeat, the weather was sunny and spectacular. We crammed around the dining table to eat our feast, all ten of us. A couple of the girls – the ones who got most of the male attention – started a food fight by chucking peas around. This annoyed those of us who didn't get the same male attention because we didn't have time for it and didn't really know how to play the subtle, confusing and ridiculous game of 'be a little bit stupid around the boys and they'll like you'. My mates were the hyper-bright, nerdy girls and trying to impress teenage boys just wasn't a game they were capable of. It's heartbreaking and humiliating, if fluttering your eyelashes at the lads doesn't come naturally. It makes me sick to my stomach thinking about it. I opted out early and decided being one of the lads was preferable to being fancied by them.

The only way to get everyone on the same page was a post-dinner drinking game. What British teenagers learn to do as a rite of passage to lose their inhibitions! What is it with teenagers and shots? Out came the sambuca. Error number 1. Teenagers and sambuca, *anyone* and sambuca, is never going to end well. I make my friends laugh and I love it when they laugh. Another shot, followed by another. And then the inevitable: the aloo gobi and pilau rice want to pro-jectile right back out of the gullet they went down. I had to bust open the old wooden toilet door, while Robyn was still on the toilet, to throw up. I was put to bed. I woke up super early, still pissed, and saw that a few of the hardcore fun bunch still hadn't gone to bed and were crossing the road to climb the hill. I grabbed a jumper and ran out to join them.

'Ahh, Anita, you stink of sick!' they all laughed and so did I. The sun was beginning to rise and we couldn't stop laughing. Up we climbed, stumbling, giggling, free and drunk, and luckily I'd thrown up and slept it off a bit so I felt invincible. It was like a scene from a movie! We got to the top of the hill in time to watch the sunrise, The Fugees still ringing in our ears. This was teenage bliss. Awkward, hungover, sicky-smelling, teenage bliss. Watching the sunrise is when I always feel at my most peaceful. 'Let's take a picnic down to the river and have a swim today,' someone suggested . . .

Thanks for this sweet little detour, Anita, but what on earth has any of this got to do with hair?

It had been just over a week since the Bubbly Aunty torture session and my leg hairs had started to grow back, just under the skin. The sane and safe thing to have done would be to have left my legs alone or exfoliate them to help the hairs grow through the epidermis. What came next was a major mistake and a scene from a slasher movie. The last thing on earth to do in this situation is to take a razor to your legs. Which is, of course, precisely what I decided to do. And I butchered them. The skin came off along with the hairs and I had blood running down both legs. I was distraught at the massacre-like scene. First came the shock and panic at the pain and blood, followed by that sinking feeling, that once again, I'd be fully clothed not having fun. Another holiday ruined by blood. Everyone else went swimming in the river on that beautiful hot day. I sat on the side preparing the picnic, too embarrassed to tell them why I couldn't swim. Because being an Asian girl means something as simple as going for a swim is never that simple.

My blonde friends were all laughing with carefree abandon, their hair barely visible. They didn't even have to bother with shaving because slightly hairy blonde thighs are delightful. I wish I could go back and say to myself: GET OUT THERE WITH YOUR FRIENDS! YOU ARE NOT BOTHERED ABOUT THE BOYS ANYWAY.

Back to beauty, because some hair for Indian women is essential to beauty – the stuff that sprouts from your scalp. Long, flowing, luscious locks all the way down your back, moving like waves and glistening in the sun. I couldn't wait to chop mine off, but cutting my hair was a big no. My long hair was lovely, shiny, silky and down to my bum. And I hated it. When I had it, it was usually scraped back off my face and pulled into a thick, tight plait. Until I was 18! It was hardly ever worn long and flowing, only at weddings and parties, and even that wasn't straightforward. At 16, I was approached by an 'uncle', someone I'd known my entire life, who felt the need to compliment me on my beautiful long hair. He told me what a fine young woman I'd grown into, what a wonderful girlfriend I could make for someone. Such a skin-crawlingly strange comment and totally inappropriate. I always knew he was dodgy; I couldn't wait to chop my hair off after that.

I wouldn't have minded it so much if I was allowed to trim it straight, so I was determined to do a bit of secret cutting in the bathroom. To see the bottom of my hair in the mirrored bathroom cabinet, I had to stand on the toilet. Of course, looking over your shoulder into a mirror to try and cut your own hair is never going to be straightforward, or straight, for that matter. I'd taken to secretly trimming away at the ends from time to time but, on one particular day, after the gross pervert 'uncle' incident, I decided to really go for it and the scissors travelled from my bum to halfway up my back and *slice*. I cut. Down it fell. At least five inches of my hair lying on the bathroom floor. I knew I was going to be in trouble. I panicked and decided the best thing would be to cut less on the other side. Down fell about two inches. Now I'd done it. I was going to be in so much trouble plus what was supposed to be a straight line was a little off . . . by about four inches. It was about four different lengths. I went down sheepishly to show Mum and Dad. Mum gave me a big thwack on my back: 'What have you done?!'

They were fuming. I was sent to bed and my punishment was that I had to keep it at different lengths, my mum wasn't going to even it out for me. Thankfully, someone at school did it for me but I was so frustrated by my stupid long hair. I felt it was keeping me from truly being me. Mum made a pact with me. As soon as I finished my A-Levels, I was allowed to cut it.

Guess where I went the afternoon of my last A-Level exam? Straight down to Toni & Guy in Bradford city centre. I felt like Rachel Greene from *friends*.

* * *

The secret code of silence around puberty in my family was so effective, so deep-rooted, so entrenched in 'we do things this way', that we didn't even think to question it – we were too scared. Scared of what, though? What dawns on me now is that none of us were even aware of what the repercussions would be if we were to break the silence. Even writing this now, in my flippin' forties, I'm wracking my brain to understand what would have happened if I'd talked about any of it to someone – other girls, other women. If I'd somehow managed to fight the stigma and openly discussed or maybe even asked a question about what was happening to me. I can't, for the life of me, think what anyone else would have done.

That is an incredible thing to think about. There's a hold over you, silencing you, shaming you, when you are a girl. The consequences aren't even known or tangible, but they are so sinister and ingrained that it keeps you in submission for life. FACK ME! The only thing that comes to mind is judgement. That if I were the sort of girl who talked openly about puberty and womanly things, if I made public the details of what 50 per cent of the planet go through, I'd be judged as a wrong 'un. A wicked, evil, dirty woman or worse, the sort of woman to lead other women astray. A troublemaker, a bad girl, a bad influence with loose morals, too free, a homewrecker, a witch, too independent, a churail, no respect, too gori, too Westernised, lost her culture, a coconut. Chi chi chi. Bringing such shame.

How have we allowed this to happen when it's half of the planet who go through it (and, may I point out the obvious, the most important half of the planet) if the survival of our race is your thing? Holy saturated sanitary towels, Batman – somebody has done a right number on us.

I can't protect little me anymore, but I can certainly arm any of you out there, if you need the armour. Let's talk!

Love Your Skin Colour and Your Nose

Tanning. A simple, natural process, whereby the sun reacts with human skin, making it darker. Melanin is the natural pigment produced in our bodies; it absorbs UV radiation and protects our skin from more UV by making it darker. Nature is perfect. It's a wonder.

In the 300,000 years of human evolution, the human body has sussed out a huge amount. The body and mind are both remarkable: giving birth, mind-blowing; if a nail drops off, it regrows, bonkers; broken bones can heal, people learn to walk again after breaking their backs, incredible; space and ocean exploration, great feats of engineering; those nutters who run ultra-marathons in the Sahara Desert, mad; the dudes who sit for years in meditation, growing beards and gnarly nails, brilliant – and, to top it all off, the skin tans to protect itself.

Yet, Asians, people who are from the Indian subcontinent – a hot land, where the sun beats down and kisses the earth and everything on it – have a major problem with tanning. I'm looking at you, **colourism**, I'm staring you down and I'm taking you down, because I've had enough.

'You wanting to be light-skinned is just like us wanting to be tanned.' No, it's nothing like that. This is far more sinister. Colourism is an insidious prejudice that begins when you're born. 'Baby is so fair', 'Baby is dark'. Already, on day one of it breathing freely, out of its mother's womb, someone – grandparents, aunty, uncle, father, mother, a passing stranger – has already made it aware of the shade of its skin. If it's fair, it will be told how beautiful it is. If it's dark, a sympathy smile. Welcome to the world. Congratulations, you've already been judged. And to top it off, you're hairy too. This corker of an issue affects both boys and girls but, of course, for women the implications are far greater. The biggest issue being marriageability. Fair-skinned girls, now they get the best price, but who will want a dark-skinned girl? A fair-skinned wife is a sign that a husband is doing well, well enough to get a bride with pale, pale skin. She's prided and paraded by the mother-in-law because her skin shows wealth, that this family have the capacity to find a creamy daughter-in-law.

What kind of damage is being done to our self-esteem and psychology when we can't even tolerate our natural skin tone? A preference for fair skin and aligning lightness with power has always existed in India, but it was perpetuated by colonialism. We were colonised by the white man, who came and took from our land to build his own – doesn't matter how many railway sleepers they laid down (and technically, they didn't do any of the laying, it was Indians who did the graft), no matter how forcefully they came, how much they took and how callously they left, we still believe that, on some level, just because of the shade of the coloniser's skin, they are superior. Come on, team, let's get real here! They were not in India doing us any favours. Now, I'm not sure anyone really remembers why there's a preference for light skin, where the prejudice has its origins. There just is.

Skin shade is relative because no matter what the general pigment of your people, this view holds true. For South Asians, class, caste and colour all intersect, which leaves dark-skinned, poor, low-caste women in an extremely vulnerable position. I'd like to say that those who moved abroad left these archaic and damaging thoughts behind but, sadly, colourism is alive and thriving amongst South Asians in the UK. It's not helped by Bollywood. In India, Bollywood stars, who all tend to be light-skinned, are paid fortunes to advertise skin lightening products. These products are seriously problematic and the idiots who take money to advertise them are part of the problem.

India is a land of many layers but it's highly prejudiced and discriminatory towards people who are poor, people who belong to lower castes and now, worryingly, people who aren't Hindu. If you're poor and spend a lot of time outdoors in the blistering Indian sun, you're going to be a few shades darker than those stepping from air-conditioned cars into air-conditioned buildings. To top it all off, people who have the most influence over the masses in India are fuelling the prejudice and lining their own pockets. They are not just preying on insecurities, they are creating insecurities to sell those products. I doubt any of the products actually do what they say on the tin, which is good, but also means the entire thing is a scam. The people being pushed to buy the creams are the brown, everyday working-class folk of India, who will never attain the insanely glamorous lives of their idols. They are all various shades of beautiful brown.

The first time I went to India, I was two years old. I spent a lot of time playing outdoors, in the dusty red earth of my grandmother's house in the village in Punjab. 'Teri kuri kali hogeyi,' my great grandmother shouted to my mum, as I was happily playing with a stray dog's puppies, 'Your daughter has gone black.' There is no word for tanned, there is no word for getting dark, the word used is black. My little brown body had tanned, naturally, so much so that both my cheeks had burned and cracked. I was yanked indoors and Vaseline was slathered all over me. From that day on, I've always been warned about the sun.

'Thupe na baeeth' *Don't sit in the sun.*

'Pith karke baeeth' *Sit with your back to the sun.*

Your 'rang' should be 'saaf': your 'colour' should be 'clean'.

This prejudice needs to be acknowledged, confronted and we really need to address it. There may be many reasons for colourism, such as successive conquerors in India being fair-skinned, both the Mughals and the Brits. Implying that darkness is bad is another prejudice perpetuated in the stories of my childhood. Even in temples, the goodies, gods and goddess are always fair-skinned and the baddies or the demons are always dark.

Weddings are where colourism really shows its ugliness in all its judgemental glory. The aunty network or as I call them, the illuminaunty, love to compare notes on shades of brown, especially at weddings. The illuminaunty don't do subtlety, they don't do politically correct.

'Girl is pretty but so dark-skinned.'

'Look at that boy, so fair, he looks like a prince.'

'Who will marry her with that complexion?'

'She will look so dark in all the wedding pictures, not like a radiant bride.'

'Her skin is so fair, you can see the Coca-Cola going down her throat.'

There's so much pressure on brides to look at their most translucent. I've seen absolutely shocking make-up, foundation seven shades lighter than the person's skin, being applied to create ashen-faced monsters, walking to their doom. Back in the eighties and nineties, when there were hardly any foundations to match Asian skin tones, options were thin anyway, so people would pick light shades which would make lovely brown skin turn a sallow grey. I've met a few make-up artists in my time who've had problems trying to match my shade, too.

Colourism doesn't just exist in the South Asian community, it's a huge problem in all of the non-white world. The skin-bleaching industry globally is worth well over three billion pounds. When I made a documentary exploring the issue for BBC1 a few years ago in 2009, Japan was the country which spent the most on skin-lightening products. Now, according to the World Health Organization, 77 per cent of women in Nigeria use skin-lightening products. Another multi-billion dollar industry created around our insecurities and the perpetuation of an insidious myth, that light skin is the most beautiful.

Bollywood movies have perpetuated this beauty myth and I believe it's now worse than ever. The actresses of my childhood were dusky, brown-skinned beauties, with big almond eyes, Indian noses and full Indian hips and a slightly plump physique – a sign of being well fed and wealthy. (Look up Rekha, Sridevi and Hema Malini when they were young.) Now the beauty ideal has changed and a lot of actresses could pass for white European, and some of them are. The look is fair skin, small Western nose, big boobs and no hips. It's not uncommon for actresses to get plastic surgery to attain the Disney Princess look. Add to that never ever seeing anyone other than white faces in the cultural landscape growing up, our self-worth was and still is taking a battering.

My nose has always been a bone, or rather cartilage, of contention with myself. I've always hated it. It's from my dad's side, it's Granny's nose. All my aunts and uncles have it, as does my brother. Our strong Roman profile. We'd sit and giggle about the family nose when we'd get together but, on my own, when I'd look in the mirror, I'd hate what I saw. This wasn't helped by often waking up in excruciating pain as my mother would try and mould my nose in my sleep. Always trying to mould me. Mum said she was shaping it so it didn't look like a pakora! (A pakora is a deep-fried ball of potato and onion – an onion bhaji, that's what my nose was being compared to, by my own mum!)

It's no surprise that I very nearly had a nose job on a few occasions and I was even offered one for free by a plastic surgeon I was interviewing in LA if I'd appear on his TV show, Dr. *90210*. He said he could fix my 'Indian nose'. I discussed it with my agent at the time, who told me it was a bad idea and that I'd be 'too pretty'. My nose adds character to my face. Too pretty? Is there such a thing? At 25, I didn't give a crap about character, I wanted to feel 'too pretty'. It seemed to me that it was the small-nosed pretty girls who were getting all the work. Pretty and white, or just white. Anyway, as is obvious, I didn't go through with it, mainly because it was for his show and would be there for people to watch forever, plus I hate the idea of surgery. Every time I think about getting it done, and it is a reoccurring desire in my life, it always happens when my self-esteem is at rock bottom. Funny that. Plus, what message would I be sending to young South Asian women with strong noses? We need to reclaim the aquiline aesthetic. Us big-nosed beauties need to step out there with our heads held high and our noses even higher. Take a deep inhalation through both nostrils and as you exhale, say to yourself, my nose is magnificent.

It doesn't just stop at skin colour or the line of your nose. In South Korea, a country that has more plastic surgery per capita than any other country, double-eyelid surgery is very popular. To give the eyes a more rounded, Western look. How has this happened? Who is setting the Eurocentric beauty agenda for us to aspire to, this cultural colonialism? Is it advertising? Magazines? Television? Is it the luxury brands that have historically only used Western women to model their clothes? Is it Hollywood movies?

Why are we being told to hate what we see in the mirror?

Can we mix it up, please? I'd like to see a broader representation in movies and in my magazines. Women of all shades, the darker the better. And while you are changing up who you cast, how about women who have depth and strength of character and something to say, not just eye candy to make the male lead look more interesting? How about we start by at least having women a similar age to the male lead? Tom Cruise will be in his eighties, no doubt still doing his own stunts, and his female love interest will still be in her twenties. And bigger woman please, women who look like they eat food. And maybe a few hairy women, too. Yes, more big-nosed, hairy women.

* * *

At 15, I put on a bit of weight. Up until then, I'd always been super active. A Little Miss Fidget, who loved to play games and sports. I was lucky I had natural hand-eye coordination and decent balance, so I'd get picked for most sports teams at school and, if I lacked the natural talent for something, my enthusiasm would fill the gap. I was not fast at all, but if a team was ever a woman down to run, up I'd step. I'd always come last in the race but I was always happy to volunteer. At 15, things changed. I lost my hockey boots (first excuse) and I'd started working at my local radio station and became more interested in drama, so my activity levels dropped off. I'd grown as much as I was going to, nothing to do with my tamarind consumption, but I was still eating with the abandon and carefree spirit of someone who has never worried about weight, at least three–four rotis a night. Actively encouraged by my Punjabi culture, which revolves around food and doesn't really have set meal times. Eat when you're hungry! There is a Punjabi phrase about roti, 'you don't count them', just keep making them until the people you're feeding have to roll themselves off their chairs.

So, naturally, becoming more sedentary and eating all my mum's lovely food, I got plumper. It was noticed. Noticed by my PE teacher. 'Come on laydeez!', she'd scream, in her long, lined, warm tracksuit bottoms and cosy fleecy hoodie, with us in our athletics knickers! Oh, the humiliation. 'Girls at your age should not have little bellies, I see little bellies.' I knew she was talking about me. It was also pointed out by one of my straight-talking friends: 'You're getting fat.' She told me straight and I respected it because I knew she was right. I hated my body and I'd never seen it like this before. I started to exercise. Every single day, I'd come home from school and start a workout. I'd step on and off the bottom step of the staircase 100 times to warm up, then head into my room to continue the manic sweat session. I'd just move as fast as I could. I was already used to dancing around in my bedroom, so this was just ramping it up to include squats, knee raises and side-stepping – basically whatever I could do in my tiny box bedroom surrounded by all my stuff. It worked. The weight fell off.

Now, let's put this into perspective. I wasn't fat. I've never been fat but for some reason the seed was sown. The seed of body insecurity. That grows as you do, so every time you look in the mirror, you think you need to shape up. There is nothing wrong with exercise and keeping fit. I'm one of those annoying people who loves to exercise. I'm a huge advocate of keeping our bodies moving as long as we can, as long as we're alive. It's vital for life. Energy and vitality and mental health can all be improved with a few squats and a jog around the block. It also means you can eat that wedge of carrot cake when you fancy. But I was never fat. It just wasn't true. Fat was all I could see, however.

As the grown woman that I am, I'd love to tell you I've dealt with all of these issues, but childhood insecurities are a pain to get rid of, not helped by constantly being reminded of my perceived inadequacies by the world around me. They don't just magically disappear. On top of that, I have a new dose of grown-up issues I'm lumbered with. My insecurities still exist, not quite the crippling, nauseating, debilitating insecurities of a teenager. They do ease up the older you get, you'll be relieved to know! I've definitely grown into the way I look and finally I'm unapologetic about my ethnicity. I've even found the power to write them down, in the hope that it will also help me beat them down. But, at 40, you start to worry about other stuff, like aging and making the most of your time and running out of time and your position in the workplace and white supremacy and the patriarchy and your relationships and whether you'll ever achieve your full potential and how to navigate your next 40/50 years before you drop dead . . . Just the massive existential stuff. No longer just worrying about how to get rid of a bit of belly. Although, that is still a worry.

I'm much less nervous about the way I look, but I've yet to have a proper beach holiday where I confidently prance around in a bikini (or even just walk in one). Sadly, I'm not comfortable in my body and I worry that I'll have spent a lifetime worrying about it and then get to 90 and wish to God I'd embraced it, loved it and owned it. Felt body beautiful. I also like to think 90-year-old me will be the wildest, carefree version of me ever, where I can do whatever the hell I want, like hang gliding in just a pair of heels or something.

Is everyone walking around feeling a little bit self-conscious? How many of us are walking around in bodies we don't particularly like? A remarkable body, with a beautiful beating heart and oxygen pumping round it, which means we can wake up and enjoy another day on planet Earth. We all need to start to find a bit of compassion for ourselves and dial down the negative monologue. And be grateful for what we have, just as we are. Keep the big important issues that we really do need to tackle but being fat, getting old, our skin tone, these are all just distractions. We are so fixated with that stuff, we are missing out on enjoying life, magnificent life. Let's all look in the mirror and love what we see, including all the flaws. I want to love all my dodgy bits, my mistakes, my fuck-ups and flaws. I want to see it all and think it's great!

So, that's the plan. To love it all, the bulges, rogue hairs, the tan, the lines, the wrinkles. Just learn to accept myself as I am. I'm still working on being the best version of me, I haven't suddenly decided I'm cured from insecurities now that I'm 40. I'm trying to be kind to myself, to really try and give myself a break once in a while. I'm trying to dismantle some of the nonsense that was imposed on my childhood brain, stop the constant pressure from an internal dialogue that constantly tells me I'm not good enough. My nose doesn't resemble a pakora and, even if it does from certain angles, who doesn't love a pakora?!

I'm learning to like, no, love, who I am. It's a good place to start, the most important place. I realised it's all been such a waste. What a waste of time. So, work with me. Own it. Step out into the sun, not with your back to it, but with head raised, arms stretched. Own it all. All your glory. You.

Yorkshire Will Always Take Your Breath Away

She. Is. Beautiful. My God, she's a stunner.

Breathtakingly beautiful. A timeless beauty. A beauty that inspires. A beauty that commands respect. A beauty so overwhelming it can make you fearful. A beauty that's both welcoming and terrifying. A wise, ancient beauty. The finest beauty, because she is so old, because she knows so much. Because she is tender and delicate and needs our care, because she is stronger than you and I and will be here radiating her beauty long after we are gone. Beauty so magnificent it touches your soul. A beauty that makes you weep. A beauty that will receive you with open arms.

She's always there, waiting for you. She's kissed by every season. Colours resplendent, not flashy or gaudy, painted by a master, the original priceless masterpiece. Golden, brown, grey, blue and more purple than you've ever seen anywhere else in nature. She adapts to her needs. She makes me ache with longing. She makes me weep with desire. I yearn to see her when I'm sad, to feel her consoling embrace. She always understands me, soothes my pain.

My deepest secrets and fears are hers, she keeps them safe. She never judges.

She knows everything about you, but you'll never know her secrets, her depths. You'll never truly know her and you will respect that because you love her unconditionally. She is greater than you or I. Her anger is a storm that will batter you into submission. She can test your love, your loyalty, definitely your patience, and push you to your limits. She can make you feel fear as quickly as she'll make you feel safe, capricious by nature. She commands our respect.

God, I miss her. I have to tell everyone I meet about her, desperate to share her wonder with the people I love. Don't just take my word for it. Meet her, experience her, she has love in abundance for us all.

My Yorkshire. Mi Yarkshar.

Like everyone else born in God's own county, I carry a pride in my heart for the place of my birth. I may have a multitude of other identities but cut me and I bleed Yorkshire. Too dramatic? Not dramatic enough, I say! Knock on any door in Bradford, doesn't matter what ethnic background, what religion or how much money they have in the bank, ask them where they're from and they'll tell you straight: 'Bratfud, innit?'

Places stay within us. Even though I'm not there, living just off the M62, Yorkshire has seeped into me for life. It has taken up home in my heart. Yorkshire penetrated my soul and I can't get it out. I'm permanently stained and scented by Yorkshire. We are so indoctrinated and spellbound by it from birth that jokes are still made about Lancastrians and being from 'the right side of the Pennines', even though the Wars of the Roses ended well over 500 years ago.[6]

Even when someone posted worms through our letterbox when I was 12. I opened the envelope very confused and Mum just threw it away and we never spoke about it again. Even when I stared at the National Front graffiti at my local bus stop every day when I was a tot, even when I was asked funny questions about my 'Indian' life and people shouted 'Paki' across the street at me. Even then. Yorkshire is different, Yorkshire is mine. No one can take that away from me. They can try, but I won't let them get anywhere near it.

What is it that makes Yorkshire folk so annoyingly loyal and what is their identity made up of that makes them so proud? The language, food, history, sense of humour, architecture, the accent, water, sense of humour, good working-class folk, the white working classes and the working-class migrants, and most importantly, the breathtaking ancient landscape. Oh, and did I mention the sense of humour? Pie and peas, fish and chips, baps and bread cakes, parkin, Yorkshire pudding, curry. Is it the soil? Soil so fine it produces the best rhubarb in the world, in the rhubarb triangle of West Yorkshire. Eating raw rhubarb nicked out of someone's garden is a sheer delight. The more face-screwingly sour, the better! There's definitely something in the water, the finest tap water in the land. It's so good, I'd fill bottles of the stuff from my mum and dad's tap to bring back south. It's nectar.

---

[6] This chapter comes with a health warning for Lancastrians: I'm about to bang on about Yorkshire for quite a bit.

I see my London media life now and how ridiculous it all is through my Yorkshire eyes. I worry I've changed, become one of those types who left 20 years ago and now loves my adopted home of the big city. I ponce around buying expensive sourdough bread. 'Over three quid for a loaf of bread? Av ya gone mad?' said Dad when I took him to my local Sunday farmers' market. Yorkshire folk don't spend unnecessarily. My friends now include east London clichés and I love them – I'm one of them! Bankrupting themselves on natural organic wine, debating coffee filtration, the latest cheese to be grown in an actual sewer for added flavour or something. But my Yorkshire eyes see it all and take it with a massive shovel of salt. I now live in an area where children and dogs are given the names Milo and Fifi! I also live in an area where, a stone's throw away, children are still on free school meals and there are people sleeping rough. I always get asked 'What d'ya go and do that for?' about moving to London when I'm in the North. They might not like the answer, but it's true: London is the greatest city on earth and I love my cosmopolitan adopted home, I think of myself as a Londoner in many ways. I love that there are people from all over the world who live there. I hear a multitude of languages and accents – Turkish, Jamaican patois, Vietnamese, French, Polish, Punjabi, Somali, Estuary, Cockney and Yorkshire – all in my local nail salon. But London is great at telling everyone it's great. It's in constant competition with other flash gits like New York, Paris, Berlin, Beijing. It needs to boast and flex its pecs to the globe.

Yorkshire doesn't have to prove a pig's shit to anyone. Yorkshire is too down-to-earth for that. She'd never really boast. She doesn't need to. If you know, you know, and if you don't know, you will, once you experience her. She's warm and welcoming. She doesn't judge you if you come as your true self, she demands that: no bullshit here, please, just you. And if you do carry an air of pretence, she'll soon batter it out of you with her disarming sense of humour. She'll look at you, listen with a deadpan stare and cut you down to size if you sound like a dickhead. Like the goat farmer I met filming once, whose opening line on first meeting me was, 'Anita, wha were that coat you were wearing on *Countryfile* last week? So blooming big on ya, looked like it were ya dad's.' I thought it was cool. That's me told.

She'll treat you, or rather, 'tret ya', like you're a member of her family. She's cultured and talented and has produced some of the finest talent in the land: the Brontës, Nicola Adams, Tasmin Archer, Nadeem Ahmed, Barbara Castle, Jessica Ennis-Hill, Dynamo, Helen Sharman, Effie Bancroft, Zayn Malik, Nina Hossain, Jodie Whittaker, Mel B, Matthew Krishanu, Dame Judi Dench, Dame Barbara Hepworth, Govinder Nazran, Andrea Dunbar . . . It goes on. Can you tell I'm a bit proud? I'm spellbound by the landscape, the drystone walls, the rolling Dales, the windswept moors, purple heather carpet. Even if they've never set foot in the Yorkshire countryside, town folk are stained by the faded grandeur of Bradford city centre, a city that was once the centre of the universe.

We'd make the pilgrimage to York whenever we had people come to stay or when we fancied a day trip. Pretty much every weekend of my entire childhood we were bundled into the boot of Dad's Rover hatchback, heading out on adventures across Yorkshire. York, the Dales, Malham, Skipton, Harrogate, Ripon, Flamborough Head, Scarborough, Whitby. Dad's a Yorkshireman so his love for the land is never in question. Mum is a migrant to Yorkshire but, like a convert to anything, she's devout and loyal. Mum lurves Yorkshire and she lurves nothing more than to show Yorkshire off: 'Wait until you come to visit WHERE I LIVE. We have BEAUTIFUL scenery, beautiful hills.'

So keen were my parents to show off their Yorkshire, they'd pick up waifs, strays and total strangers to take on weekend jaunts throughout my childhood too. Like the family who approached Dad in Bradford city centre to ask where they could get the best Indian curry. They were originally from Suriname but lived in Holland. Suriname is a former Dutch Colony in South America. In the 19th century the Dutch did a deal with the Brits for indentured labourers from India after the abolition of slavery. So much for the abolition. As a consequence, Hindus now make up around 20 per cent of the population. More of that massive British history that no one talks about – just how many Indians were moved around the globe for work and now cannot trace their ancestry. How about we start telling some of this history in schools? From 1834 to the end of the World War I, Britain had transported about two million Indian indentured workers to 19 colonies, including the West Indies, Fiji, Mauritius, Sri Lanka (then known as Ceylon), Trinidad, Guyana, Malaysia, Uganda, Kenya and South Africa.

This family were on a road trip through the UK and someone had told them to head to Bradford for authentic Indian food. They were so lost! Getting an 'authentic curry' in a curry house in the eighties was as authentic as the Indian guy in *Short Circuit*.[7] The only place to get real authentic curry anywhere in Britain, as every Asian will tell you, is in an authentic Asian home. Dad suggested to this family of complete strangers, that he'd just met on the street, to head home with him and his wife would cook for them. Just like that. Standing on the street with total randoms, he invited them home for dinner. He didn't consult Mum, he didn't need to – he knew she'd be fine with it and would happily prepare a feast. Not only did they eat with us, my parents insisted they stay the night and even gave up their own bed for them. They admitted to my parents they were a little scared spending the night. No shit. They'd obviously never come across an overbearing Punjabi family before! They were overwhelmed by the experience and their kindness and returned the favour when we spent a weekend in Holland with them.

There was always a steady stream of various students, doctors and nurses, usually from India, that Mum would befriend and, the next thing you know, we are taking them along with us on a Sunday adventure to show off our beloved

---

[7] He was white! Look it up.

Yorkshire. If you love a Sunday lie-in, my house was not the place for you. Sunday was anything but a day of rest. It was a day for adventure regardless of the weather – in fact, the wetter the better! Blackpool, the Dales, the Lake District, any number of beautiful northern destinations for a day trip.

Sunday adventures across Yorkshire are the happiest memories of my childhood. I've been asked on numerous occasions what qualifies me to be a *Countryfile* presenter (well, apart from the obvious – I'm a presenter, but for some reason this is often not enough). I've never birthed a lamb or owned a pair of wellies, but my love for the land is deep and runs through me. There are so many places I'd love to take you, so let's get going.

Saltaire, frozen in time – we could walk the streets of the perfect Victorian village created around the mill built by Sir Titus Salt. We could even pop into Beatties (not Betty's) tearoom, where I spent a summer as a waitress, having to boil up pigs' trotters in a giant pot, with a hangover from Hull, not hell, to celebrate Yorkshire day. (Of course there's a Yorkshire day!) Serving bacon butties in the shop to council workers in hi vis vests, who loved it when I served. The rule was two rashers in a large bap, but this was too stingy for my greedy Indian eyes so I'd ram in an extra couple when the boss wasn't watching. Then I'd spend the afternoon serving cream teas to a steady stream of artistic locals, American tourists and well-dressed retired couples off to see the Hockneys in the mill. I'd chat to them all. The lead singer of Terrorvision's mum popped in for tea and I dined out on that for a while.

Finish up that scone, there's more sightseeing to do! We could head out across rolling Dales scattered with sheep, peppered with villages and market towns tucked into the dips and crevices of the hills, the kind that transport you to another time. Not overly manicured or wealthy second home spots, this is rustic and real, proper *Last of the Summer Wine* territory. Along narrow roads with expertly hand-stacked drystone walls on either side, with only enough space for one car. So narrow you hold your breath if there's oncoming traffic. This is England's rural heartland with a raw natural old-fashioned beauty. I'd take you to Bolton Abbey to cross the stepping stones across the river Wharfe and I'd show you where I fell in on Alina's birthday party aged six and had to go home in soggy knickers. We'd walk through the woods on the other side following the river and, if we're lucky, maybe spot an otter. This is the same river the monks of the priory would have walked along when Henry VIII booted them out. It's a history and nature tour too!

Then we'd go up a bit higher. We really couldn't miss the wild and untamed moorlands, exposed and inviting, sometimes hiding in heavy clouds. We'd have the right gear on so you'll be cosy. Your nose will be cold, being kissed by the weather, reminding you what it feels to be alive. We'd stomp across the moors, over bumping mounds of soft purple heather, wading through muddy marshes, splashing through streams. We could walk for miles and miles, under a grey sky that highlights every branch and twig on leafless winter trees, until the sun starts to set and the silhouette of the landscape appears on the horizon. Distant hills and crags are revealed against a bright navy blue sky, with the North Star winking at us. Give me a dawn or give me a dusk, when everything is a little twinkly and the world is full of magic, so we realise how magnificent it really all is. This, to me, is heaven.

On to Whitby. My favourite place on earth. On my 30th birthday, this is where I wanted to be, with its ruined Abbey, cobbled streets, pier, lighthouse, aging whale bone, Dracula legend, vintage sweet shops and silversmiths selling Whitby Jet stone jewellery. It's the perfect coastal fishing town where, on a hot summer's day, a wasp might try and share your pint and seagulls your fish and chips. The best bit about going to Whitby is the drive across the North York Moors, up the east coast. The landscape opens up and it becomes otherworldly and freeing. To this day, that drive takes me out of myself. All the different colours between the sky and earth, purple heather, green bracken, grey rocks and fluffy cream hardy sheep dotted around, make my chest expand just thinking about it. The road through it is smooth and exciting, an opportunity for the more adventurous to put their foot down.

We knew we were going on an extra-special and extra-long day trip to Whitby, or anywhere in Yorkshire, if Mum was up at the crack of dawn and in the kitchen preparing a picnic for the day. When I was a kid, my mum's picnics were something I dreaded. That's because it was a picnic very different to those found in the *Famous Five* books I loved to read. No melt-in-the-mouth shortbread, no ginger beer, no tomato sandwiches (no sandwiches of any kind whatsoever), no lashings of anything – just the threat of a lashing if we didn't get the hell out of the kitchen.

We would either travel in the van (we always had a van, you can't run a factory without a van), or our car depending on how many people were coming on the trip. We have been known to cram 'em into the van. My dad was probably suspected of smuggling illegal immigrants, but we were really just on a trip to Whitby. An ordinary family saloon can take five passengers comfortably and legally; a car owned by Indians in the eighties, however, has the capacity for eight people at least. Driver, front passenger, as many as you can squeeze onto the back seat and all the kids in the boot. Kul and I were regularly relegated to the boot of our maroon Rover hatchback. Quite a flash motor back then, a sign that the business was flourishing. We all loved that car. Plus, the boot was very comfortable, especially once all the coats had been shoved in, as they made a lovely soft furnishing. It was like having our own den and we could giggle and fight quietly enough not to catch Dad's attention.

'Chalo! Chalo! Chalo! Come on, Kids. Jaldi jaldi!'

'Tehro.' Wait. Mum had forgotten something. Dad huffs and rolls his eyes.

'Mein achaar pulgai.' I forgot the achar.

Not the pickle! Anything but the dreaded pickle! The jar of stinky pickle is tucked in with all the other snacks and we're off! (Pickle is an essential part of an Asian feast, but my God, it's going to kick up a stink.)

Before we showed any guests the sights and sounds of Whitby, it was time to eat. Out came the dreaded picnic and Mum had packed *everything*. Parantha, essentially a stuffed and then fried chapatti. You can stuff it with spiced grated cauliflower, gobi wala parantha, Asian radish, mooli wala parantha, butter or plain parantha and then the classic Aloo or potato parantha. That's right, it's a spiced carb-on-carb bonanza and there's nothing better than sitting round a kitchen table having them freshly prepared and slid onto your plate, hot off the tava. Pickles, bottles of Coca-Cola, disposable plastic cups, a flask of chai, more disposable polystyrene cups, disposable paper cups. A few homemade samosas, chutney and the all-important ketchup. Samosas and ketchup is the ultimate combination and you'll find it everywhere: dinners, birthdays, engagement parties, parties of every variety, absolutely at weddings and part of a Punjabi picnic. If you've not tried a samosa with ketchup, you've not lived. This picnic sounds amazing, doesn't it? For me, it was a curse. Growing up, most of us want to fit in, not stand out, but we might as well have been a rare species being watched as part of a David Attenborough documentary. Put on your best Attenborough voice and continue to read:

'Aah, we are in luck, here they come, the lesser-spotted *Asian Family*, rarely sighted in these rural northern idylls, but when they are, they are often in wondrous large groups. To watch so many of them appear from one family saloon is like a magic trick. They just keep coming and the last to emerge are their young from the boot of the car – oh yes, you can see them gasping for air, no doubt someone will have let off a final flatulent flourish just before their exit, you can tell by the speed in which they are trying to clamber out.

'They speak to one another in a very loud combination of English and Punjabi. They talk to their young with angry shouts to stay in one place, the young responding with a combination of obedience and face pulling at each other.

'They are parked up on the seafront, with a clear view of what they, like many other humans, have come to enjoy, the ocean. If we are lucky, we will be able to observe their unique feeding ritual. Let us watch for a while. Yes, the basket is being placed on the bonnet of the car and the females in the group are preparing what we hoped we might catch a glimpse of: the display of the wondrous Punjabi picnic.'

For little me, these picnics were a social disaster. A public humiliation of the highest order. We were always going to stick out wherever we went, what with us being 75 Asians crammed into one car in the British countryside. All the Punjabi picnic did was shine a spotlight on us even more. Hello, Britain, here we are with our colour and our food. I hate to say it, but I was ashamed. I didn't want to stick out, I wanted to be seen like everyone else, I wanted to blend in. I liked who I was, I just didn't always want the added extra Indian layer. Nothing would stop us from having a good time, but you'd always notice people staring at you, maybe even pointing, probably discussing our presence.

* * *

Now, things are very different for me. I've grown up. Not only am I proud of my difference, I celebrate it. I wear it as my superpower. I have an innate understanding of two worlds, two cultures, histories, heritage. I can move seamlessly from one to the other, feeling as though I belong to both and neither, and can feel powerful in my own skin. I've never felt more powerful. I want to do everything to help change the landscape, so the next generation don't feel as though they are the outsiders. And things have changed: samosas have become the perfect accompaniment to any picnic, Punjabi or not.

A funny thing happened with my experience of the childhood family picnic, though. As soon as I'd take the first mouthful of food, all those stomach-churning feelings of being self-conscious just faded away. Truth is, some people may have looked at us, some may even have said racist things to each other about us, or to us, but most people didn't care. Some may even have been smiling at the sight of an Asian family out at the seaside. Everything disappeared with food. It's got a magic power. My parents never once made us feel self-conscious. We were just like everyone else. Now, no food brings me more pleasure than the stuff I grew up eating. The Indian food lovingly prepared by my mother, that I now cook at home and shamelessly put into Tupperware and take into parks in London for a summer picnic with my friends. I'm now so obsessed with Indian pickle I make it myself. I have a cupboard full of them: ginger and turmeric, lemon, chilli, mango, carrot, even bitter gourd pickle. The more tangy and potent and ponky, the better. Now, nothing beats a Punjabi picnic in my beloved Yorkshire.

Half-Arsing a Job is Not in Your DNA

The weekend is when my parents' energy kicked into warp speed.

Saturday was market day, so still a work day. As well as the factory, my family have always done markets. Market trading was big business in the eighties, especially up north, before cheap high street shops and mega supermarkets turned up and consumed the lot. I loved helping out on the market. It was either that or stay at home and clean the entire house, which was our Saturday morning duty. Hoover top to bottom, dust, polish, clean door handles. Yup, I'll take standing around in the cold all day long over cleaning the house. Although cleaning wasn't the worst bit, it was having the cleaning inspected by Dad that was terrifying. If it wasn't done properly, we'd have to do it all again. Dad is a perfectionist. He is like my best mate now but when we were kids, he had a proper temper on him and it felt like any one of us could spark it at any given moment.

Come wind, rain, sun or snow, we were market trading at weekends. Not fair-weather, posh, fancy London markets, proper 'this is our livelihood, we turn up even if we sell nothing' markets. We prepared for the bitter cold in the winter by wearing the right gear. Basically, skiing clothes. Salopettes and Moon Boots, with handwarmers shoved into every pocket.

The first job was always to set up the stall. Most market stalls now are already built but, back then, you'd have to bring your own, slotting cold metal rods together on a freezing day, bbbrrrr! A sheet of tarpaulin over the top, industrial crocodile clips to hold it all down, rails erected, coats hung, prices on and we were good to go. 'Come and get your winter body warmers, cheap at twice the price,' I'd shout. Not that the clothes traders ever shouted. I was just imitating the fruit and veg boys and Gordon the egg man, who had the loudest voice in Shipley: 'COME AND GET YER EGGS AS BIG AS YER HEAD. TWELVE DOZEN EGGS AS BIG AS YER EDD.'

Market traders are some of the most quick-witted people I have known, so it's a great training ground for charm and sales, which came in very handy for one of my first ever presenting gigs, chatting to randoms in Covent Garden. To get a sale, you've got to be ready to chat and negotiate. As long as a profit is still being made, there's no harm in the customer believing they've got a great deal. If it works well, everyone is happy. But some customers can test your patience. There was a woman one weekend who was insistent my dad was too expensive, and she could get a jacket cheaper in Kirkgate market.

'£22.99! I can get it for a tenner in Bratford!'

Dad had had enough. 'How much is the bus fare to Bratford?'

'20p.'

'Well, here's 20p, go and buy it from there!' he said with a smile.

She bought the coat.

This is where my mum got her Yorkshire education, having to try and get her Indian head around the Yorkshire sense of humour. A massive culture shock for her.

'Ey, Lucky, when ya ganna leave Bill? You r' too gud fer im. I'm ready when you are.'

'All these pretty Indian girls with ugly Indian men, when ya ganna give him the elbow?'

It was the eighties! Mum took it literally and Dad had to explain it was a joke. 'What kind of joke is this? If someone said this in India, there would be a big punch-up.'

The food at Shipley Market was a treat to look forward to. The reward for freezing my ass off all day as a child. A currant toasted teacake, saturated in butter, with a cup of hot instant coffee for breakfast. Lunch would either be a massive baked potato with cheese and beans, or pie and peas from the caff, a traditional West Yorkshire delight of a hot pork pie, with mushy peas and mint sauce. My favourite stall was always the sweet stall. It looked like the most fun to work on, weighing out quarter pounds of the sugary delights. Strawberry Bon Bons, Black Jacks, Fruit Salads, Flying Saucers. My teeth ache just thinking about it.

I always loved helping out on the market. Talking to people, helping to sell, taking the money, wandering around looking at all the other stuff people were selling. All the market traders knew each other. Traders did the rounds of various markets in the area, so you'd see the same faces again and again. I helped for years and my reward for working at the stall was not financial. There are no financial transactions between Asian parents and their children. We never got pocket money, never got paid. This was my duty. Part of being Indian. When I'd casually mention that Sarah or Anne got paid a pound to clean their dad's car, Dad would just laugh, hand me the bucket of soapy water and the sponge and add, 'There better be no streaks!'

If I wanted cold hard cash, then I needed to get a job. Being skint was not an option, because I'd seen a pair of trainers I really wanted and Dad refused to buy them. I decided I needed my own money so I'd never have to ask anyone to buy anything for me or have to rely on anyone again. I certainly didn't want to burden my parents with my demands. I needed financial independence. At 14, two opportunities to earn came my way. This was my first taste of: if you want something, go and get it. I got a Saturday job at my dad's mates' supermarket and I started working at my local Asian radio station. The major flaw in my plan of making money, however, was being employed by Asians! The supermarket paid me a pound an hour. A POUND AN HOUR. Even in 1992 this was criminal. The job didn't last long. Apparently my black nail varnish was scaring the customers and I wasn't getting paid enough to afford any nail varnish remover, so I quit. I definitely didn't get paid for a long time at the radio station, either, but eventually I was given the grand sum of around £5 an hour for a couple of hours a week. As it transpired, the radio station gave me much more in the long run than any kind of retirement fund. It was the gateway to my career and the rest of my life, it gave me an extremely cool hobby at a very young age and I found something I really loved. Plus, working for nothing gave me good grounding for my first years of working in TV! Note to self: I needed to stop working for Asians. Although, as it would turn out, I'd be underpaid for many, many, many years to come, Asian boss or not.

My parents had focus and energy and were doing everything right and, yes, we were comfortable. A nice house in an affluent, predominantly white area, a car, two kids in private education. And then in the early nineties, everything changed.

'When will we be normal kids? When will the factory close so we can go home straight after school?' I once asked my mum. A prophetic question. The end of the eighties and the huge recession under Margaret Thatcher was the beginning of the end. Within two years, by 1990, my parents lost it all. Expanding the business, a couple of orders being cancelled, the bank refusing to extend a loan and manufacturing moving to China and Taiwan with prices we couldn't compete with meant that the business my parents had built from the ground up was now coming crumbling down.

With the shop gone, the factory had a lock put on it. We lost the roof over our heads. Money was tight and we moved to a small suburban semi in a slightly less affluent area and now drove a beat-up old car. A car I would not allow in the school gates. I'd get my parents to drop me off down the road and walk the last stretch of the journey! I was ashamed. Now I wasn't just the Asian kid in a very white school, I was going to be the poor Asian kid, too.

My parents did their best to keep the stress of it all away from us. There were arguments, huge blazing rows, but this was normal, pre-factory and post-factory. If my parents didn't have a row in a day, there was something very wrong. They loved nothing more than a blazing row. My dad was a balance of fun and furious. Consequently, Kul and me spent most of our childhood afraid. In fear of the rows, because Dad's voice was big and booming. We were definitely not the quiet Asian family. I'd often wake up in the night to Mum and Dad arguing. I never knew what they were fighting about, I'm not sure they did either. I took to sleeping with my fingers crossed because, if you cross your fingers, squeeze your eyes shut tight and pray they won't fight tonight, it might come true. They still fought and I'd wake up with crooked fingers.

My mum was never a frivolous spender and delicious Indian food is very cheap to cook, especially when you shop at Asian grocery stores. My parents never spoke about money in front of us kids, so I don't remember feeling as though we had less than before. But I was aware that things had changed. It had seeped into the atmosphere. I didn't ask for birthday presents and Christmas presents – Christmas holidays off school were enough of a treat, we didn't need presents on top of that. I'm not telling you this for you to feel sorry for me, we just didn't do gifts and didn't expect them or demand them.

The only time it really affected one of my choices was when I'd been selected to go on a Yorkshire Schools expedition to China. I was 15, my first year of GCSEs, and when I heard about the selection weekend in the Dales, I instantly said hell yes. China to me was the most exotic place on earth. India was normal but China was the land of kung fu, Shaolin monks, chicken chow mein and . . . my doppel-ganger. When I was tiny, I didn't believe that God could have come up with so many different and unique faces and fully believed that we all had a doppelganger somewhere on earth – mine lived in the land of myths and magic, China. This must have been due to the steady diet of kung fu and Bruce Lee movies and watching *Monkey*.

The selection weekend was gruelling, including a 3am wake-up to climb Ingleborough, one of Yorkshire's three peaks, plus group tasks, solo tasks, and on the last day we had to prepare a skit in our little groups to perform in front of everyone. Naturally, I directed ours and gave myself all the funny lines. I loved every single second of it. Being out-doors, being adventurous, being part of a team but also making my own choices, being away from home – this was heaven. There were a lot of kids but only a few places on the expedition. They asked us what groups we'd like to be part of, should we be chosen to go. I put down mountaineering, but what I actually wanted to put down was trekking, I just didn't know the difference. All I knew was I wanted to be in the mountains, as far away from people as possible, totally immersed in nature. I got selected and was giddy with excite-ment. My first real, proper, faraway adventure. It dawned on me the first time I met the rest of the mountaineering group that I might have made a mistake. There were six massive 6th form boys and three girls, two of whom were solid hockey playing types, properly hench, and Vicky from school, known to me as Perfect Vicky. We did the introductions and went around the group to find out everyone's climbing experience.

'We go to the Alps every yaar.'

'We holiday in Scotland and have climbed Ben Nevis.'

'I'm planning base camp Everest.'

When it got to me, I actually said, 'I've climbed a ladder.' At least they laughed. And yes, of course I was the only non-white face that weekend.

We began the training sessions. Every weekend there was something different to climb. We did Scafell Pike in the Lakes and I was the slowest of the group and nearly flew off a summit in 85 mile-per-hour winds (they had to tie a rope around my waist and attach it to the group leader so I didn't die). My gear was crap compared with everyone else's, but it really didn't matter, I was in my element. Turns out, mountaineering was precisely the group I wanted to be in. The sense of satisfaction of getting to the top of a mountain and seeing the view (if it wasn't in a rain cloud) was magnificent. I felt like my mind was clear in the mountains. Nothing else mattered. It was just me, the peak, my legs, my mind, the peace of the great outdoors and my rucksack full of snacks: a marathon, some Kendal mint cake, cheese and cucumber sandwiches in a white bap (that's a bread roll to anyone south of Sheffield). No parantha and pickle this time! I also had another powerful motivation in the form of a lovely, floppy-haired ginger lad who was super dreamy . . . But we'll get to that. And to Perfect Vicky.

There was just one small problem. If I was going to get to China for the larger expedition, I needed to raise money to fund the trip. The small amount of 3,000 big fat pounds! I knew the parents of the other kids would pay for them. I had my job at the radio station that paid me the grand sum of fuck all. So, this £3,000 I had to raise was really the biggest mountain of all. I knew it was causing my dad extra stress. My parents were super happy I'd been selected but I also knew there was no spare cash. Floppy-haired ginger lad was actually going out with Perfect Vicky, so I made what I thought was an adult decision and backed out of my trip of a lifetime. A simple truth about being poor: expensive trips to China are off the agenda.

It's strange how, as a kid, I was so able to let things wash over me. I didn't want to make things about me. Not when Mum and Dad had so much on their plates. I learned to fend for myself and to be hyper aware of causing the least amount of stress. I wondered how I could make everything better for my parents, and once I'd made my mind up, that was that. Power forward and don't look back! I mean, I flatly refused to look at anyone's photos when they got back from the trip – I'm not having it rubbed in my face, thank you. Thank God there was no Instagram back then. I had this amazing capacity to think forwards and put anything bad out of my mind, because if I did think about it, I'd be upset and I wasn't sure how to deal with being upset. Being upset was another emotion I pushed into a dark corner somewhere in my mind.

After a couple of failed attempts at reviving the business, my folks had to start again from the bottom. And they were not too proud to do whatever they could. At first, the only jobs available were in a nursing home for Mum and working in a nightclub for my dad. In a strange way, it was the best thing that happened for Mum, as it liberated her. She was educated in India and had done a secretarial course, so her typing skills were fast. She went on an employment training course and felt having an Indian accent would mean she'd find it very difficult to get work, but she met white British people who could speak well enough but had no basic reading and writing skills, failed by the British education system. This gave Mum the confidence she needed. She may speak with an accent, but she can read and write fluently in three different languages. She retrained and went to night classes at a local adult education centre, where someone lovely saw how smart, skilled and helpful she was and encouraged her to apply for jobs, helping her fill out her CV. Eventually, after a few years, she landed a job as a liaison officer, an interpreter, at the Bradford Royal Infirmary.

With her many languages, love of people, powers of persuasion and boundless energy, Mum was in her element and this job really was the making of her. Then through a very nurturing and encouraging Indian consultant at the hospital, she was given the opportunity to work on a twinning project with a hospital in India, specialising in boys with haemophilia. This hospital has become Mum's life's work – she goes every year and tirelessly continues to raise money for them. With her natural gift of the gab and lovely radio voice, Mum also got a show at a new Asian Radio station that had just opened in Bradford. After hearing they were looking for presenters, she turned up and knocked on the door. She's utterly fearless.

Dad is both charming and has great chat and tried his hand at a variety of different sales jobs and was always coming up with business ideas. They were doing whatever they could, whatever it took, to keep us afloat. And what about the two sets of school fees they had to pay every term? They could have taken us out of those schools but for my mum, this was NOT an option. They'd worked hard to get us into those schools, me and Kul had studied hard to be there, too. Getting us the best education, as they saw it, and the best start in life was the whole point of their existence. Every single penny they earned went to our schools and I will never forget that. I think Dad's always been a bit bitter that everything he ever earned went towards me and my brother. He's definitely kept a tally! Whatever your opinions may be about private education, this for my parents was their way of giving us a boost in Britain: by infiltrating the system middle-class white folk used to get ahead too.

Mum, my Rottweiler of a mother, my warrior queen, went to see both my headmistress and Kul's headmaster and explained the family situation during the worst of it. Dad was very withdrawn and hurting at this stage and it took him a while to get back out there. He was even too proud to sign on. Mum was prepared to do whatever it took to keep us in school. I'm pretty certain Mrs Warrington at Bradford Girls Grammar School and Dr Smith at Bradford Boys had never had a meeting like it, and had certainly never met a woman quite like my mother. I know my mum has the capacity to go full Bollywood melodrama at the drop of a hat – and both schools came to an agreement with her so we stayed where we were. The money they were saving for our future, the cash they had saved in the bank and some of Mum's wedding gold all went towards paying for the rest of our education. Mum was never one for spending, we were her only priority. We are constantly told by her to never be afraid of dealing with a situation, never presume you are defeated before you've even put up a fight. Even if you fail, at least you gave it a go. Failure teaches us the greatest lessons.

Dad's life eventually changed after an offer by an old friend. Remember Kamala Aunty, who used to sew for my folks? Their hard work had paid off, right royally. Their small shop had grown into the third largest independent retailer of electrical goods in the country! They offered Dad a job as general manager. They are more my dad's family than his actual family. It must have been a devastating, earth-shattering, dark period of fear and panic for him, feeling lost and with no control. Imagine a potion of humiliation, depression and shame, with huge amounts of anger and pain thrown in for good measure. And sadness, so much sadness. It had gone, everything they'd worked so hard for. It all sank. They had to let everybody go. It wasn't until the factory closed and my parents hit rock bottom that I truly witnessed the power of who they are and the metal they are made of. Where do humans get their incredible capacity to survive at all costs? Our ability to thrive in the darkest of situations? I'm in awe of my parents. My God, they've worked hard.

* * *

The thing about all the jobs I've ever had, whether they paid me or not, is I couldn't do anything half-arsed. If I was going to do it, I gave it my all. What I absorbed from my parents is their abundance of energy and general zest for life. I've watched them graft and never moan. I didn't understand the concept of a lie-in or that you might have a day to loll around and do nothing. As a consequence, I find it very difficult to do nothing now, but I'm trying to go easier on myself. I think we all need to do that for ourselves, from time to time.

I'm consequently also terrified of parenthood. I'm terrified I'd mess my child up, that they too would find life a heavy burden at times, and a relationship with me too complex. But then I wonder what that must feel like, to know that you could risk your life and give up everything to make sure your child survives and has the chance to thrive. That love. My parents could have been so much more, done so much more. Mum wanted to act, and Dad wanted to join the RAF and become a pilot. Neither had the option to pursue their dreams. They got married and that was it. They were duty-bound. Very quickly, me and my bro turned up and then their priority was us.

Asian kids are brought up with a sense of duty to their parents. Whether you like them or not, even if they weren't particularly good at being parents, you still have to do what's right and look after them until the day they die. I have always had this sense of duty in me, compounded by witnessing everything my parents did for me growing up. I feel a deep sense of guilt that they suffered so much for us, that I couldn't help when I was a kid, that I couldn't make things better for them. Children who watch their parents suffer often feel misplaced guilt. (I don't know this because I have done years of therapy, I know this because I heard it on a radio phone-in.) I know my parents feel immense guilt that they didn't give us the stable and calm childhood they know we should have had. I made them leave Bradford three years ago. I found them a beautiful house near me with a gorgeous garden. They call it their dream house and it's the least I can do for them. Now is their time to relax and enjoy their life. Maybe have a lie-in or two, if they want.

People often ask where I get my drive from. It's pretty simple: I get it from them. My childhood was tough, tougher than I allow myself to remember. Being foreign and working class in Britain always means a tough life, especially when there's no peace at home. I got frustrated writing about this period of my childhood and couldn't understand why the words, the stories, the memories weren't flooding back. I'd blocked them, like I did at the time, too. This was the period in my life when I turned inwards and created my own world. I started living somewhere else, in my bedroom, and in my mind. Planning my escape.

Every Woman Deserves
a Room of Their Own

Knock before you come in!

Welcome to my bedroom. Welcome to my domain.

My bedroom was my world. After the factory closed, this is where I retreated and disappeared to. I created a place of sanctuary for myself, a place of discovery. I'd spend hours doing all the important things a teenager does: listening to music, watching my TV and reading the *NME*. It's where I would dream, create worlds in my head, escape to wherever I wanted. A whole life happened, past, present, future, in this little box room at the front of the house. (Unbeknown to me, it was preparing me for life in lockdown, 30 years later!)

The door would close behind me and this was all my space. Up until the age of 11, I shared a bedroom with my brother. Once I was into double figures I decided I wanted out, becoming Little Miss Independent. My days of watching *Thundercats* and playing Decathlon on the Commodore 64 were over. I picked up my copies of *Smash Hits* magazine and my two teddy bears and relocated. I was so proud. This felt important, a significant literal move in my life. A step towards my eternal search for independence and freedom. My own space. No one else to share it with. Just mine, all mine. Maybe this was about having some kind of control in a life I felt I had no control in. I could have had it sooner, but my mum's brother had visited from India and stayed with us for a year, AN ENTIRE YEAR. It's very common in Asian families for relatives to come and stay for indefinite periods of time. Now he was back in India and I claimed the room as my own. My territory. No one was allowed in without knocking. When I say no one, I mean one person: my little bro, Kul. Mum and Dad did what they wanted. There was no respecting of privacy – another basic tenet of Asian parenting.

At 11, you are probably expecting me to describe the room as beautifully pastel coloured with soft furnishings, floral curtains, a blush pink carpet, photos of friends, family, puppies and ponies. A dolls' house in the corner and an immaculate desk with organised pencils and crayons and a lovely neat pile of beautifully illustrated fairy-tales. A lot like the 11-year-old bedrooms that belonged to my friends.

My teenage bedroom was NOTHING like this! I finally had my own domain and I hooked this space up in my own haphazard, makeshift way. The décor changed over the next 10 years of course, but importantly, my parents allowed me to do what I wanted with it. New Kids on the Block posters turned into New Model Army signs, wallpaper became wall graffiti (I went through a period that involved writing all over the walls). The baby blue colour scheme became black: black ceiling, weird black wallpaper, black radiator, plus candles dripping wax down empty bottles of Black Tower lined the windowsill. There were piles of files, piles of books, copies of *Smash Hits* became copies of the *NME*, a small shrine to Kurt Cobain, an exhausted school uniform slung over a chair, socks and stripey tights clung to my black radiator. I'd regularly smoke the joint out with sandalwood, patchouli or rose-scented agarbatti, much to my father's annoyance. He hates the smell of josticks. Regardless, Mum lit them religiously every morning before her daily prayer meditation and every time my bedroom door opened, a plume of jostick smoke would waft out. There was a permanent fog in my room. I had a Body Shop lip balm that I got as a present, a bottle of Body Shop dewberry body spray and a black eye-liner, and that was the extent of my make-up. (I didn't even own a lipstick until I got my first proper presenting gig on Channel 5, aged 24!)

I never had a wardrobe. Just an open-plan shelving unit in front of my bed, where I hung a few clothes and folded a few jumpers. I didn't have tons of clothes, but I loved what I had. My baggy shirts, baggy hoodies and baggy jeans were staples, basically anything that resembled a big bag! I began shopping at the army surplus store, like all the fashionistas. I was desperate for a pair of Dr. Marten boots but they were too expensive, so Mum, who really could not fathom what the hell was going on with her daughter, Mum who wanted me in pink dresses, Mum who would lightly try and encourage me to put on some lipstick (to which I would just scowl and ask why I'd want to make my lips shiny), Mum who spent years wishing I'd get a handbag with a complimentary pair of heels, took me age 14 to the tiny army surplus store at the top of Leeds Road to buy me a pair of big black boots. They cost £35, I remember, because I was so grateful they were being bought for me. My dad called them my bovver boots. I put yellow laces in them and loved them and lived in them.

My room had personality, it was daring and original, and I was forever being told to tidy it. The main bone of contention was the clothes. They had a habit of sliding down from the open-plan shelves and crawling all over the rest of the room, along with schoolbooks and files, my uniform and stripey tights. Once, I came home to a completely empty bedroom. Everything gone. 'I've been robbed!' No, I hadn't. Dad had shoved everything, every single thing in my room, into black bin liners and put them in the garden. Anything I needed for the next day I had to go out and get. Homework, uniform, clothes, my one lip balm. It was his way of getting me to tidy up. It worked for that day, Dad's twisted sense of humour. At least he had just put my stuff in the garden – Mum would take my things to give away to charity, without even consulting me. I guess it was a good lesson in non-attachment. I've subsequently been very good at getting rid of things: clothes, diaries, boyfriends. There was no space for hoarding, attachment or sentimentality in my house.

My cultural education happened in my bedroom. Friends at school had generations of white, British culture to inherit, passed along through various members of the family. Stuff everyone just seemed to know, like The Beatles' back catalogue, going to the theatre or watching ballet, being surrounded by books and learning about literature and poetry. The things my parents were passing on to me were generations of cooking knowledge, ancient Indian wisdom and stories, a love of Indian music, fluency in Punjabi and Hindi, an ingrained work ethic and a love for travel and adventure. All great and fully appreciated by the time I'm 40, but at 14, in nineties Britain, they were redundant. How was any of that stuff going to help me in any social situation that didn't involve impressing aunties? How on earth, if you don't have people around you to feed it to you, do you get the knowledge you need to blag your way through polite British society? First, you thirst for it and then you search for it and then, you learn, fast. You soak it up from wherever you can. My TV and my radio were two vital access points for me into other worlds.

A lot of things changed for me when I turned 13. Big, tectonic plate shifting. I was officially becoming a teenager, Mum and Dad were closing the factory and I'd been ditched by the cool girls at school. They grew up and I didn't. They were the most mature young girls you'd ever met and at 13, they'd discovered boys. I was a long way off and I think I cramped their style. So, I was out. But before they dumped my ass, they did give me a parting gift that changed my life. One of my friends, Anne, had taken a cassette from her elder brother and brought it with her on a school trip to France. New music? I definitely wanted to hear it. It was a homemade Smiths' compilation, with The Queen Is Dead on side A and a collection of other Smiths' and Morrissey songs on side B. I borrowed the tape to listen to it on the coach on my Sony Walkman cassette player, complete with foam orange headphones. My tiny, underdeveloped pop brain exploded.

What was this incredible sound I was listening to? British music that gave me the same feeling of melancholy and comfort as the ghazals of my childhood! Music that seemed to soothe, that took me away from the world around me and seemed to understand my teenage pain and frustration. I could drift into another world, carried along by Johnny Marr's chord variations and lyrics that soon became lodged in my brain, after hundreds and hundreds of listens.

I loved The Smiths. I thought they were singing for me. The misfit, the alien, the lonely outsider in their room. I thought they were mine for life. I was entering phase two of becoming my teenage self. My miserable teenage self. Music had always been of great importance to me. Waking up at the age of two in my parents' car to start singing along to 'Gapuchi Gapuchi Gum Gum', a classic song from the heyday of Bollywood in the late seventies. Rallying other toddlers to learn my very basic dance routine to 'Let's Get Physical' by Olivia Newton-John in the playground at nursery. Listening to songs on the radio and remembering the lyrics and the melodies off by heart. Always performing in my mind, creating a dance routine to Nik Kershaw 'Wouldn't It Be Good' and Starship's 'We Built This City'. Standing right in front of the TV, nose pressed to the screen, when *Top of the Pops* was on, so it felt as though I was almost in the studio when I danced along, dreaming of pop stardom.

The moment I pressed play on that Smiths' tape may well have been the precise moment my latent moody, angry, serious, intense, 'deep', annoying teenage gene was activated. I'd gone from a relatively happy, tree-climbing, bouncing kid and metamorphosed into moody, spotty, confused teenager. New Kids on the Block were dead to me! No more fantasies of running away with the boyband. Now I wanted real music, music that made me feel something – that made me feel grown-up. I wanted music that transported me somewhere safe and magical, both alien and familiar at the same time. The only cassettes I had were compilations of songs I'd recorded off the radio, usually the top 40 countdown on a Sunday night on Radio 1. This was my only way of gathering music back then at 13, with not a penny to my name and no pocket money. (Asian parents don't do pocket money.)

I was a little brown lass listening to The Smiths and if there were any others in Bradford like me in the early nineties, I hadn't come across them. I connected with Morrissey's lyrics, as a lonely Asian outsider, a misfit who felt I didn't belong anywhere. The Smiths eased my teenage pain, I felt they understood my experience. In their music and his lyrics, I thought I found someone I could relate to. I found the universal in Morrissey's experience of growing up in a migrant Irish Catholic working-class Northern family.

It's all coming together now! I had music made for me, I had a new teenage attitude, I had my own space. The creation and expansion of my world took place in my tiny room. I was the master of this literal dark universe.

I said let there be light.

In my room was my old, ugly box TV, way too big for the room, with no remote control and a bent metal hanger as an aerial. It would always need a jiggle around to try and get a clear signal, the colour was never right the entire time I had it, but it was good enough for me to stay up and watch late-night Channel 4. There was never any issue with me having a television in my room – it was seen as an essential in our house.

I said let there be communication.
The only phone we had in the house was in the landing at the bottom of the stairs and this just wasn't going to do. Not for my private conversations. I connected a cheap telephone with a very long wire to the main phone, then ran the cable up the stairs, round the hall and all the way into my room. My lair was beginning to take shape . . .

I said let there be sound.
The all-important combination radio, cassette and record player that stayed with me from 11 right through to my first year at uni. I played my first ever vinyl on this piece of technology, a gift from an aunty as I never had money to buy my own, Sister Sledge – 'Frankie'. It's a classic and I still know all the words and, of course, my self-choreographed dance routine.

I said let there be (out-of-tune) tunes.
I had a small Yamaha keyboard that I could never play. I'd sing along to any tune on the radio, attempting harmonies as though I was a lost member of the band, and I would pretend to play the keyboard at the same time. I now have an upright piano in my home that I can't play. But still, in my mind, one day I will be a concert pianist.

I said let there be mood lighting.

There was a simple pendant light in the middle of the room with a small sky blue tasselled light shade. To create a dimmer ambience, I draped my polyester dressing gown over it. It dimmed the light, yes, but also looked like someone had hung themselves in my room, so I lifted the bottom and wrapped it around the rest of the light. Then I went downstairs for dinner. I returned a couple of hours later to the smell of burning polyester in my room. That day, I could have destroyed my own kingdom. And burnt down the entire house. So, I eventually said, let there be health and safety checks.

Let there be a dance floor.

In this room, this tiny space, I'd dance. I'd dance my own freeform choreography, fiercely, fantastically and like a fool. In this room I was anyone I wanted to be, and I was frequently Kate Bush. I'm still frequently Kate Bush.

Let there be comfort.

I had a raised single bed, with drawers under one side, a small cupboard on the other and a pull-out desk in the middle. The desk could come all the way out, which meant I could crawl underneath, a den within a den, when I needed to hide away from myself, and make myself really small.

Let there be pain relief.

Sometimes, things got a little too much in my house. It was a hotbed of arguing, the disagreements deafening. I was a teenager, so had a ton of emotions and no idea how to deal with them, anger and sadness that comes with growing up, feeling confined with no power to change anything. So, sometimes, I would meticulously unscrew the blade out of my pencil sharpener and use it to cut myself – a small phase of self-harm. It's strange to write down, it's even stranger to think about, because it's so buried away in my past and not something I spend any time thinking about or dwelling on. But it happened. It's important for me to tell you because I found being a teenager really hard. Really, really tough. Overwhelmingly difficult, sometimes. I thought I was tough enough to take on everything and conquer the world, but I was also in a lot of anguish and feeling a lot of pain and felt terribly lonely most of the time. So much of my life was out of my control. I had no influence on the things going on around me and it seemed that every adult I knew was unhappy, stressed or angry.

Stepping into school, I'd switch into school mode. At school, I never, ever, thought about my home life. School was an escape of sorts and I was a master at compartmentalising my life. Still am. I'm super skilled at switching off emotions. But here's a little thing I've learned about emotions – apparently, you can't switch them off. They just morph into something else, another emotion, and then somehow these undealt with emotions can just turn around and bite you on your ass at some point down the line. Your own emotions turn on you! And when there's so many bubbling away, so much confusion about what the hell is going on around you, so you feel totally trapped, well, then it's a war. Then something will implode. And I did. The only time I felt I gained some control over my life and felt some kind of release, felt something, was in those moments when I'd sit in my room and cut myself and watch the blood slowly appear from under my skin. I found it both terrifying and satisfying. I felt alive and present and, in those moments, thought about nothing else. Nothing. I just focused on the pain and the blood and it was a sweet relief from the rest of my life. The sharp pain would bring me sharply into that moment and that moment only. And it was my secret. Mum once saw my forearm covered in scabs and scratches but neither of us said anything. I didn't want her to say anything. I didn't want anyone to know. It was just for me. I just wanted to get away, find quiet, find peace, find a life for myself.

Writing this feels so exposing, even now. As raw as those wounds. I'm giving something about myself away, something important. But it feels equally important to share. I was confident and I was always busy doing lots of things and I had a fantastic mask. It wasn't even a fake mask, it was legit, something I was able to slip on so skilfully, I wasn't even conscious I was doing it. Everyone around me was unhappy. Everyone was angry. Everyone had expectations. Parents, school, friends. On top of that, it's a part of my personality that I feel like I have to take care of everyone else, too.

* * *

Even though cutting myself was a release, it also made me feel great shame. I still feel that shame, telling you. It is hard.

But it's also vital not to feel shame around talking about mental health. Mental health wasn't a term I was aware of for so long, and yet mental suffering is rife in my family, and more widely in the South Asian community. I hate the thought of other young people going through pain and mental anguish on their own. There is support out there. You can reach out for it and get help. You don't need to struggle on your own. If you feel your family won't understand, or won't want to hear it, find someone caring to speak to. You can't keep emotions bottled up. Those feelings will fester and the stench will be unbearable. If you want to live a whole life, at some point you have to unearth your feelings and face them down. Overcome that fear and take your power back.

Just like so many things in my life right now, I'm having to re-examine so much of what I took for granted. Morrissey is just another piece of the wider system that I thought was one thing and turned out to be something else. Turns out Morrissey would never be able to see the universal in my story. He'd probably find everything about my story offensive. Bloody typical. My most formative years, and the music I invested so much time in and gave such meaning to, were never for me in the first place. I spent years devoted to this man and his music. When friends at school moved on, recognising there was more to life than sitting in a room listening to *Strangeways Here We Come*, when pretty much every Asian person I knew took the piss out of me for loving The Smiths, I didn't care. How could I give up on music that had such powerful meaning for me?

That I loved? It's somehow grotesquely fitting that I find Morrissey's political views abhorrent and ridiculous. Not to mention illogical. Showing support for a far-right party and he doesn't even live in the UK, plus he's from a family of migrants!

What a massive let down. I totally picked the wrong saviour in my teens. In a way, though, he did me a favour by making me open my eyes to the reality of the world as an adult too: 'Anita, some people don't like the look of you and that's it. You make them nervous about their own existence and place in the world.' I have to recognise the reality of the world around me. Don't get complacent, question everything, don't rely on anything, especially not what you thought you knew. But it's difficult when so much of the world is dominated by white men and so many of them make music I love! They run the shop, don't they?

However, there are so many other powerful voices, so much important art, that says something meaningful, that connects with my experience, that I can find comfort in and these artists needs elevation, they need the spotlight shone on them. They must be celebrated. We need more of them, get to hear from them. Thankfully, my thirst for culture, art and finding meaning continued and there was so much more waiting for me beyond Morrissey. Also, luckily, I'd been well trained in non-attachment from an early age too.

Give Yourself a Break

So, I never had a boyfriend. At least, that's the story my parents got. Until now.

When it comes to matters of the heart or sexuality, Asian kids of my generation are often screwed. And I don't mean the fun kind! No boyfriends or girlfriends allowed. Ever. But marriage is a MUST. So how the heck do we learn about relationships?

The problem pages of *Just Seventeen* were pure porn to my sheltered Indian eyes and the only brown couples I saw on telly were on *The Bill* and usually involved a domestic abuse storyline. The only place I experienced any kind of romance was Bollywood. Every Saturday night, we'd rent a (usually dodgy) VHS copy of an Indian movie. Bollywood is the name the West has given to the all-singing, all-dancing genre of Hindi cinema. It's mega. They churn out more than double the number of movies as Hollywood every year and it has a global following wherever the South Asian diaspora is, but also in China, Russia, Peru, Nigeria, the Middle East. The storylines and slapstick comedy have universal appeal. Every film is a love story, where boy meets girl, they can't be together because of the SHAME it will bring, but after a healthy splattering of incongruous song and dance numbers with at least seven costume changes, mothers whose only purpose is to cry and put up with a casual bit of domestic violence (slapping women is the only way they'll learn, right?), spoiler alert: true love always wins out and/or someone dies. At least, that's the Bollywood I grew up with.

I have a love-hate relationship with Bollywood. The films of my youth were over the top, farcical melodramas. Most of the stories revolved around male characters and women were inserted to look pretty (and nothing like the average woman on the streets of India). These films were designed to be pure escapism. A three-and-a-half-hour marathon of a movie, where you suspend your disbelief and overlook any continuity mishaps. The song and dance numbers are inserted willy-nilly and often have no relevance to the story. The storylines are Shakespearian in scale and they are filmed in impossibly beautiful locations (the Swiss Alps were a favourite spot in the early eighties). Mum LOVES these movies.

'Come on, Mum, that was just ridiculous. AS IF a man can jump off a seven-storey building then jump back onto the roof, backwards.'

Mum's standard response: 'Well, your silly dishoom dishoom English films are the same. Tom Cruise and James Bond, they never die. Plus, my Hindi films always have a moral, a life lesson, they are teaching us something.'

Yes, Indians love a morality tale.

As fanciful, daft and sometimes annoying as these movies were, I also loved them. In these movies, Indian women were beautiful. OK, they had no voice or agency but, my God, they were beautiful! Yes, I would secretly imagine myself as a trapped princess in a Rajasthani fort draped in silks and jewels, dancing from one palatial room to another, like the Goddess Waheeda Rehman in my favourite film from 1965, *Guide*, or wistfully staring out of a jali window across the desert. Dreaming of life beyond – maybe by jumping out of the window, landing on a horse and galloping away into the sunset, off to a music festival in the desert, with both Keanu Reeves and River Phoenix. I'd play a DJ set and dance till dawn . . .[8] It's my Bollywood movie fantasy, so anything can happen.

What Bollywood provides the sexually repressed and culturally prudish is wholesome romance with dash of wet saree to keep the boys happy. It was entertainment you could watch with the entire family without having to reach for the remote, with nothing filthy happening that might give young impressionable minds any ideas, like kissing. For Asian parents, the unabashed romance of Bollywood films was a harmless outlet for teen desire and, more importantly, a way to prevent them from acting on those feelings. My parents didn't need to invest in any kind of restraints for me though. I'd come up with all kinds of genius solutions to my

---

[8] India in the nineties had no such thing as music festivals. Now they have them all over the country, including in palaces in the desert. When, 30 years later, I was filming my Bollywood documentary for the BBC, the producers did wonder why I was SO insistent on the rooftop dance sequence. I lived out my filmi fantasy.

boy-less predicament. First, I really didn't notice boys until I was about 15/16. I also recognised, or at least I thought I knew, convinced myself even, that boys didn't really fancy me. Having a boyfriend behind my parents' backs seemed too exhausting to organise, all the subterfuge and secrecy, plus the soul-destroying games you need to play to be noticed by boys. Which to me looked like they involved not saying much, giggling a lot and showing flesh. I was highly opinionated, and laughed if something was funny, but *only* if I thought it was funny. I preferred to keep most of my body covered up, draped in layers and layers of floating, oversized tie-dye dresses, with my dad's shirts thrown over the top for extra bag lady effect. (I even wore my dad's trousers to a club once, the crotch was down to my knees. It was the early nineties, but I'm not sure anyone else was rocking their dad's trousers back then.) I'd made the decision early on that I was going to be wearing the trousers in my life. Nope, boys were definitely not going to fancy me. I don't think I wanted them to either. What are you supposed to do with that kind of attention?

Growing up, there were many contradictions and complications to my romantic life. I definitely fancied boys, I absolutely fantasised about having a boyfriend, but there was no way on earth I was going to have a relationship in real life. Being friends with the lads was a much more comfortable space for me to inhabit. I wanted to be their equal, I wanted to be treated the same as them. I didn't want to be patronised, or patted on the head or the bum, or have to wear pretty frocks to go out on dates. My interpretation of young relationships was girls giving away their power just to make the lads feel good about themselves. I found the whole idea of teenage romance exhausting, painful and humiliating.

I went to an all-girls school, so for a long time the only boys I came into contact with were the kids on my street, family friends and the boys at my temple. There were a couple of boys at the temple who tried to profess their love for me when I was a teenager, brave souls they were, approaching the girl who clearly didn't give a toss. Even if I had fancied them, what would we have done? Had dates every Sunday at the Gurdwara? Touched socks under the table while eating langar? There were boys all the girls at the temple fancied, older, with gorgeous floppy hair, and they hardly ever came unless it was a special occasion. They seemed to have lives – and that's really what I wanted to have, that freedom to choose.

It was with my best mate at the temple, Harpreet, that I'd spend hours dreaming up fake romances, discussing bhangra, RnB and the predicaments of being a brown girl. Conversations I could never really have with my best mates at school. She understood the Asian girl code and our parents never knew what we discussed, ever. They also never knew that we stole miniature bottles of booze from her dad's corner shop, to secretly drink in her bedroom . . .

If my mum got a whiff of me even giving an Indian boy a second look, she'd think it was the signal to start planning my wedding. Boys were off the agenda, at least in the real world. I lived my love life in my head instead. I created elaborate make-believe scenarios with the boys of my dreams.

Keanu Reeves and I were going to somehow meet and we'd ride off into the sunset on a Harley-Davidson, or maybe even jump into his time travelling phone booth. Bill and Ted for life! This may still happen, right? Or I was going on tour around America with Anthony Kiedis from the Red Hot Chili Peppers or Mike Patton from Faith No More, or River Phoenix. I even went through a brief Rahul Roy phase based on his one successful film, *Aashiqui*. I wasn't fussy. Boys at this stage were just my escape mechanism to the life I actually wanted to live. Like being on tour in the States, on stage, performing, making money, being my own person. I really didn't want to set up home with anyone. Marriage and babies were not part of my exit strategy to liberation. Becoming a rock star was my route out, or acting in movies, or being on stage, travelling somewhere, anywhere, free to do whatever I wanted, whenever I wanted, with no one to answer to. The closest I'd got to rock star status was singing a solo of 'In The Bleak Midwinter' in the choir at York Minster.[9] Rock'n'roll!

My first experience of a boy liking me was on a school trip to France, in the second year of senior school. I was part

---

[9] Yes, I was that cool. Choir took me on tour to sing in glamorous locations like the school hall and Bolton Abbey – come on, don't tell me you weren't a little bit impressed with York Minster. I even convinced my mate Al it was cool and got her to join: 'We get to have days off school together.' She was sold. Al was tone deaf but successfully mimed the entire time she was in choir. The choir was of the highest standard.

of a cool gang back then, possibly the coolest. They were sporty, healthy and wealthy. These girls were probably the most mature and self-assured 12- and 13-year-olds you'll ever meet. They all looked so confident and stylish in their clothes from Dash and Benetton and then there'd be me in jeans too long for me, tucked into my high-top trainers (no brand), a pink jumper, black hooded anorak made by my parents, a long messy plait and a fixed brace straightening my teeth. It would only be a year before these girls would drop me from their crew. Ditched in a cruel double geography after lunch. I walked in just before class and they hadn't saved me a space, and that was it. Why this heartless dumping? Well, they'd got into boys, and boys were into them, and I was cramping their style. This would be my first real taste of rejection. Luckily for me though, the oddball outsider girls were always open to taking new recruits. With this crew, I didn't need to worry about boys for a few years. This new crew of misfits were the coolest girls in the *world*.

But, *retournons au Français*. A group of local lads on mopeds had discovered there was a group from an English girls' school residing in their small town. Perfect Vicky somehow got chatting to the lads and next thing you know, eight girls were dangling out of a ground-floor window, talking to four boys on mopeds. Vicky was well into the leader of their pack, Giles, pronounced Geeel, and he seemed to be well into her. This scenario goes to prove that feelings can cross language barriers, or at least straight-up teenage lust can. The shortest, youngest-looking French lad (he looked about ten) to my surprise said he had a crush on me. ME. WHAT?

I was pushed to the front of the window. *Er, bonjour, comment t'appelles-tu?* I had basic French, enough to be able order a pastry, the important stuff. He spoke no English, so I led the conversation. As he opened his mouth to speak, a sunbeam struck metal, sorting out his teeth too. *Je m'appelle Thomas.* End of conversation. What you really want to hear is how we kissed and our braces got stuck together, right? Nope, no chance. This really was the first time a boy my age had smiled at me. It was kind of thrilling but utterly terrifying.

Back home, France and Thomas were a lovely, fun-filled, sweet memory. Until I got some news that made the blood drain from my entire body and was going to DESTROY MY LIFE. Vicky had stayed in touch with Geeeel and Thomas wanted to contact me. What the hell for? I mean, seriously, dude, was I the first girl you'd ever met with a brace? Vicky said she'd given Geeeel my address to pass on to Thomas.

YOU DID WHAT?!

NO NO NO NO.

I have Indian parents. I do not want to be receiving mail from boys in France. This was a disaster on a grand scale for my teenage self. Every day, I'd try and intercept the mail, which was impossible because I had no idea when the mail came and I spent all day in school. Then one day I was home alone with Dad and he showed me an envelope and asked me what it was. The blood drained out of me, my legs turned to complete jelly. Vicky had properly stitched me up. I opened it. His handwriting was atrocious and the only English words he'd learnt for the purpose of the letter were:

Anita.

I love you.

Thomas.

WHAT THE ACTUAL . . . . This guy was a maniac and now I was having the worst day of my life. I had to explain that I had no control over the fact he was some kind of obsessive lunatic, or maybe he was just being French. I can still feel the heat coming off my face from that day and the combination of utter fear and humiliation. Dad listened and then he just said, 'You're lucky it was me who opened it and not your mum.' And that was the end of it. Dad seemed pretty cool in that moment. Or maybe he realised that his child was a young naïve child, that this was not a big deal. Or maybe he filed it away and thought, better keep a close eye on this one . . .

So, you know by 15, boys are still not my priority. This didn't mean that I wasn't noticing or even fancying them. God yes, I was, but I'd watched enough Bollywood movies to know it was always going to be too much drama, plus why would anyone fancy *me*? Also, it just wasn't allowed, so I curbed my real world desires, convinced romance was not my bag. Until, that is, I had my first ever snog on the staircase in Tumblers (the local club). If I'm telling you this tale, I might as well give you all of the juicy gossip that's stayed with me all this time. My first kiss was with a lovely ginger floppy-haired sixth former from the boys' school, called Zac. This is going to come as a major shock to my parents and I may never be allowed home again:

'Yes Ma, it's true, I kissed him.'

Camera flicks to mother's face, her eyes widen, mouth opens in shock. Camera flicks back to Anita.

'I kissed . . .'

Camera back to Mum. Back to me.

'I kissed . . . a ginger!!!'

Extreme Bollywood style close-up on my mother's face, as she screams.

'NAHEEEEEEEEEEEEEEEEE!'

We'd met when I was selected to go on the mountaineering expedition to China. Zac was dreamy and talked to me. Can you imagine? He really seemed to like me and was kind and funny and found me funny. Plus, he was fit, with floppy hair. The hair was always important. I told him I fancied him (yes, I know right, what a flippin' contradiction: one minute I'm not into boys, the next I'm just stepping up to them to tell them they're hot). I mustered the courage to just tell him I was into him, and I've got to give it to my younger self, I was direct and had guts. Go me! And how did he react? Did he say the feelings were mutual and would I like to go to Andy's Records then Burger King, or maybe get a cheese and onion pasty from Thurstons with him next weekend (dream date)? Did he say, how about we go for a lovely walk across Ilkley Moor, then a trip to Betty's for a cream tea (dream man) or even just get a bag of chips? Naturally, none of the above.

Sadly, he had to break it to me that he didn't fancy me and was seeing Vicky. We get it, Vicky, you're hot! Big sigh. Let's be real for a minute, why the hell would he fancy me?

Left: Check out this gorgeous lot! Nanaji and Naniji, my grandparents on Mum's side.

Below: Nanaji's first wife, Pritam Kaur. We still don't know what happened to her during the Partition of India.

Left: My grandad, Kebal Ram, from Dad's side – this is his actual passport pic showing him exactly as he landed in Blighty, in 1953.

Right: My mum and dad on their wedding day with Gran (Dad's mum), already lending a guiding hand on how to make roti!

Left: Look at my mum and dad, only 19 and 23! Yup, Mum's older. On their honeymoon in August 1976. Bloomin' icons!

Sombre for such a happy day – but guess who's about to turn up and make them smile…?

A collage of Anitas…

Left page: The good old days, when it was just me, Mum and Dad! Loving that eighties décor – and at the very bottom is me (far right) pondering life, on my very first trip to India, age three. Can you spot baby Anita on a tractor, too? I've been preparing since birth for *Countryfile*.

Right page: And then Kul came along. Bloody cute though, I'll give him that.

A classic Punjabi picnic, complete with pickles and eating on the bonnet. Take me back!

Epic wedding in India in 1984, when I was seven. This is my aunt (masi) with her new husband, and me in the middle. She looks thrilled!

Left: In the Dales with the family – look closely and you'll see, instead of looking up at the gorgeous scenery around me, I'm just really interested in the snack in my hand… Oops.

Right: Blackpool with Mum, Dad and my two aunts. Gorgeous, gorgeous Blackpool.

Playing around with Kul, Mum and Dad.

Below: Centre stage as Mary in Bradford Elm Day Nursery, 1980. Where it all began.

Above: A picture of innocence, a picture of sass… Oh, how times have not changed!

Left: There is no age limit on sleep-overs. I stand by that til the end of time.

Right: With my gang, aged 20, with free-flowing eyebrows! It's the nineties.

Above: Hockey stick? Check. Awkward first day of school family photo? Check.

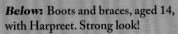

Below: Boots and braces, aged 14, with Harpreet. Strong look!

Left: Check out my New Kids gallery… I was a FAN, all right?!

Right: Adventures in the motherland with Al, aged 16.

Right: Grooving at my wedding on 1st November 2009.

Left: My life, my heart, my Rafi.

Right: YORKSHIRE! And breathe.

I was, no doubt, devastated, and this situation would have added to my 'no one is into me' narrative, but the great technique I had developed to deal with heartbreak back then was to just shrug it off and walk on. It's worked for me so far and, look, I'm only having to write a book in my forties to figure out that maybe my own internal dialogue has been quite hard on me . . .

After half a watery cider (all the booze on tap was watered down at Tumblers), I was heading down the staircase and who should be on his way up? None other than dream boat ginger Zac. By this time, the alcohol had started to have an effect. I had a little buzz on, enough for me to lose the few inhibitions I had left. As I crossed him on the staircase, he stopped to ask if I was OK (what a guy!). 'Yes, I'm fine and I understand completely,' I said, slightly swaying because of the booze and because the DJ had just dropped Nirvana 'Smells Like Teen Spirit'. Then to my surprise I said, 'I don't mind if you don't want to be my boyfriend, but can I kiss you?'

There it is, girls and boys. I straight up asked for my first kiss.

Cue slow motion. The lights fade. Spotlight is on us. Portishead 'Glory Box' begins to play as our eyes meet, my bum-length hair is blowing in the mysterious indoor breeze and our heads move slowly slowly slowly towards each other.

Needle scratches off the record. Back to reality.

The staircase is brightly lit, my bovver boots are sticking to the carpet, the smell is a combination of beer and sick and stale fags, and people are trying to get past us on the staircase. And then a ten-second snog happened. I had a SNOG! The one thing I never thought I'd have, not for many years to come at least. My feet felt like they'd lifted off the ground, it was dreamy and so satisfying that I'd asked and he said yes. I felt so powerful. I'd soon discover that this is usually all girls need to do and boys rarely say no. I had to cut my moment of bliss short though because the dancefloor was calling. 'Smells Like Teen Spirit' was blasting out of the speakers and I needed to go and jump and scream for joy. I was slightly tipsy and had kissed a boy, precisely the reasons my parents were afraid to let me out. They didn't need to worry though, this little moment of experimental joy wasn't enough for boys to become my thing, not really, not in real actual life, not yet.

* * *

Crucially, this is a romantic fairy-tale for non-romantics. I did not ever believe a handsome prince was going to save me and make everything OK and, it turns out, I was right. Anita, no handsome prince will save you, but you must work on selecting the boys you allow in! Or at least spend some time thinking about the qualities you'd like them to have. I was so content with living in my head, living my alternate dream life, that it would go on to mess up my future choices. I didn't even realise I had a choice, so convinced was I that no boys were into me, that when any did show any interest in the not too distant future I was so grateful, I'd just end up in a relationship. I had developed zero critical faculties when it came to the opposite sex. I'm just going to take a minute to have a word with my younger self and if you need some friendly (if slightly skewed from my perspective) advice, it's for you, too.

Well, 16-year-old Anita, you'll be thrilled to hear that at uni and beyond, boys do fancy you. Maybe not always the ones you fancy, but that's OK. You will have secret relationships. Sorry to reveal this to the world/your mother but, NEWS FLASH, a lot of Asian kids are having more than just 'fraaanships' with people out there.

You might not need a prince, but at least believe in yourself. Don't keep going out with the first guy who shows you any attention because you're so grateful for the attention. For all your sass and confidence, and drive to succeed and do well at work and everything you put your mind to, you are properly shit when it comes to boys. What you want from a partner requires some level of critical analysis. Have some.

Jo, one of our smartest friends, had a checklist: *educated, listens to great music, well-read, wears cool T-shirts, has interesting friends, fit*. At the time, you thought what a crazy idea, I'm just going to meet the man for me, it's going to be totally organic and natural and I'll just know. NO NO NO. Jo is a genius. Always have standards because you are incredible. What is this crazy pressure society puts on all of us to be in a relationship, this crazy pursuit to find 'THE ONE'. Please spend some time on self-reflection. I know you are scared, I know looking into the past terrifies you, but you need to face your fear because it's holding you down, it will consume you, corrode you from the inside. Yes, your outer shell is tough but the corrosion will begin to eat away at that too. You'll smile smile smile on the outside, yet internally there's a deep hollow. Making other people smile is also not the answer. As much as you love doing it, and 'doing the right thing', fuck 'em. Don't be afraid to find your true power, and your true power lies in being you. Don't worry about making everyone happy, because you'll wake up at 40 wondering who the fuck you are.

I thought tight clothes and make-up were frivolous and daft and being sexy for boys was a waste of time. I was a massive prude in dungarees. I was, and remain, such a prude that I refused the first proper magazine shoot I was ever offered because they wanted me in lingerie – the editor called me up in disbelief! I remember the conversation and how he couldn't believe I was saying no. I said I couldn't believe it was a genuine idea for a shoot. I was prepared to walk away from the entire magazine shoot rather than have my photo taken in my pants – not even *my* pants, someone's selected fancy pants. They changed the brief and my briefs stayed covered up! Now, although I still have body confidence issues, I've learnt to love dressing up AND dressing down. I feel as OK in heels as in wellies, in trainers or in clogs. None of it makes me any less. I. Have. Power.

You Don't Need to Compromise on Your Own Happiness

A major factor in not being one of the lusted-after at school was the fact I was brown. No one really fancied the brown kid back then. In Bradford, no one thought brown folk were cool. We knew we were, but the rest of Britain hadn't seen this yet. Back then, we were all just Pakis. Even brown kids didn't fancy the brown kids. I know, some kind of crazy next level issues, right? 'I've never fancied an Asian girl before you.' This has been said to me by Asian boys at least three times. Is this meant to be some kind of compliment? Am I supposed to be flattered? Ooohh, lucky me, this guy with self-loathing identity issues has picked me as the chosen one. Stroll on, mate.

Asian girls think all Asian men are mummies' boys (which is usually true) and Asian boys think all Asian girls are square and boring (which is far from the truth), but I think it's much more than that. Both Asian boys and girls come with Asian families and that means a ton of baggage. Big family bumper packs, buy one get 500, multi-generational, jute sacks of baggage. It's bad enough having to deal with your own families Indianness, sod having to take on someone else's too. Not when all you want is a stress-free teenage romance.

Throughout my life I would go on to be fetishised by white boys:

'Oh, you're so exotic.' I'm from Bradford.

'I'd love to go to an ashram with you.' Yeah, drum n bass clubs are more my sanctuary, or a walk on Ilkley Moor.

'You could be my Indian Princess.' No, no, I really couldn't possibly. I'm not here to fulfil your Empire fantasy.

Turns out, I'm not alone in feeling sexually isolated as a teenager. Not that I wanted any actual sex. Brown kids of my generation are very much later developers than the average white kid. In 2017, Durex compiled a global list of 44 countries and the average age people lose their virginity: India was second from the highest age, with 23 the average. The UK was at number 19, with age 18. If British Asian was a category on the list, we'd be right at the top with NOT UNTIL YOU ARE MARRIED!

Had I grown up in India, maybe I wouldn't have felt like I was missing out so much. Maybe everyone in India develops later and having imaginary boyfriends and girlfriends is the norm. Certainly, the idea of dating is relatively new over there and even then, openly, only amongst the urbanised upper middle classes. India is a deeply conservative society but from what I have seen, young urbanites in Mumbai are certainly making up for lost time, but ultimately marry who their parents approve of.

For most Indian girls and boys of my generation, boy-friends and girlfriends were a no-no. Romance? Denied. Sexuality? HAI HAI HAI. SEX? Chi chi chi. Ney ney ney.[10] The shame of it. So, to get around the small problem of no dating, we simply lie to our parents. (Although from what I saw was going on around me, it was clear boys had it much easier than girls.) Who's that boy on the phone? Oh, just a friend. They could never know he was a boyfriend. You'd be locked away, have your ass whooped or worse, be married off!

A friend of mine always had an eye for the lads. I'll never forget the description of her first French kiss and how he'd licked her braces and how she couldn't wait to get back to school for more. When she went to uni, no longer forced to wear the terrible dowdy outfits her mum picked, she'd turned into a beautiful swan. Everyone noticed, particularly the boys, and she loved the attention. Her Indian parents, meanwhile, were completely panicked by their sassy, sexpot stunner of a daughter, so they let her finish her degree, then found her a husband. Just like that, so she was no longer their problem to worry about. Her brother, however, left

---

[10] There's a lot of repetition in Punjabi for added drama. We also like to rhyme. Boys woys, girl shirls, friend frund, drink shink and, one of my all-time faves, party sharty. My mate once had a sharty party on New Year's Eve and had to hide his pants behind the U bend of the pub toilet. It's a top-secret story but I have to tell everyone I know and now you, because sharting is inherently funny, unless it's you doing it.

home, did whatever the hell he wanted and eventually married a white woman – but that's to be expected. It ended well for my friend, she was happy to get out of her parents' house and you'll be pleased to hear her husband is lovely.

What you need to know about my own mum is that she thinks of herself as an open-minded Indian mother, because she'd say, 'You can marry anyone you want, aaaaannnyyyybody, you are lucky I'm so open-minded, other girls' mothers are much stricter than me, you can pick the person you want to marry . . . as long as he's Indian.' This was her obsession – marrying, and marrying Indian. She was liberal enough to allow me to pick for myself, but also told me 'no one knows where to start with you' (like I was going to let anyone else do it) as long as he was a boy from a family from any state in India, which was really useful in suburban Bradford. The worst crime I could commit would be to bring home someone non-Indian.

What's the worst that could happen if you fell in love with and wanted to marry someone who didn't fit your parents' expectations? For some Asian girls, falling in love with the wrong man is a crime. Back in the 1980s, I used to lie on my granny's sofa pretending to sleep but actually listening to my two aunts have a good old gossip about which of their friends had run away from home, usually with a boy. Probably to escape a forced marriage. Punjabi parents disowning their daughters was commonplace when I was a tot. Mainly because they'd dared to make their own choices about their lives. There is no such thing as unconditional love in an Asian household, unless you are a son of course. Here's the deal: you bring shame, we disown you. You don't even need to bring home a person as shocking as someone white, black, Muslim, Hindu or Sikh (depending on your religious perspective) for Bollywood-style melodrama to ensue. Even someone from the wrong caste can result in children being outcast. A person who has the same religion, same food, same language, same culture, same customs – you are the same sodding people, but three generations ago your ancestors did a job that Britain decided would help define you and now here you are refusing to speak to your own child because they made their own decision about who they want to spend the rest of their life with. Utter madness.

What's the worst that could happen? The worst? The worst is the worst. I knew someone whose husband was doing time for killing his own sister because she'd fallen in love. A so-called honour killing. I fail to see the honour. Shame shame shame on those who treat their daughters like chattel. Who place the burden of being the families' pride on their daughters, who suffocate their existence, who crush their souls, who believe their only use is to bear sons and make roti. Shame on you, I say. I've seen so many crushed wills, I watched all my aunts and cousins bury their own wants and desires to keep their parents' heads held high. I too was filled with this nonsense. The moment you marry is when parents can breathe a sigh of relief and proudly watch their daughter – the one so many said had too much freedom and would end up marrying white, or would run away – have a traditional wedding and marry someone Indian. Fulfilling her dharma, her duty. That's the moment they wait for. As though bringing up a daughter is an act of danger and trepidation, a great, heavy joyless burden, until you can finally say she belongs to someone else.

Marrying within your culture is the ultimate, then there are degrees of acceptance depending on who you go for. To marry white is often accepted, probably because Asians aspire to whiteness. Although there's the threat of the watching, judging eyes of the community to keep you on track ('Give her too much freedom and this is what you get'), we still feel to be married is a level of acceptance and, for the fairer-skin Indians, a way to vanish your identity, should you want to. There will be beautiful fair-skinned, mixed-race babies and everyone will live happily ever after.

Then there is what is rarely ever accepted, that will put Indian Hindu or Sikh families into a tail spin – to marry Muslim, to marry black, to marry black and Muslim, and to come out as LGBTQ+. The levels of prejudice within the Asian community are shocking. Don't get me wrong, things are changing and more and more families are happy to accept their children and the choices they make, but for every family whose son or daughter has come out as gay or married who they've wanted, there are many more who could never bring themselves to do this for fear of abandonment.

Pre-colonial India had very different attitudes towards sex and sexuality. When did we, the land of the Kama Sutra, where gender was always fluid and not binary, become so uptight? Was it when the British, with their colonial attitude and Christian morality, turned up? With an audacious sense of superiority and their shock and disgust at the sexual expression they saw? It was the British who added the petticoat and blouse to the saree. They also quickly put a stop to any homosexuality by making it illegal. Killjoys. We took that colonial legacy and ran with it, and haven't stopped running.

So how on earth then, if marriage is the ultimate goal and you're not allowed a relationship, are you ever meant to meet someone? In my family, up until me, every single person (well, every single woman at least) had an arranged marriage. My uncles left home and married white women, an easy solution to their own identity issues, removing themselves from their ethnicity, free to do what they want. Oh, the privilege of having a penis! The way the system worked was, you stay at home until your parents find a suitable person for you to marry, you have a big wedding and, if you are the daughter, you then move in with your in-laws.

My mother's generation got on with it because they accepted the system and had zero other options. But the world was changing, rapidly, and within one further generation, children born in the UK wanted to have some choice in the small matter of who they were going to spend the rest of their lives with! This meant an easing up of the system. Now, 'arranged marriages' became 'introduction marriages'. Your parents, along with the illuminaunty, would find suitable matches to introduce you to and you are, amazingly, given the opportunity to say no.

The illuminaunty have been the reason for most Indian marriages for centuries.

The illuminaunty is global.

The illuminaunty knows everything about everybody. Knowing everybody's business is their business.

The illuminaunty establish where each family falls in the pecking order based on religion, wealth, education, culture, class and sadly, for years, caste. They then sit back and go through the rolodex of families in their busybody brains, brains with a capacity to store a vast amount of other people's information, until they find another family who is a suitable match.

Mr and Mrs Sangar, self-made business people, looking for a match for Harpal, their dentist son, who lives at home and drives a Porsche. The calls will go out, word spreads, all the rolodexes from Birmingham to Bradford, Toronto to New Jersey, Delhi to Jallandur, begin spinning. Now, the illuminaunty have upgraded to WhatsApp. Messages are shared around the world in seconds, biodata pinging into smartphones, along with a daily photo of a flower or a cheru-besque toddler, with a platitude printed across it or a quote from Buddha or an ayurvedic treatment, until . . . We have a match! Mr and Mrs Sera. Also self-made business people. Their daughter is very pretty and fair and homely and is also some kind of scientist . . . but no one really knows the details of what she does, because she is very pretty.

Picture this family set up: Granny, the matriarch, is the decision maker, the ball breaker, looms over a large extended family where everyone must do their duty. Spoilt sons, who don't have to worry about a career or bettering themselves as it's all handed to them on a plate and who think they can get away with anything because they usually can, will be protected by Mummy. The high-achieving daughter needs to make something of herself because she's not a son. Arranged marriages are to young, beautiful and suitable women, women who will fit your family's culture, who smile a lot, say very little and, this is a must, bear children. She must be the right sort of girl, because she will be a reflection of your family. If you're LGBTQ+ the family, if they know, will keep it hidden from everyone. If you choose to marry someone not deemed to be suitable – let's say, free-thinking, independent, Muslim, black – then you are Out.

The family I am actually describing is the highest in this land. Gatekeepers of the Church of England. The one and only Windsors. 'You know the Vindsors? The royal family? Totally Asian.' When Meghan and Harry decided to bring up their child the way they wanted and to live their own life (let's face it, that's really all that happened), they were stepping out of the joint family network. The finger of blame was sadly and predictably pointed at the new bride, the woman who didn't fit in, who (wait for this, it's truly shocking) had her own mind. It feels to me, as discussions about Meghan and Harry rumble on, like I'm watching another cliched Indian soap opera. Family sagas about 'disruptive' daughters-in-law have kept India glued to their small screens for decades. So, you see, Asian family traditions and culture aren't so alien to this land.

I opted out of this system, and this was a great source of consternation for my aunts. At 16, I was at a wedding. Don't ask me whose wedding, I have no flipping idea. I went to so many growing up and very rarely knew whose I was attending. Indian weddings are more than a family affair – you invite everyone you know or everyone who has invited you to a wedding. Most of the time, at weddings of the eighties and nineties, no one knew who was coming or going. You'd easily have 1,000 people on the guest list. The reception would take place in some kind of school hall/sports centre/community hall, with rows and rows of tables, Coke bottles, packets of crisps and peanuts, bottles of Bacardi and Johnnie Walker Black Label and a buffet big enough to feed Britain. A gate-crasher's paradise.

This one particular wedding was a seminal moment in my life. It was the wedding where I swore never to attend another wedding. I was dressed in a simple cotton kurta top with adidas trainers. I was ahead of my time and definitely followed no rules when dressing in Indian clothes. If I had to wear something Indian, it had to be super simple paired with my adidas shell toes, a design classic. Mum hated that I was in trainers but she also knew she wasn't going to get me in heels. She had lost the battle to try and make me girly by the time I was six. I was sitting next to my mum, tucking into my second packet of Walkers cheese and onion, when the illuminaunty clocked me. Had they spotted my shoe choice, they may have thought twice about approaching. It looked like they moved en masse as one single entity. A blob of shimmery sarees and enough gold to sink a ship, all whispering 'kussur pussur, kussur pussur', gliding towards us, like a horror movie monster. Five sets of beady kohl-covered eyes all peering at me. One set of eyes spoke to my mother while the other four continued to stare at me.

'Kuri ki kurdiyeh?' What does the girl do?

'Kuri di ummar ki?' How old is the girl?

'Munday bhaterey hayge ah.' There are plenty of boys.

'Can she see that I am sitting right here, Mum? Tell her I'm only 16.' I walked away fuming. Fuming was a semi-permanent state for me then, you may recall. 'Don't mind them,' my mum would say to try and calm my outrage. 'It's just our culture. But . . . they did mention a boy who rides a motorbike and one family has a fleeeeeeeet of Rolls-Royces.'

'The aunty network sounds great,' my single white friends in their thirties would later say to me. 'It's so hard to meet people, why not have a system where someone has gone through a basic checklist before you go on a blind date?' Maybe the illuminaunty need to branch out into other cultures.[11] Maybe they could create a marriage bureau app and call it PREETINDER? Their tagline could be: '200 per cent success rate . . . Love comes later.'

* * *

'It's all about adjustment and compromise' is a sentence I've heard a lot in relation to how to make a marriage work, but interestingly, it always comes from women. The expectations placed on women are enormous, regardless of what

---

[11] The illuminaunty should have been deployed to do track and trace.

culture you belong to. As someone who hates to disappoint people, I've really taken on the pressure to try and keep everyone happy. I have been moulded from birth to try and be the right sort of girl. A girl that is successful and listens to her parents and makes them proud and makes sodding chapattis and, crucially, marries the right sort of boy. Basically, to be it all, to have it all, to do it all.

The illuminaunty marriage system does work for a lot of people. Not everyone finds it a chore. But for some of us, these expectations don't accommodate or make space for what you want to do with the only life you have. To do what might make you happy and allow you to make a few mistakes along the way as well. There's no safety net if you fuck up! The stakes are huge – if you mess up, then you get the booby prize and a big bucket of fetid shame is dropped on your head. So, you live in and move between different worlds if you want to have any kind of romantic life before marriage. It's a life based on a need-to-know basis. How much do your family need to know? Your friends? There's the life you build for yourself, if you're lucky enough to be able to, and the life you want your family to know about. That's how you have to roll. Shifting in and out of worlds. Imagine skilfully navigating your life like that! South Asian kids of my generation are masters of disguise.

If it's happiness you desire, you ultimately have to do what you want. Plus, I'm SO OVER SHAME. Little Anita, do yourself a favour and try and see through the bullshit, keep going down the road of liberation as hard as it may feel, keep walking towards the light. We are the first generation who are having to learn to live between worlds and cultures. Some of us, painful as it may be, have to upset the apple cart to change the world and make it easier for others. We have to stick our necks out and speak out. We need to find our courage and power, to make it easier for others to turn around and say, 'Nah, you're alright. I'll just do me, thanks. If I want a Rolls-Royce, I'll buy my own.'

You Will Party, Whether You're Allowed To or Not

Asian kids are adept at living multiple lives and lying to our parents. This is a basic survival technique if we want any kind of social life whatsoever. Sometimes I think Asian parents would be happiest if their children just had no friends. My parents did their utmost to try and curb it.

'Mum, Dad, can I go . . .'

'NO.'

'Can I . . .'

'No.'

'Can . . .'

'No.'

I've stood up so many mates because I'd say yes to every invite going, knowing full well the answer from my folks would be NO most of the time. And remember, I had 'liberal' parents. It's easier sometimes to not bother having friends. Or at least keep yourself a little aloof.

But teenagers will always find a way to party. To get around not being allowed out at night, the nineties spawned a phenomenon in the UK called the Daytimer, a club night during the day. While the rest of the country were raving after sundown, Asian kids, whose conservative parents would not allow this in a month of Sundays, especially not the girls, came up with a cunning daylight, midweek solution. Girls, heading to school or Bradford college, would jump on buses in their modest, parent-friendly outfits, then at the back of the bus a salwar would become a pair of jeans and bright red lipstick would be expertly applied. The best RnB, hip hop, garage, soul and bhangra tunes, Mary J. Blige, TLC, Soul II Soul, Tupac, LLCool J, Achanak, Bally Sagoo, all played while Bacardi and Diet Cokes were sipped and secret ciggies puffed away at. Girls and boys hooking up in their best garms, stand-offs between Sikh boys and Muslim boys, the odd fight. And dancing, non-stop dancing. They'd start at lunchtime, finishing at about 6pm. Then, enough Wrigley's Juicy Fruit was chewed and The Body Shop's White Musk applied to get rid of any lingering evidence, and you'd make it home in time for roti. Parents none the wiser.

My world was that of Bradford Girls Grammar School and my friends were middle class and white, so day-timers were not on their radar. And why would they be? They were allowed out at night and no one, anywhere, was paying attention to or even cared how teenage brown kids were getting their kicks. There had been a British bhangra scene growing in the UK since the seventies and it is now global. But, strangely, it's still hidden away as a sub-culture, a youth movement, that only us brown kids seem to know about, 40 years on!

Even if I'd wanted to go to a day rave (and believe me, I did, especially as my brown mates from the temple seemed to be having the best time), once classes began, my school gates were closed and there was no escaping until the end of the day. So, I had to somehow convince my parents to let me out at night and give me a bit of freedom. Why send me to a school where you want me to assimilate but then ruin my social life by never letting me out with my friends? A social life which, by the way, had thrived up until I was 15. Sleepovers were a regular activity my entire school life – I went to every birthday party, weekends away, the odd authentic camping holiday – which was more than my Indian girl friends at the temple were allowed. It's only when boys and Tumblers came into the picture that there was a slight bump we had to navigate. And not just my parents – every parent at the school.

Being around alcohol wasn't the problem, not really. We'd been going to the pub as a family forever. Often, we were the only brown family in our pub in the Yorkshire countryside. My dad loves the pub and he taught us to love it too. Much to my mother's annoyance. Our favourite pub in Bradford was called Macrory's, a small Irish place down a set of Yorkshire stone steps, cavern-like, and every Sunday they'd have a live band playing so we'd go along for a drink and a sway. Dad would have a Guinness, I'd have half a Murphy's, Kul a coke and Mum a Baileys on ice. Or Dad would take Kul and me to Calico Jacks in Little Germany, where he taught us to play the fruit machines and how to shoot pool, while giving us great pearls of wisdom for life: 'The game's not over until the black is potted.' And my favourite: 'Only go to the pub if you can afford a round.' Giveaways signs of Dad's misspent youth!

Tumblers was the only club in Bradford that would serve underage drinkers and for parents, girls and boys together with alcohol, unsupervised, is a problem. Tumblers was THE place, a club where we were free to hang out with friends at night away from our folks, where I could spend hours dancing away to all the music I loved. No longer couped up in my bedroom, here I could express myself fully. I'd let my bumlength hair down and mosh until my head felt like snapping off my neck. Whiplash was an unfortunate consequence of a night headbanging at Tumblers. Headbanging? What on earth was I thinking? It was only a brief dance phase, which my neck is now very happy about.

Getting to this heavenly dive bar in the first place was always a mission. First, how do we get our parents to agree to letting us go? Depending on the leniency of your folks you'd have to come up with your own home exit strategy. For some it was just easy: 'Ya sure, daaarling, just let us know what time you'd like Daddy or me to come pick you up in the Range.' Others had slightly older boyfriends from the boys' school that their parents were happy about. Actually excited that their daughters were in a relationship! They were on another planet. 'Ya sure, daaarling, Freddie picking you up, OK ya, he's borrowed his daddy's Merc, OK good, ya sure stay over at his, then Daddy or me will pick you up in the Jag.'

Those of us whose parents were a little more old-fashioned had to come up with the 'I'm staying over at Robyn's house and we are going to Tumblers, Robyn's parents will pick us up'. Robyn was the most sensible and trustworthy friend I had, she would usually garner a positive response. If this failed, you'd just tell them what they'd want to hear. 'I'm off for a sleepover at Robyn's', omitting the detail that you'll be swinging by Tumblers. My naughty friend Katie would often jump out of her bedroom window and sneak out. She asked me to stay over at hers a few times but Katie was too wild for me, she wore make-up and had even had sex. Utterly terrifying.

But getting out of the house on any night out had to be a well-timed masterplan. How do I put on my outfit for the night and leave the front door without smelling of curry? When Mum was home, 99 per cent of the time she was in the kitchen, cooking. Apparently, curry can only be cooked in vast quantities, which I can now attest for. The food was for us to eat as a family, or because we had guests coming round for dinner, or just in case anyone decided to turn up for dinner, or to feed the neighbours, for her colleagues at work, for people at Bradford Cathedral, or the milkman, or postman, or Jehovah's Witnesses, or anyone who Mum sparked up conversation with, or anyone who knocked on the door: 'You can have some if you want'. I'm sure if I said, 'Mum, everyone who's reading my book wants to taste your dhal,' she'd say, 'No problem, darling,' and start getting the pans out. Friday and Saturday evenings were big cook nights. The smell of Mum's tarka for aloo gobi, matar paneer or chicken curry permeating the entire house, with Dad opening all the kitchen windows and door as he hated the smell.

When I now make Indian food, the food I grew up with, I love the smell that fragrances my home, making it smell *of* home. Back in the mid-nineties, however, curry was killing my vibe. I did not want to be the Asian who actually smelled of curry in the pub so the last thing to do before leaving home was a change of clothes: Dad's trousers, baggy shirt (probably also Dad's), a dab of patchouli oil on my wrist and dash out out out the front door.

All to get to this grimy club, where private school kids in Dr. Martens and oversized jumpers drank watered-down cider or cheap vodka with orange cordial (I'm gipping at the thought), and bounced around the dancefloor to the Sultans of Ping. Finally, music blasting out of loud speakers with space to dance that wasn't the living room or a wedding reception. My musical world was expanding.

* * *

Music is my greatest joy, my first and longest love affair, my best friend, my confidante, my consigliere, my sanctuary. Music has defined and shaped so much of my life. I've met some of my greatest friends because of our shared passion for tunes. I've walked away from otherwise lovely people because our musical taste simply isn't compatible. Harsh, I know! But totally reasonable.

It's through music I was able to feel and express all my emotions and change my mood. I didn't even have to do anything, just press play and it would work its magic, allowing whatever feelings I had a problem expressing otherwise to simply pop up and exist. And I couldn't get enough. Music is a master soother. My musical education started in the womb. Mum sings and has a beautiful voice, and she sang all the time. The songs of her childhood brought her comfort in Bradford. The best and sweetest singing was saved for Kul and me, and we got our own intimate private concert every night. We weren't read to as kids, there weren't many books in my house, but we were told stories and my mum sang. She sang Hindi lullabies and a song so moving I have never been able to listen to the original without bursting into tears. Music did, and still does, really help me release emotions I didn't even know were there.

When I was finally old enough and allowed to go out with my friends (to dance, laugh, jump around, sing at the top of my lungs, literally let all my hair down, get whiplash, release stress and all those pent-up emotions, discover that listening to music and dancing with a crowd of people makes up a rare collective experience in a life that can otherwise feel solitary), I was instantly sold. I'd found my sacred space, a place I could lose myself. The dancefloor.

Embrace Your Inner Drama Queen

My world was being formed, I was starting to take shape. But I still didn't really fit in anywhere. I was always holding something of myself back, apart from in drama class.

I adored drama and English at school. I hated having to read aloud in class, which is strange to think about as it's a major skill required for my job now – just goes to show you can overcome fear. When I was 13 and studying Shakespeare and the Brontës, I'd dread the moment the teacher would call out my name. My heart would pound from the beginning of the class. I couldn't even concentrate on what was being said, all I could hear was my own internal dialogue, 'don't pick me' 'don't pick me' 'don't pick me'. It was somehow different to performing, being put on the spot like that. It felt so exposing and I didn't feel I was as good as everyone else. I've always said how confident I was at school and I was, on the surface, but underneath I was a sweaty-palmed bag of nerves trying to adapt and fit in, so much so that I could hardly focus on the words in front of me.

But performing, that was different. No desks to tie my fidgety ass down, no sitting in silence in front of a stern teacher. No, this was the opposite of double geography. Maybe it was getting to play the principal role in my nursery nativity that gave me the bug for performing. Yes, in Bradford Elm Day Nursery in 1980, there was a little brown Mary. That's some forward-thinking nursery. Or maybe it was a way to channel my boundless energy? Drama suited me – I felt comfortable and at home. I was obsessed with the improv TV show, *Whose Line is It Anyway*? I studied speech and drama as an extracurricular activity. I'd get my folks to drop me off at the Alhambra Theatre and its adjacent Alhambra Studio in Bradford to watch plays, on my own. Bradford was a hub of arts and culture, for me at least, because that's what I was seeking out. I was hungry for it.

I didn't know anyone else who wanted to go and see The Tara Arts adaptation of *Cyrano de Bergerac*, set in India and starring one of my favourite Indian actors, Naseeruddin Shah. I wasn't pretentious, it was just my thing. I just wanted more than what was around me. Maybe I was aspiring to be pretentious. Tara Arts was a vital discovery for me. It was a touring South Asian theatre company from London, who would take Western plays and set them in India. They told stories through another lens and I saw life through another perspective. I saw myself in classic tales. What they brought to life on stage was pure magic. Their stories empowered me. Even something as simple as being in a theatre space with older brown faces who all loved theatre, who were unapologetic about their ethnicity and their identities, empowered me. I loved being around these arty farty literary types with their jeans and kurtas and hand-embroidered Kashmiri shawls casually draped across them. 'Is she Punjabi or Bengali?' Mum used to wonder out loud. Bengalis are seen as the cultured intellectuals of India, the opposite of the Punjabi stereotype. I was internalising that spaces where these stories, my stories, were told, were hidden in pockets that I would have to search for.

I did a lot of things on my own as a teenager. I could be a right loner, but it was a simple and enjoyable pleasure. Much easier than having to organise a group excursion and it involved little convincing of the parents. I spent hours in the Bradford Film and Photography Museum, wandering round the exhibitions, particularly the photographic ones. Soaking it all up for myself. Not waiting for anyone to tell me or show me, opening my own eyes to the world.[12]

I joined the Bradford Playhouse Saturday morning drama class at 14, a tiny theatre and cinema in an area called Little Germany. This area is full of beautiful architecture and it's called Little Germany because most of the stunning buildings were built by German wool merchants who came to the city in the late 1800s, when Bradford had a thriving wool trade.

There were no purple leotards here, no jazz hands, no singing or dancing, this was straight up theatre. Although, there was an upright piano in our dusty, dark little rehearsal room, and a few of us girls would stand around and make James play while we'd sing Beverley Craven's 'Promise Me' on

---

[12] The galleries in London are now my sanctuary for solo wanders. Galleries, cinemas and theatres are great spaces to spend time alone, places you can hang out with no one and not feel like a total weirdo for doing it. Don't lose this when you grow up, young Anita! Just go. Make time for yourself. Solo dates nourish your soul. Spending time alone, quality time enjoying your own company, is an essential life skill.

loop. It was the crew of kids I met here that really made it for me. They were not my friends from school, they were not my Asian family mates, this gang was a bunch of misfits from all over Bradford. There were a couple of older girls, maybe 15 or 16, super naughty, with tattoos and they smoked! Oooh, if only I could be that wild. There was a tall boy with shocking black hair who wore a floor-length *Matrix*-style leather jacket, pre-*Matrix*, with a Sisters of Mercy T-shirt and nails always painted black. There was the lad in the Dead Kennedys T-shirt too. The kids here were either naughty or nerdy, or a bit of both, but what connected us was that we were all outsiders in our own worlds. Here, somehow, this oddball bunch came together. It's the magic power of theatre, daaarling, the comradery of that space.

So much of my life was always filled with an undercurrent of dread. Going to school, being at home. But not at drama class. I don't remember anyone making anyone feel self-conscious and we were doing plenty of out-there, embarrassing stuff. We had a Russian teacher give a session on Stanislavski . . . I mean, we were teenagers! We had another session in mime, where we had to crawl across the floor and pretend we were trees, and I never remember feeling self-conscious. We all probably felt like complete wallies, but we were wallies together. If we were all at school together, we'd never have been friends, but here we were, thick as thieves.

In 1992, we were invited to go to a European drama festival in Germany. Forty-eight hours later on the coach, finally we arrived in Erfurt – a city which, only five years earlier, had been in East Germany. The trip was funded by an arts grant, which is why all the misfits were able to go, as most of our parents couldn't afford to send us. The hotel was a first for all of us: a cavernous Eastern Bloc building, a terrifying, huge, concrete monster. It was basic by all our standards and, at 14, most of us had no hotel standards to compare it to yet. The rooms were huge and sparse. There were no showers, just baths, and concrete, blood-stained floors (at least, I imagined them to be blood-stained). We attended mime, physical comedy, circus skills, pantomime and mask-making sessions. I remember rolling around on the floor like a marooned seal for a lot of them. Thankfully, none of them required too much language, as it became obvious we were the numbnuts of Europe. Everyone had some English, apart from the East German kids, but they were the first generation to live in a united Germany, so we'll let them off. The kids from Luxembourg were communication wizards, holding conversations in pretty much every European language at the same time! The Spanish only ever seemed to appear in a circle playing hacky sack or in a circle around a guitar, and their English was based on soft rock ballads. What the heck did we, the UK contingent, bring to the party? Nirvana T-shirts, aloof attitudes and really fussy but basic taste buds. For Sarah, the food was too foreign, so she ate pasta with ketchup for the entire trip. We were also all given a piece of steak for dinner at one point. I wasn't supposed to be eating it, Hindus and Sikhs don't eat the sacred cow and I'd never really eaten a slab of cow before, although I had no real beef with beef. My parents were never really that strict about the whole no beef thing.[13] We just never cooked it or talked about it. As it is, I had nothing to worry about. Turns out none of us had eaten beef on this trip, it was horse steak.

The days were spent making friends through hand gestures and facial contortions, which I'm pretty good at, as I have a very expressive face. It's useful when interviewing someone or for a good reaction on the telly. This trip was liberating. I was free, there was no family and no school friends either, with no judgement, just a little gang that I felt part of. I also tried my first real taste of alcohol, a Budweiser, on a tram. I felt pissed after half a bottle and got up to do impressions, terrible impressions, which signalled the beginning and end of my career as an impressionist.

The wonderful thing about acting is that the experience is bigger than the individual. It's why I always wanted to be in school plays. Even just sitting in the wings, in the darkness, watching the others on stage performing, creating a world, using an ancient artform, that takes both the people on stage out of themselves and the audience to another place. It's been said so many times about the feeling you get when 'treading the boards', but it really does get under your skin. I will never lose that itch to create, to be part of something, to tell stories.

Drama was the perfect space for someone who could effortlessly put on different hats depending on the situation.

---

[13] We never cooked it at home and Mum claims she'd never eaten it. When I reminded her about the burgers she made, her response was, 'But they are hamburgers.' You can see how easy that mistake was to make. 'Ham' burgers and homemade chips was a regular 'English' dinner for us.

It was the perfect place for someone who finds it hard to express emotion in real life to go and let it all out. Playing at make believe was such a gift, especially when my make-believe life was so much easier than my real one.

* * *

Oh, to not be flippin' self-conscious! What I will tell you, younger me, is not to forget your passion for drama. We can't let imaginary voices and worries about 'what people might say' get into our heads. Remember what it taught you, what you felt like, when you managed to rid yourself of those feelings. It's hard, though, not to constantly be in a state of panic about what people think when it's a script you've heard over and over again your entire life. 'What will people say?' You have to get out there and play nonetheless, play with everything you've got, because you have no other choice.

The trip to Germany with the misfits was transformative. I loved that I was there as an individual, with individual and unique skills, not part of any clique but still part of a team. The time I spent in the tiny, dark and dusty studio theatre in Bradford may well have been some of the truly happiest hours of my life.

I came back from Germany full to bursting, the same but changed, grown by my new experience. Dad picked me up off the coach and on the drive home he told me that Mum was in Birmingham with her sister. My uncle had died by suicide. Drama was a place I could rid myself of all the feelings I didn't know what to do with and take my mind off my real life. And it was sorely needed.

You Can Love Home
But Also Desperately Need
to Leave

When I think of Bradford, the weather is always grey. The mood is always melancholy.

Everything I did when I was younger was to work towards my exit strategy. To be somewhere other than where I was. Not to get to 'that there London', that possibility wasn't on the horizon, not just yet. When I was young, my dreams were really only to get out of Bradford, and not even that far. Just to the converted barn halfway between Baildon and Ilkley would have been fine. Just beyond the outer ring round would have done. I was itching to get out.

I loved Bradford and hated her too, in only the way a Bradfordian can. It's like that feeling of knowing someone so well you can see their flaws, they can really wind you up, but you still love the daft bastard. That's how I feel about Bradford. I carry so much shame as it is, the last thing I need is to add the city of my birth to the list as well. Bradford has been described as a shithole, but it is mine. And to call it a shithole is really doing her a disservice. Plus, you can only get away with calling her a shithole if you are from there. Bradford gets bad press but she made me. She cultured me. Bradford's fortunes have changed in the last hundred or so years, from one of the wealthiest cities in the world to somewhere associated with poverty and deprivation, race riots, book burning and a permanent promise of regeneration, which never seemed to materialise. Even in my lifetime, I saw shops and department stores slowly pack up and leave the city centre. I've also known people from Bradford to lie and say they're from Leeds. Can you imagine feeling so crap about your hometown, you pretend to be from Leeds? Not me. Bradford and proud.

The population of Bradford is just over 500,000, with 63.9 per cent white British and the largest proportion of British Pakistanis in the country: 20.3 per cent. (So large, it was known as Bradistan when I was growing up.) British Indians make up 2.5 per cent, so I really was an ethnic minority in Bradford. In my time, the city had become quite segregated in inner city areas, mainly due to white flight – as more Asians moved in, white families moved out. Growing up there, it seemed everyone had an opinion about the place, whether they'd been or not. Usually it was negative, which only strengthened my love for her.

Knowing Bradford and generally the culture of a northern city gives you a completely different perspective and understanding of life, especially when you move to London and realise how different things are. It gives you the edge. It gives you an understanding of England fully, the land beyond the

M25. Leeds got all posh and swanky with a Harvey Nichols and Manchester has always thought it was IT with its cocky swagger, even before Selfridges opened up. But can either of these places claim to have Britain's biggest pound shop? No. Didn't think so.

I loved Bradford but I really couldn't wait to get out.

My dream wasn't even just for me. It was a dream for my entire family. I wanted us all to live in the converted barn between Baildon and Ilkley. I wanted us all to have space. Away from our predominantly white suburb. I wanted to look out of my window and see the horizon and not just the cul-de-sac opposite. I was so bored of knowing my neighbours' movements, week in, week out. The mundanity of suburban life.

Monday – Andy at number 3 goes to cricket.

Tuesday – Judith gets dropped off after aerobics but always spends half an hour talking to her mate in the car before going in. Which I always found very strange. Just invite her in for a cuppa, Judith?

Wednesday – Val goes to Asda or, as we call it up north, Asdas.

Thursday – Jack practises his golf swing in the front garden.

Friday – Pat's granddaughter comes to stay. (She was mixed race, which I thought was thrilling. I was fascinated by mixed-race relationships. Probably because they were painted out to be such a taboo. Something my mother had already drilled into me was not an option.)

I'd sit at my window, music on to drown out the fights downstairs, watch suburban family life and feel numb. My home was claustrophobic. My only sanctuary was my little box bedroom, which was a swirling mess of feelings and homework and worries and plans. In my room I was always in my head. Dreaming of the places I would rather be. My alternative lives. I lived in America sometimes. Somehow, America was brighter and sunnier and seemed a more equal society to my eyes. I consumed so much American culture in TV shows and movies, hip hop and dance music, MTV. Failing getting on a plane to the US, Leeds or even Manchester would have done. The bright lights of these exciting big cities with their opportunities. As a teenager, these cosmopolitan cities felt full of hope compared to my Bradford. I needed more than Kirkgate market and Wimpy.

The day I passed my driving test, aged 17, may well have been the most liberating day of my life and I knew exactly where I was heading. Now I didn't need to ask for a lift, I didn't need to wait for the bus, I didn't need to ask anyone to pick me up. No friends, no family, just me, my beat-up Vauxhall Astra and a selection of cassettes. The day I'd been dreaming of had finally arrived. I was outta there. At 17, I probably drove like a bit of a maniac. With no one else in the car with me, I pushed it more than was safe. Which really wasn't that fast as the car started rattling over 40 miles an hour. I was a bit of a teenage speed demon. Driving for me was independence. Driving is freedom still.

The journey to freedom takes me from home through Bradford city centre, past the imposing edifice of Bradford Town Hall, the iconic Alhambra Theatre, past my mum and dad's old shop and the factory. Traffic lights are red on the steep hill, so I attempt clutch control and hope and pray no cars pull up behind as I might roll backwards. I just about find the biting point, I push the accelerator too hard, but I'm off again with a jerky vrooom. There's the eighties concrete block of the Arndale Centre and up beyond the seventies single-storey indoor John Street market. I know these streets, I've pounded them my entire life. I don't need a map, I've memorised the route. It is in me through osmosis. Today, I'm seeing them all from a new perspective, in my peripheral vision. Today, my eyes and mind are focused on driving, buzzing with excitement, adrenalin coursing through my veins, riding the edge between the pure terror of being in complete control and on my own for the first time in my life and the pure exhilaration and excitement of being in complete control and on my own for the first time in my life. I've waited for this moment. Dreamt of doing this. Onwards to my destination!

I've been a passenger for this journey since I was in the womb, so instinct kicks in with each gear change. Once out of the city centre, I go past the Victorian terraced houses of inner-city Bradford, curry houses, newsagents that sell fruit and veg, Asian women's clothing shops, and I drive further past the larger magnificent Victorian homes around Manningham Park, made of sturdy yellow Yorkshire stone, once homes for wealthy merchants, now large enough to house extended Asian families. Keep going, not there yet! Things are beginning to open up though as we round the corner and descend another hill. Got to keep an eye on my speed, driving through new build housing estates for the upwardly mobile middle classes, full of Asians who'd done well and their flash cars parked on concrete driveways, then slip into a lower gear to get up the steep hill to the more affluent villages in Baildon, Eldwick, big solid homes behind Yorkshire walls, with driveways and large gardens with stunning views. These areas are predominantly white in the nineties. Then, all of a sudden, the road opens up to reveal what I've been driving like a maniac towards: the West Yorkshire countryside.

You only need to do this drive for 20 minutes in any direction, from pretty much anywhere in Bradford city centre, and your eyes open a little wider and your lungs breathe a little deeper as you leave the urban sprawl behind and the magnificent splendour greets you with a nod of the flat-capped head and an 'Ey up?'

If you head up to Shipley Glen or Baildon Moor for a run around, as we often did as kids, you can see Bradford sitting in its bowl beneath you. Rows and rows of terraced houses, peppered with 'those dark satanic mills'. The mills that built this city, that fuelled the city, that choked the city, that created communities, that are the reason I am a Yorkshire lass. The mills that kept us locked to the concrete and stone and are also the reason for our need to escape. That used to cough up a right mess but now just sit there quietly and proud, polished up and turned into art galleries and fancy flats.

It's on these same moors that Bradfordians have been escaping to get away from the oppression of the city since the Industrial Revolution. But I'm not stopping just yet though. Not this time. My destination is a little further still.

The road opens up before me with Dales and sheep and the odd farmhouse on either side. My music gets turned up too.

For this journey, I need music to fuel my energy, music to match the surroundings, the soundtrack for this moment had to be just right. Will I play Rage Against the Machine? My Jungle mix tape? The Smiths compilation I've been listening to for the last four years? The Prodigy, *Experience*? Nah. Not today. Today, I push the cassette in, rewind it a bit, oh no, too far, fast forward a smidge, rewind a smidge, back, forwards, back, forwards, until I find the beginning of the track or near enough anyway. Predigital, everything took so much longer. But it had to be cued just right. Music born of the same land as me. Today, for this epic drive, my soundtrack has to be Bradford's finest, New Model Army.

There's the converted barn to my right, but today, I haven't got time to imagine me and my family living in it. I'm now officially on the move, squeezing through Burley in Wharfedale and slowing down to give the Hermit pub a little wave, then, just up a little further, on top of the moorland over a couple of cattle grids, I see her grey craggy face, giving me a knowing smile, in the distance. Awaiting my arrival. As she does everyone. Well aware we all need to break free from our concrete prisons and come seek her embrace. Ilkley Moor. The Cow and Calf rocks.

The car judders to a stop. I slam the door shut with a tinny clunk. Do I go left for a slow walk up the path or do I go right to scramble up and over the rocks as I always did as a kid? No-brainer. I bust a right and walk towards the pile of fallen rocks that make for a perfect scramble up to the top of the crag.

'I knew this day would come. I've been waiting for you,' she says. (It's my story and in my story, the moors talk.)

At the top, out of breath, I turn to take in the view, out to the horizon, over the posh little town of Ilkley, and just stare and breathe deep. Let it all go. It's November and the weather is as moody as you like, but this is my kind of weather, I can handle this, I'm in my comfort zone. Grey, mysterious, a bit chilly, threatening to rain. The scene is just as I'd imagined it. I knew for a long time that the minute I could get behind the wheel of a car, I'd head to Ilkley Moor for a walk. On my own. No company, just a solitary teen-age Indian lass from Bradford walking, looking, breathing and maybe lying down to watch the clouds. I couldn't wait to make the pilgrimage. To experience this place in a new way, without my family or friends, without the distraction of a conversation or a laugh and a joke, without having to keep someone else entertained, holding a little cousin's hand, without the distraction of wanting to see the pleasure and joy, sometimes even the fear, in their faces. An aunt from London actually cried with fear climbing to the top. There aren't too many hills in Southall and Ilkley Moor was proving to be a bit of a culture shock for her. No having to console and convince visiting aunties that they won't fall off the top or be eaten by a werewolf this time.

Today, I was here to have her all to myself. No sharing. I do what I always do and read the graffiti etched into the millstone, over a hundred years of names carved into the rocks, leaving their mark, adding to the magic, the names saying they too loved this place. Every time I'm there I think, one day I'll come back with a chisel and add my own name, stake my claim to a piece of the moor, add to its history: 'I was 'ere.' But I never remember to pack my chisel – I don't have a chisel.

This place has meaning but, more importantly for me, it has feeling. It's the reason I made a beeline for it. Anytime I set foot out here on our family weekend adventures, the noise of the rest of my life got dialled down – not muted completely, just dampened. The weight of the world left at the traffic lights in Shipley. Here, all four of us relaxed. Here, my parents smiled. Nature worked its magic and healed us and soothed us, giving us all a shoulder massage. A bit of respite before heading back to the pit of Bradford. These moors were our group family therapy sessions, totally free and available on tap.

I wanted it to myself this time though. I needed to get away from everyone, everything, up here on my own. It was a place where I didn't need to wear a particular mask, didn't need to put on any kind of face. The dutiful daughter, the marriage counsellor, the protector, the clown, the outsider. I didn't have to worry about anyone else, I didn't have to consider what people might think of me, I didn't need to make anyone else feel good about themselves, trying to be what everyone else expected. I was always so aware of other people's feelings, considerate to their needs, and was always conscious of making sure everyone else felt fine. I always approached the person on their own at a party, I befriended the new girl at school (whether they wanted me to or not). I was resilient and self-assured from a young age because

211

I'd had to be and I was happier thinking about how other people felt rather than how I was feeling. Much easier to talk about someone else rather than yourself. Because I was always fine, remember?

I didn't need anyone to look after me or make sure I was OK, that was my survival narrative. My parents always presumed I was OK. Being considerate meant I would never want to upset anyone, so I often never did what I wanted or even said what I was really thinking. I'd just agree to make others feel good. Go along with something even if I didn't want to, dumb myself down to massage other people's egos. In the process, I completely disregarded my own feelings. I've continued to do it my entire life.

But up here on my own on the moor there was no expectation of me, I could just be. This time, the outside noise dialled down once again but it kept going all the way down to mute, to nothing, just white noise. It may have started to rain, I may have let myself cry. No one can see you crying in the rain. I didn't cry much as a teenager. It wasn't just 'boys don't cry' in my family, girls didn't cry either. Now I cry at anything, making up for it – all the tears I collected in a reservoir and the dam has finally broken.

On this day, all I was left with was the thing I least understood, that scared me the most: my deepest feelings. Sadness, loneliness and the excitement of all the possibilities, all crashing around together usually, but now still. There was always comfort in my loneliness, because I was confident in my own ability to look after myself and I liked my own company. The fear I felt was a fear of stagnation, of things never changing, a fear of being trapped, a fear of not being able to live the life I want. And at 17, I knew I had the world ahead of me. Back then, the fear didn't scare me, it didn't paralyse me, it just fuelled me. I had energy and urgency pumping through me at a speed that matched my driving and it was this drive that powered me forward.

I walked and walked as my inner mantra repeated and repeated and repeated: 'I will get out of here. There's a whole world out there. For me.'

I just wanted to live my own life and not have anyone tell me what to do. Don't we all? I wanted to find a place where I could just be me. Express myself. Enjoy myself. Be myself.

I didn't fit the mould of anything around me. Not at home, not at school. Whatever shape it was, it wasn't Anita-shaped. I was free-spirited and open-minded and curious as hell. I was a loud-mouthed gobshite, with a fuck ton of opinions at school. I was a frustrated, angry teenager and yet trying to be a dutiful daughter who did everything right at home. I'd sucked out everything Bradford had to offer at this point and I was stifled by the 'community' around me. I really didn't want what everyone else had. I didn't want to 'settle down'. I wanted out of the suburbs, I wanted to explore life and have adventures. I hated what was expected of me. I had had enough of the patriarchal rule over my life and how it was being upheld and perpetuated by women. I wanted to find my voice and find my people. There had to be more like me out there somewhere. I wanted to define myself. I wanted to have some fun. I wanted freedom.

I flippin' well needed to get out.

Work Harder Than Everyone Else and You Might Have a Shot

It's 1996 and things can only get better.

'You're heading for two Es, Anita.'

This is what my form tutor said to me when I went to discuss possible university applications. I fancied sitting the Oxbridge entrance exam, but I'd not been selected as one of the top tier of girls who would be groomed by my school. Most of the girls had already been groomed by their parents to make sure they headed straight to either Oxford or Cambridge. That's the kind of thing the aspiring, wealthy middle classes know about. That's the kind of thing private schools are geared towards. You've been taught Latin from the age of 11, given self-belief by the bucket load, and you are trained to know exactly what's expected of you in those interviews. Plus, you will have studied piano and ballet and horse riding and violin, you'll be able to talk with ease about your extra-curricular activities and your expensive skiing holidays and your work placement at your godfather's investment bank. I don't think it has changed since.

'Dad thinks I should study law at Cambridge.' Indian parents aren't short on aspiration.

The teacher basically laughed in my face. So how did the Punjabi lass from Bradford get to work in television, I hear you wonder.

I'd been working at my local Asian radio station for a few years and already I knew that I really loved it. But I didn't think I could get a career as a music radio presenter on Radio 1. (That was so far away and, as it transpires, would always remain far away.) It was simply a great hobby for a girl who couldn't sit still, I mean THE perfect hobby for me. I was put in a soundproof room on my own, with a microphone to say what I wanted, and two hours to play music. It doesn't get better than this, whether people listened or not – and they did listen! I was there as much as I could be. I hosted a bhangra show which I subverted into an Asian underground show, blasting Fun-Da-Mental, Bally Sagoo and the KK Kings out to shopkeepers, housewives and taxi drivers across West Yorkshire. I couldn't get enough. During my holidays I'd present five days a week, on either Breakfast or Drive Time.

Then I watched the brilliant film *Bhaji on the Beach* when I was 15. It was a monumental moment in my life. I'd never seen anything like it. This film for me was every-thing. It was made by two Indian women – written by Meera Syal and directed by Gurinder Chadha. It was the story of a group of Asian women from Birmingham going on a trip to Blackpool to escape their lives. This film was fearless and covered so many important and relevant issues within the Asian community. I saw myself for the first time. I was so overwhelmed by what I saw that I wrote a letter to Meera Syal to tell her what I thought about the film. A handwritten letter. And I bloody critiqued it. I think I told her that not all teenage girls wanted to impress boys. I was such a nun. Amazingly, Meera wrote back. It showed me Asian women can write, direct and star in British movies! We don't have to wait, we can create our own stories. I wanted to do that. My thinking was as simple as that: if you see it, you can be it.

I'd recently had a . . . debate, let's say, with my dad, about what I should study at university. He thought I would naturally be applying to study law. Now, I loved the idea of being a barrister and presenting cases and arguing in court and *L.A. Law* was one of my favourite TV shows at the time. But I realised I didn't want to study law, I wanted to be in *L.A. Law*. I suggested I study drama. This was quickly put to bed as a ridiculous idea. What was I going to do with a drama degree? Act? Ha!

'When was the last time you saw a successful Asian actor in the UK . . . apart from Art Malik, on the TV? Even the guy who played the Indian in *Short Circuit* was white!' For a long time, there has been the stereotype that Asian kids are encouraged to only study a few set things. 'You have a choice to study law, medicine, pharmacy, accountancy, dentistry, business, IT, absolutely your choice, no pressure, your choice, but it has to be on my list of subjects chosen for you, by me. Your choice though, remember, no pressure.'

Not everyone conforms, because there are plenty of Asian builders out there too. Education is of huge importance to the Asian community. It is a way out of poverty and the above careers are not only well paid but well-respected professions.

To be a 'professional' gives everyone a great sense of pride and you have some kind of authority and respect in a land that's not your own. You can afford the house, the family, the Mercedes or BMW. You know you are smart, smart enough to make it in a foreign land, despite the odds being stacked against you. When our parents and grandparents arrived here, not all were uneducated. Some came with degrees and professions, but those hard-earned bits of paper that many sacrifices were made to gain did not have any value here. Our families had to do menial and manual jobs to get by and they were not too proud to do whatever they had to do to provide a better life for their kids, so they in turn wouldn't have to do the same jobs. I'd watched my mum's little sister arrive in London with a first-class MA in English, one of the smartest women I know, work as a seamstress all the hours God sends while raising her family. Her daughter studied law and is now a very successful businesswoman. For Asian parents, watching their kids succeed makes it all worthwhile. It was the entire point of the immigration exercise. The traditional career paths were 'encouraged' to make our lives easier.

It does mean that if you try and suggest something else, like maybe your heartfelt passion, you are looked at in a patronising way, smiled at, and then an instant change of expression happens: a frown, with a short, sharp 'NO', is the end of that conversation. Or a 'study law/medicine/accountancy first, so you have something to fall back on'. Ideas of getting into other industries, where we would have to fight tooth and nail, are shut down instantly because it was obvious from the landscape around us that these were not places where people who look like us can gain any success. Most of us didn't even realise the variety of jobs out there that we could potentially do. Even if I had studied drama, the chances of me getting any kind of success would have been so slim. The roles for Asian women are few and far between. Only now is the landscape just beginning to change, slowly. Thankfully there is now an army of Asian kids who don't want to go down the 'traditional' chosen careers path and I would actively encourage this. Follow your passion. Those industries are crying out for you.

Education, work, was meant to be freedom. It's where I put all my chips to get out. After doing some research I found the best media course in the country at Leeds University, a four-year degree studying broadcasting. I thought I'd stick with what I already knew a bit about. It was highly competitive to get onto this course, mainly as it offered a coveted six-month placement in industry. This was gold dust. There were only 30 places on the degree and the entry requirements were an intensive interview process plus two As and a B. I was happy and Dad was happy.

And then: 'You're heading for two Es. I suggest you do not apply to Leeds,' was what I got from my tutor.

I went home a bit upset that evening. This is where my dear mother's never-ending well of positivity came into its own.

'Don't listen to her.'

'What?'

'If you want to go to Leeds, then apply for Leeds. At least get the interview and see what happens. The teacher doesn't know everything.'

So, I did. And I got an interview.

I went dressed in my tweed blazer (I was wearing tweed long before *Countryfile*), the lapels covered in badges, mittens on string threaded through the arms. Very practical solution to not losing gloves, I've always thought.

I loved school, I loved learning and I was bright and quick. I grasped concepts, always had an opinion and loved being involved in discussions. My problem was I just never really studied enough at home, because home was complicated. I'd managed to coast through most of my schooling and get ten GCSEs, but A-levels needed me to knuckle down. I didn't. I didn't have a photographic memory and neither did I really have the space and peace where I could sit and study. My mind wasn't focused, it was preoccupied with looking after my family and keeping peace in the home. I worried all the time about my parents. I shouldered the responsibility of keeping everyone else happy and making sure everyone was OK. The burden of the eldest daughter. I'd go between the living room to hang out with Dad, the kitchen to help Mum and my brother's bedroom to make sure he wasn't becoming too much of a hermit, always wanting to protect him. I think my parents relied on me. I was the go-between. The peace-keeper. The UN. Or, at least, I tried to be, keeping the peace by keeping everyone upbeat. I needed to make sure that they were not too upset, sad or lonely or, crucially, angry. I was and am loved by both my parents and enjoyed spending time with them. But I had the ability to change their moods, par-ticularly Dad's. Their marriage consumed me, I was like a parent watching two kids who could play up at any moment, and it was my job to keep them distracted and entertained.

Even though I was gasping to start my own life, I didn't have the time to focus on what I needed to do. I had to grow up pretty fast and I lost interest in schoolwork. I'd leave things to the last minute. I thought my brain would retain information I'd understood in class. I'm not really sure what happened to me during my A-levels. I guess when your home life is a bit topsy-turvy, kids react in different ways. I was reading novels, listening to music, watching films and TV, sneaking out to the pub, anything but studying history text-books. It's strange that I have very little recollection of those two years. Just the odd fuzzy memory. I remember falling asleep in a double history tutorial, probably because I hardly had any sleep that night. Maybe I'd stayed up watching telly with Dad, maybe I'd got sucked into late-night radio in my room, maybe because Mum and Dad had had a barney in the night. My forehead was on the desk when the teacher, who was sitting directly in front of me, actually very kindly, considering, woke me up. I remember wanting to study French but the teacher talked me out of it, even though I was a natural at languages. In hindsight, she probably didn't want me in her lessons. Some teachers really didn't like me.

I can never forget A-level results day. I opened the envelope and . . . B, B, C, D. A flippin' D. FOR DISASTER! I was destroyed. Looking at them now, I guess they are not that bad. Especially for someone who didn't study. But back then, I might as well have got four 'U's. My school was geared towards academic success. And I'd ballsed it. My crew of mis-fits, my brilliantly clever best mates, every one of them got straight As. Jo was off to Cambridge, Robyn to Oxford, Al to Goldsmiths, Rach to Manchester. They'd done what was required of them. They hadn't missed the point of A-levels. They'd got their heads down and studied hard and were now reaping the rewards of getting onto the courses they wanted. Idiot, here, felt like a right idiot. I went home and I cried. I cried and I cried, and I never cried back then.

* * *

The next few days were a blur of ringing round unis to see if I could get in anywhere through clearing. It was a disappointing, dark and miserable few days. My entire life had been gearing up for university. This was going to be my lift off moment and I'd messed it up. I was annoyed with myself for not working harder, I was annoyed with myself for not proving the tutor wrong. I was annoyed with myself for now being annoyed. I was humiliated.

I had four days of walking around under a dark grey fog, then a letter arrived from Leeds University. 'We know you didn't get the grades, HOWEVER, we would like to offer you a place on the course based on your interview.' I could not believe my luck. This doesn't happen, does it? How bloody jammy was that? I'm the jammiest git on earth. I'm the jammiest jamfaced jamhead in jamland. I obviously talked a good game, mixed with a bit of charm and my authentic love for TV, all skills required to be a top presenter as it happens. I'd bagged my place. And guess what? I was the only brown lass on the course.

There's so much pressure on Asian kids to succeed academically and I felt a huge amount of shame after messing up my exams. I'd failed my parents and failed myself and I even felt I'd failed my super smart friends. The truth is, I was struggling and had probably been struggling for a while, but no one noticed. I didn't know how to ask for help, and I still don't. Probably because I don't want to burden anyone with my problems. My school wasn't set up for any child other than those who came from middle-class backgrounds with parents who had time – time to invest in what their kids were up to. I don't think my school ever knew anything about my home life. No teacher ever asked me about going to the factory, or losing the factory, or how or where I was doing my homework, or what time I'd gone to bed, seeing as I was falling asleep in class. There was no emotional or pastoral care whatsoever. Only my English teacher showed some concern because I was one of her best students and my work was slipping. I think my parents believed that this is what their money was going towards, a school that kept an eye on our education because they were too busy just trying to survive, working their behinds off.

Home life was chaotic. My parents worked all hours and we worked too. I didn't have a set bedtime, a nightly routine, so applying myself and doing my homework was not always an option. But what I learned from this little bumpy episode of my life was resilience and tenacity. This was the launchpad that showed me I had to work and work hard. I had a gift, I talked a good game and this had opened a door for me. Finally, I wasn't in school anymore and I was off to redefine myself. This time I was going to work harder than anyone else . . . and have some fun while I was at it.

Freedom is Complicated

'You can cut your hair when you're 18, after your A-levels.'

It was a promise Mum had made. The exams were over. I'd got my place at uni. My bum-length hair I'd had my entire life, my lovely Indian locks I'd had a love-hate relationship with, were finally being sacrificed. I was off to be whoever the hell I wanted to be. To discover who the hell I could be. My long plait was not coming with me, it was weighing me down.

'You've lost your beauty,' I was told by an aunty after the chop, but I didn't mind her bonkers comment. Being complimented on my 'beauty' was not top of my agenda. I had an entire brain to expand! Also, our worth is not determined by the length of our hair. Long-haired girls are seen as dutiful as well as beautiful. Short-haired girls are seen as spirited, independent, rebellious. Yes, to all three of those. Plus, when I say I chopped it, it was still down to my shoulders! But my beauty had gone, apparently. On with the rebellion!

Leeds is only 10 miles away from Bradford so moving away from home involved a negotiation. I wasn't backing down from this one and I won my case. Damn, maybe I was suited to studying law after all. For Asian parents, letting their kids leave home, particularly their daughters, is a major deal: 'You are giving her too much freedom.' My mother would even repeat it to me when she was particularly cross: 'No other Indian mother would give her daughter so much freedom.' Everyone has a right to freedom. Unless you're a Punjabi daughter. Then you can only have as much 'freedom' as you're allowed by your family. You are not free. You are controlled. It is not your privilege to choose any aspect of your life. You do not have self-determination. You will do what your parents think you should. 'We your parents will decide, and then your husband will decide, and that is your life.' Sounds like a right shit set up to me.

It's not this extreme for everyone and certainly wasn't for me, but I felt this was the weight around my neck. And let's face it, my parents were trying their hardest with me, but I was doing my best to resist. This was the subtext of my entire existence. Freedom is precisely what I wanted and, as a human being, freedom is my right. There's so much attachment to the families we are born into, so many complicated layers that keep us bound to them. But if you take a step back, you can see that you are free. Just walk away and choose the life you want. It will be hard, but you can do it. And if they love you, they'll come round. The problem with Punjabi families is you don't know what variety you are going to get. The variety that won't speak to you ever again or the variety that will physically abuse you, to keep you in line. Both possibilities exist. As do the more reasonable varieties, I must add, but it really doesn't make it any easier.

My entire life was spent in the pursuit of making my own choices, good or bad. I wanted to experience life and to discover who I am, and this was all going to happen away from home. My parents were so excited for me, particularly Dad. This must have been just what he wanted for himself. The opportunity to study and find out who you are. To live and experience growing into an independent person. Dad loved calling me 'the student' and his new line about me from then on about anything I did was 'typical student'.

Bring home washing – typical student.

Look a bit scruffy – typical student.

Get out of bed – typical student.

Eat – typical student.

Breathe – typical student.

Mum was just delighted because she was convinced I would finally meet some 'Asian friends' and, in turn, discover her elusive dream son-in-law.

Freshers' Week is the craziest week in an undergraduate's life, with every university society throwing open their doors, with parties and cheap booze and hormones flying all over the city. In 1996, students head out in hunting packs of at least 25, all dressed identically: boys in an array of Ben Sherman shirts, hands in pockets, trying to walk with their manliest stride, all chanting 'lager lager lager lager'; girls in baby doll dresses, with pencil-thin eyebrows, all chanting 'lager lager lager lager'.

Nothing about it appealed to me. It scared the life out of me. So I went to precisely zero events, not one party, not one club. With my mother's voice ringing in my ears, I did go off to find other brown faces. I did try out an Asian society bash, but, oh no, this place was not for me! I was underdressed for starters, I didn't have any Prada or Hugo Boss or high heels. These kids knew how to dress, I was just lowering the tone. A couple of lads who'd never met me before kept referring to me as 'sister', which I found really peculiar. Just ask me my name! I'd never been in a room full of this many Asian kids who I wasn't related to. It felt like being at a bad wedding. It just wasn't my vibe. I felt like a total outsider in this room. Sure, we had things in common because of our ethnicity, but I'd come to uni to broaden my horizons. Not to find a husband. Plus, this wasn't my world – for starters, where were the white folks?!

I retreated back to the sanctuary of my student flat and watched drunk students stumble past my kitchen window. I was much happier being in, talking and listening to music and getting smashed in my own space, than going out to get smashed in a meat market . . . I saw the spotty lads my housemates would bring home after a night out. You're alright, thanks. I was not about to put myself in a place where the object is to get off your head and then get off with a bloke. I already knew what rejection felt like in the teenage game of who's the hot one, so I opted out.

Brilliantly, due to a very slow social life back in Bradford, I felt zero FOMO. Thankfully, it didn't take me long to find a bunch of boring bastards who were just as happy staying in like me. The crew I befriended were all outsider oddballs too: the Italian/Scottish girl from Turin with her espresso machine and love for Metallica. At 24, the 'mature' student from Ireland who introduced me to Guinness. The Belgian who would sprinkle dried rosemary on his Safeway economy burgers, like a gourmet chef. And the half Belgian DJ from Hull, with the best record collection I'd ever seen in my life. For us, a top night out was always in the kitchen. We'd congregate to listen to music and cook. Cook-offs were our favourite pastime. We'd watch crowds of students file past the window on their way out to down sambuca and have sick-flavoured snogs, while we'd discuss how much seasoning our tomato sauce required.

It was in these kitchen sessions my palette began to expand: I discovered proper cheese for the first time. Cheese and red wine. Cheap red wine. The cheapest head-pounding plonk available. Two-bottles-for-a-fiver cheap. And cheese. Proper English cheese. Like Stilton. I'd never eaten Stilton in my life. Why would I have? The only cheese we ever had at home was Kraft cheese slices. A stinking-ripe Stilton would NEVER find its way into my mother's shopping basket, or really any Asian shopping basket I know. Asians generally don't get stinky cheese. This was a baptism by mould. We drank and we ate and the more cheap plonk we drank, the more cheese we ate. It got to the point where I was gouging out just the blue veins, the really salty, crusty funky bits, like a wild, cheese-crazed animal: rookie error. In the morning, I woke up with the most shocking and unusual taste in my mouth. My tongue was still fizzing and sticking to the roof of it. I wasn't really sure if I could still feel my tongue, so I had to keep sticking it out like a yawning puppy, to make sure I hadn't killed my taste sensors. The air in my room that morning would have killed anyone entering. I was at uni for an education and I was getting one.

I introduced my gaggle of gourmands to my world, too. Of course, Mum had packed me off with little jam jars full of the essential spices and two large metal cooking pots, one big enough to feed a small army and the other big enough to make rice for the whole of my campus, plus a small pressure cooker, which terrified me. Pressure cookers always terrified me, you never know when they are about to blow. I started simple. A crowd-pleaser: chicken curry. I'd begin the process, chopping my onions, as my other housemates were getting tanked up on bottles of Diamond White cider. I'd watch in amazement, learning the ways of the teenage mating rituals all from a distance. I just couldn't bring myself to join them.

It was usually me and the DJ from Hull who would end up staying awake, chatting longer than the others. This guy was cool and kind and bloody interesting. A teenage boy who knew about records and books and films and theatre and was happy to sit and chat about music into the night. It didn't take long before I stumbled into a very innocent relationship with the guy who was essentially my best mate. (Don't tell my mum and dad. Inappropriate boyfriend number one.) Of course, this relationship was a complete secret and a constant source of inner conflict for me, because I knew I'd never be able to tell my parents. Although they were never going to find out.

* * *

I was considering leaving out any of the bits of my life that involved dating white boys. There would be quite a few blank pages. Don't panic, Mum, not LOADS, but a few. There was always the slight issue that any white boyfriends fundamentally didn't understand a huge part of my identity, one I had a conflicting relationship with myself, but which was me nonetheless. 'Why can't you just tell your parents about us? Can I come round for dinner?' The reasons why they couldn't were subtle and complex, but none of my boyfriends were sophisticated enough in thought to understand that other cultures roll a bit differently to theirs.

Wanting romance and exploring your sexuality is part of being human. Our ancestors, who were busy writing the Kama Sutra and getting busy, knew all about this. For me, though, normal dating, the kind all my non-Asian mates were doing, had me in a pit of guilt, all the bloody time. Seriously, constantly. I can make light of it now looking back but, my God, even writing it down is both terrifying and liberating. Asian kids don't talk about relationships, ever, not my generation at least. I was in a permanent state of turmoil, always afraid that I was letting my parents down. The guilt, fear and anxiety followed me everywhere.

I knew I wasn't allowed to do it. To date anyone, really, but definitely not someone who wasn't Indian. Our strict Asian parents made it all the more tempting by banning it, so it's their fault, really. All that repression, what did you think was going to happen? Some of us were never going to toe the party line. But the inner conflict does mess you up somewhat. Here I was, finally with some freedom. But that freedom was always going to be complicated. All the control and manipulation I'd experienced growing up, 'What will other people think?', 'This is not how girls behave', 'You are lucky you have such a lenient mother', to list a few of the classic one-liners, had only gone and flippin' worked. I was guilt- and anxiety-ridden. Crippled by it. How on earth was I going to be the right sort of girl at uni? The one I was expected to be, or the one I wanted to be.

So, boys are not my forte. I was forging ahead with my education, trying to make (kind of) astute decisions to progress myself in the right direction. When it came to lads, however, I had no critical faculties whatsoever, often dating the first bloke who would show any interest in me. Was this because I had zero confidence in myself and zero belief in my attraction to the opposite sex? Was it because I was so grateful for the attention? Was it because brown kids were not desired, not openly anyway? Was it because I'd never been taught that you are allowed to have standards and think about the qualities you want in a person? Was it because everyone else seemed to be hooking up so I thought it was the thing to do? Was it because I was just an average young woman, making plenty of dating mistakes, going through a process of trial and error as everyone else did? Or was it because my only criteria for a man, the edict that had been ringing in my ears since the beginning of time, was that he HAS to be Indian?

Did my mum feel she had to go on about this all the time because my world was so lacking in colour? 'Hmm, not many Indians here,' was her comment on dropping me off at Leeds. My mum loved all my friends, she loved that my world was middle class, but she also feared that my world was a bit too white.

Find Your Sound

Most of the DJ's student bedroom was taken up by two Technics turntables and speakers. A classic student bedroom of the late nineties. Tuition fees were not introduced for another two years, but in 1996 we were the first year to be offered student loans which, for me, stacked up to 12 grand's worth of debt. A lot of money, but compared to what students owe now, it seems like pennies. It was obvious the day the first student loans kerchinged into student bank accounts, as that was the day ludicrously large Hi-Fi systems and speakers were seen being shoved into tiny student bedrooms.

This is where my musical education picked up speed at a rapid pace. Two years earlier, in 1994, Goldie had released 'Inner City Life', UK Apache had released 'Original Nuttah' and our ears had been opened to something so incredible it could have been from an alien planet. We'd stepped through a musical portal into a world of sound we had no idea could exist. In this student bedroom, we watched movies and listened to all the latest drum n bass and jungle records, hip hop, jazz, funk, soul, neo soul, techno, house, rave. Synapses were being formed and were firing at a rapid pace. This is what I wanted in my life. This is what had been missing. I'd been searching for more art and culture and inspiration but now I had other people to open my eyes and show me what else was out there to discover. Music was filling an infinite well inside me and it just made sense to me. Music was still how I connected with emotions I kept shuttered, how I released emotions I couldn't understand. I liked the people who also loved music, they were my kind of people, people I had something in common with for starters, who I could sit in a room with and not have to speak to if we didn't feel the need. It was an exciting education learning about new music and artists which, only a couple of months before, I had no idea existed. Not only was I a fast learner, I was top of the class. I'd found my thing, I'd found my escape! Quite simply, it made me forget about everything else and be happy.

It's such a magnificent, overwhelming, spiritual feeling when you discover an incredible new tune or album, when you hear it for the first time and then share it with people who you know will appreciate it. You want to watch their eyes widen and heads nod up and down, see a warm smile creep across their face. Connecting to music is transcendent. I couldn't get enough: Andy Weatherall, Ashley Beedle, Björk, Ry Cooder, Fela Kuti, Miles Davis, Talking Heads, Fleetwood Mac, Buena Vista Social Club, Portishead, PFunk, G-Funk, 4hero, Herbie Hancock, Nina Simone, Gilles Peterson, DJ Shadow, Tom Waits – to name a fraction and give you a sense of the vibe. No genre was left undiscovered! I was introduced to independent record labels like Blue Note, Rawkus, Ubiquity, Nuphonic, V Recordings, Metalheadz, Trojan, Warp and discovered the world of record shops. I became the little Asian lass with the green JanSport rucksack spending hours in Crash Records, Mr Jumbos and HMV.

We were nerds, who loved nothing more than nerding out about music. The best part was bringing home an album and listening to it in its entirety, all in one go. An album was put on, inlay sleeves were studied for information. Who did the production? What label was it on? What were the samples? Then we'd go and buy the original song to hear where the sample was taken from. This was a world in which I was content. I was at home here. I felt safe. My ears could hear it all, the layers of production, the twiddly bits and the heavy bass and the strings and even the silences, and it all moved me. Music wasn't just something to have on in the background at dinner parties, it was the guest of honour. It was the main event. It was pure pleasure to find other people who could happily sit and just listen and hear every inch of the tune, and let the music take us wherever it wanted. To just absorb ourselves in it. Music is in my bones and if you feel it too, you know what I'm talking about.

I spent a lot of time inside, listening to music, but I wasn't a complete hermit! I also went out. Oh my God, yes, I went out out. It is 1996, remember, and we're heading into the age of technology and dance music. I still didn't have a mobile phone or a laptop at this point but I had a Saturday job at Miss Selfridge, was still doing my radio shows in Bradford and had my flash new uni mates – I was going through an awakening. My mind was nourished by the music, my soul

by the food and my body by the world of underground club-
bing. The holy trinity complete.

The club world became my temple. Dance music, house,
techno, drum n bass all are meant to be played out loud,
in dark underground clubs. Hip hop is meant to be heard
played live on decks by some wizard in baggy jeans and a
cap. And all this music is made to dance to. I was drawn to a
world on the fringe, but it felt like the centre of the universe.

In underground clubs, I felt safe. In these clubs, no one
cared where you were from or what you looked like. There
were people of all shades and flavours and, to the untrained
eye, most people dressed to sweat, in simple jeans and a
T-shirt. But subcultures are all about insider knowledge. In
these clubs, the jeans and the T-shirts were always branded,
and were usually hard to get hold of – Japanese brands like
Evisu and Maharishi. The clothes were expensive but also
street. In these clubs, people gathered for one reason only:
the music. B-boys and B-girls met skater kids, met house lov-
ers and techno heads. In the drum n bass club, everyone was
part of the 'junglist massive'.

The two ways of connecting in a drum n bass club are
through the music and through dancing. On these dance-
floors, I always managed to find my space. It didn't matter who I was next to, I didn't even have to dance near my
friends. I just needed to lose myself in the tunes. In the um
ka umka um ka umka of the beat or the waaaaaa waaaaaaa
waaaaaa of the bass. You'd always find the usual suspects, the
girls in sexy, skimpy outfits, looking hot and a little self-conscious, the cool guys who danced at half time, stepping from

foot to foot, usually with one eye on the girl in the skimpy outfit, the kids who came with wicked moves, ready to bust them out, ready to be seen. There was always a group of head nodders around the DJ booth, who refused to take their very expensive mountaineering coats off, and the one kid who had done a few too many Ecstasy, dancing four times as fast as everyone else, arms flailing.

In a club, people can take off their Monday-to-Friday masks and be who they want to be. In a society so geared towards achievement and economic success, they need a place of release. And dancing the night away is so much better than downing 10 pints and getting into a fight. Music allowed me to take my mask off too, to not pretend to be anyone other than a person who liked rhythm, sounds, melodies and dirty basslines!

I went to clubs to watch the DJs too. I'd get excited about hearing their set. I'd leave the club desperate to get my hands on the records that were played, as soon as they were released. I was immersed in this scene. I found my home. I belonged. No judgement, no expectation, no one to impress . . . in this space you come as you are. And I did. In my baggy trousers, my DC skater trainers or adidas shell toes, a hoodie, a Helly Hansen fleece and my rucksack. The rucksack came with me everywhere. Even on the dance-floor. What was in the rucksack was always a mystery, even to me, but it was always heavy and always a requirement. I didn't go anywhere without it. Plus, it gave me a bit of extra space on the dancefloor so no one could get too close for comfort.

I loved the connectivity between strangers in a club, congregating to worship at the altar of the DJ, letting the music move them to express themselves, to let their bodies move as they wish and as freely as they want, to smile and feel euphoria. It was a ritual. Nobody cared where you came from or what you had. Up until then, my entire life felt like I was constantly under someone's gaze, being told how to behave and what was expected of me. At this point in my life, I didn't feel like I fitted in anywhere. I was too white to be brown, too brown to be white. Too rebellious, too loud, too demanding, too angry, too opinionated. There was no place I'd found where I fitted, where I could be myself, where I felt comfortable just being me. I didn't know who I was, I was still trying to figure it out, but at every turn it felt like I was being told that who I wanted to be wasn't possible. Like I was always on the outside looking in. At home, at school, at the temple, it felt like every environment I walked into was trying to shape, mould and bend me to fit. But I just didn't. It's a crazy idea that we should always fit in! So small-minded. So reductive. Sometimes you just don't.

I just wanted something different and, finally, on the dancefloor in a club, I could express myself. Freely. Coming from a small community in Bradford where everybody seemed to care about your business, and a school where I always knew I didn't fit the mould, it was a huge relief to be in a space where none of that mattered. Only your love of the music. I felt a sense of belonging like I had never felt anywhere else. Club culture defined a generation but also made me realise I had the freedom to define who I was. It was hands-in-the-air liberation.

In drum n bass clubs, black kids mixed with white kids mixed with Asian kids. Somehow, the music unified across culture and class. The Criminal Justice Bill had been passed in 1994 to clamp down on the illegal raves that had been happening since the second Summer of Love in 1989. But it didn't stop them happening. Kids will always find ways to party. My first ever general election was in 1997 and the tide had turned. After 18 years in government the Conservatives were out and Tony Blair sauntered in, singing 'Things Can Only Get Better', flying his 'Cool Britannia' Union Jack.

While Britpop was fully endorsing the establishment, another movement was happening elsewhere that I was far more interested and invested in, because it affirmed my existence like nothing else. It was happening for a small select group of us who were in the know and those of us that were part of it were blessed to have been there: the Asian Underground. There was an Asian Underground music scene, unashamedly confident and uncompromising, not pandering to what anyone expected from brown musicians, a uniquely British sound. Producers were putting the music I had grown up listening to, classical Indian music, the tabla and the sitar, maybe some Indian vocals, and mixing it with electronic dance music. Also in 1996, the BBC had commissioned a brand new comedy series, *Goodness Gracious Me,* which started life as a radio series before transferring to TV. It became an instant cult classic. Yes, an actual Asian comedy on mainstream TV, showing the world how brown can be funny, clever and relatable. We could not believe it.

For the first time in my life, I had a sound that was all for me, that I understood fully. I had producers and musical heroes who looked like me. This music wasn't just being listened to in Asian pockets around the country. Major labels began signing British Asian artists, Asian Dub Foundation and Cornershop, Nitin Sawhney, Talvin Singh, rebellious and political and raw and cool. They were doing things on their own terms. This had nothing to do with pleasing the white music industry or our parents, this was a sub-culture, a coming of age for second generation British Asians. Had we finally arrived? Were we at last putting our cultural mark on Britain? Were we carving out a space?

I got myself on student radio to do a weekly dub and Asian underground radio show. I teamed up with a man who owned a record shop in the Corn Exchange, where I was buying these sounds coming up from London.

London. I had to get myself to where the rest of the world seemed to be. I couldn't wait for things to head up north to me anymore. I was impatient. This meant booking a ticket on a National Express and heading down the M1 to that there London. I had some dreams to chase.

* * *

My passion for music started at home. I loved so many different styles of music but just like the rest of my life, it was compartmentalised based on who I was with. The music

I listened to with my Indian family was the Bollywood classics of course, but I also found myself staying up late with the adults at dinner parties, adoring ghazals, poetry set to classical music. Jagjit Singh is one of my favourite voices of all time, I can spend hours alone in his company. I loved qawwalis, devotional Sufi songs, and there's nothing like a bit of bhangra to get me onto a dancefloor at a family party. (I am Punjabi, after all.) Then there's also the sweet religious sounds of beautiful shabads, bhajans and kirtan I would hear on a Sunday morning. The complex raags and rhythms of South Asian music that I took for granted, soaked into me before I heard my first blast of Western sounds.

My love for music just grew and grew throughout my life, and is still growing. I absorb myself in global melodies still. Wherever in the world I travel, I have to sample their music, to pick up some of their local vibes, head to a club or a record shop, listen to local radio. If a song or piece of music comes on that my ear tunes into, I'll stop a conversation mid flow to direct everyone's attention to it. If you hear a tune that blows your mind and you're desperate to share it with someone, I'm your girl. To this day, one of my favourite pastimes is hanging out in my room listening to music, planning a DJ set, or even creating a mix which I imagine I'm playing out in a dark, sweaty club, or in a field somewhere, sending the crowds berserk with my selection. I'm an epic bedroom DJ.

If You Don't Do It,
Someone Else Will

Music. Radio. TV. The Universe. These were my goals. I'd found my place and now I had a mission. I wanted to head to the epicentre and surround myself with music. At that time, there really was only one place: the BBC.

My degree offered the Holy Grail: a six-month placement in TV. An opening into a world that seemed a million miles away. This was gold dust. An opportunity to get your foot in the door of a notoriously difficult industry to get into. (Unless, of course, Daddy is the boss.)

I was already working my ass off at three different jobs to afford uni: data imputer at GE Capital (if you've ever applied for a store card on a Saturday and had to have your credit checked, I was the person telling you whether you can get that dress on the never-never or not), part-time radio presenter (not that this paid) and my new absolute favourite, bartender at the West Yorkshire Playhouse. There were placements around the country and a few based at the BBC. Some of the kids on my course were already discounting London because they knew they couldn't afford it. There was only one placement I wanted and that was at the music department at the BBC. I wasn't very good at giving myself room for manoeuvre, so this had to be mine.

My tutor had other ideas. 'I think you should apply for the placement at the BBC Asian Programmes Unit, in Birmingham.' Hmmm. I wonder why he thought of that one for me? I wasn't offended or surprised that he'd suggested it, I simply set him straight. There were two reasons I wouldn't be doing that.

1. Because I love music and THE ONLY placement I want is in the music department at the BBC.

2. I'm related to far too many people in Birmingham, so there's no way I'm going there.

That's right, Howard, you just got told! Imma head for London, you're not going to pigeonhole me! (A few years later, the Asian Programmes unit would be instrumental in helping my career, but I wasn't to know that back then.)

I trained like a warrior for the interview, like an assassin, like Bruce Lee preparing for a fight. I'd been prepping my whole life for this! I walked into Western House (renamed Wogan House now and home to Radio 2 and 6 Music) and felt a rush of excitement looking at everyone working away at their desks. This is actually the place where they make TV!

TV, radio and music were my specialist subjects. During the interview, I discussed my thoughts about the underground East Coast hip hop scene in the US and I clocked the BBC producer had not the foggiest what I was on about. He was obviously smart enough to recognise that I was just the person who should be working on his programme. I was plugged in, knew my stuff and was confident in my taste, maybe even a little cocky. And guess what? Yours truly only went and blagged the blooming placement! I was off to work at the BBC, in music, on a BBC2 music show called *The Ozone*. A whole six months getting paid absolutely nothing and I could not wait.

This was my introduction to life at the bottom rung of the ladder in TV. You get paid nothing and you're bloody grateful for the opportunity because, if you don't do it, someone else is prepared to do it for less. After a couple of months in London, down to my last pennies, I managed to get them to at least pay my travel costs. And you ARE truly grateful for the experience. I was prepared to do it. What else was a student loan for?

The Sunday before I was due to start work, I moved into a tiny attic room in a house I was sharing with six other housemates from university. We were living all the way out in Hendon, a north London residential suburb, seven miles from the centre. It's a great location if you want to jump on the M1 to head north or have easy access to the M25. I was there because we knew nothing about London geography and it was dirt cheap (for London). It was so far out, I might as well have commuted from Leeds. We were giddy with excitement though, the first night in London on our own, and I was about to start a job in telly. We needed to celebrate, so we did what British students do better than anyone else: we got shit-faced.

BLEEP BLEEP BLEEP. My alarm went off at 7am and I woke up with a shock, still fully dressed, lying on top of my bed sheets. I could feel my tiny brain bouncing around in my skull. Somehow I managed to get through my first day by nodding at everything people were telling me and sitting in the toilet when I needed a time out or to micro-nap. I spent the entire day swallowing my own saliva and counting down the minutes before I could next lie down. Note to self: do not go into work hungover EVER again, especially not on day one.

I was in London, with no connections, no money, at the bottom of the bottom of the bottom of the pile, and it felt great. At no point did I think, look at me, this Asian lass from Bradford, working at the BBC. I just thought this is where I need to be. Even though I was the only person like me in the entire department, back then I was confident that I belonged there. It was only music, what's my race got to do with that?!

My job was mainly to call in music videos from record companies and do the tea round at least 75 times a day. Within a week, I was already running my own parallel side hustle. I was ordering vinyl from all the record labels I loved and calling up the clubs I wanted to go to at the weekend and blagging guest list by saying I was coming down to do a reccy for possible filming locations. No one wants to queue for a club. This was London in 1998, the heyday of celeb haunts like the Met and Atlantic bars in central London, where Oasis, All Saints and every artist at the time were papped stumbling out of most nights of the week. But I wanted a spot on the guest list for some of the dirtiest dance joints: 333, Mother Bar, The End, Bar Rumba, Blue Note in Hoxton. Really, the last place I wanted to be was at the celeb hangout. I did go to the Met Bar once and I met Björk in the toilets. Washing my hands and side glancing Björk washing hers is a moment I'll treasure forever. The two of us, tandem hand washing.

This was it. The ultimate. Everything in my life had been leading to this point. I was in my element, full of energy. I offered to help everyone with everything at work. Keen and totally green. There was another, more highbrow music show called *Inside Tracks* being filmed in Maida Vale every Sunday that I'd heard about. I asked if I could be involved and help out. The producer said if I wanted to turn up every Sunday morning as their runner, I was more than welcome to work on it. Who's going to refuse free labour? I was skint, but a student loan, plus a student grant, plus buying the cheapest sandwiches (and pints) you can find, living as frugally as possible, could sustain a year in London. It's also handy to mistake your bank manager for your dad . . . My bank manager called me up to discuss my finances, or rather lack of, while I was working. It was a northern man who said hello, so I naturally said, 'Hello, Dad'. This stranger became invested in my adventures and increased my overdraft limit for me. I was quids in.

I was swanning around at record label events, heading off to launch parties for albums and new young pop acts. These were a great place to get fed sweaty finger food and have a couple of drinks for free. I was watching and learning as well, the whole time figuring out how the hell TV works and how those in the entertainment industry roll. I was learning that everything is casual: the dress code, the conversations, the sexism, the racism and the regionalism, all casual. Young runners were thought of as fair game back then. Jokes about being from up north were regular, but I was expecting them. I played along: 'All kids have to do a shift down the pit before school', 'Toilet? We have buckets up north'. Sexism was just part of the culture around me. As a northern brown woman, I had already absorbed that to get on, I needed to just get on. Where's the line between 'cheeky British slap and tickle comedy' and some bloke at work telling you he likes you in tight T-shirts? We were a nation who had women with their boobs out in a national newspaper – daily!

I was learning about dodgy older TV producers who take a shine to young naïve runners. Note to young self: when approached by this breed, do what your title suggests and run.

I was keen and full of energy but totally naïve. Then there were the self-styled rock stars of the office, the maverick male directors (anyone would think they were creating Oscar worthy feature films rather than five-minute TV items about East 17). The no-nonsense series producer who gave me stern looks (never make eye contact with them). The moody producer who was hungover every morning and would get me to go and buy his fags and a bacon and egg butty, but I'm not sure he ever knew my name. The bouncy researcher who LURVED pop music, all pop, only pop, who'd enthusiastically tell the music PRs how much he adored S Club 7. I'd sit in the corner wondering if we were listening to the same music . . .

Music PRs were the friendliest (bordering on patronising) women on earth, husky-voiced, good time girls, who oozed confidence and sex appeal and were always out out and always blonde. I was also learning London slang. When one Hip Hop music PR (Nihal from 5 Live in a previous life) signed off a phone conversation with 'OK, Homes', I was slightly confused and replied, 'OK, Watson.' The learning curve was steep. I was mates with everyone, but particularly looked after by a crew of awesome women, Katie, Jo and Kim. They'd buy me the odd beer and teach me how to navigate my new TV life in London. I was the youngest person in the office, but I felt as though I was in Neverland, as no one in TV had to grow up, it seemed.

After my six months was up, I'd got to know enough people (proper hustler) to be offered a job, an actual paid job, as a junior researcher on none other than . . . *Top of the Pops*. I got a job at *Top of the Pops*. Even writing that now seems surreal. My commute to Elstree Studios was now from a student cesspit in Lewisham. A seven-bedroom house, with 15 people crammed into it, where no one had washed up or cleaned the bath since the eighties. It had some kind of dungeon room in the basement, with someone living down there who no one ever saw, and one girl who only ever seemed to wear her dressing gown. Typical students. My job involved working on an offshoot programme, filming and interviewing artists and bands backstage. The excitement would begin at the start of the week and would build to a crescendo on Thursday. The buzz would start after lunch as bands would begin to arrive, get taken to dressing rooms, then be brought out one at a time to rehearse in the studio. I was all over it. Free rein to run around the place as I wanted. The best person to have on side is always the floor manager. Then you can sneak into the back of the studio and watch the rehearsals from behind the cameras.

The kid who watched *Top of the Pops* religiously every week, dancing right up close to the TV, wishing I was dancing in the studio, was now actually there. JLo, Destiny's Child (in their original line up of four), Cher (who didn't rehearse on stage but watched someone else go through her steps, what a genius), Red Hot Chili Peppers, Eminem (who had to dye his roots on the day), Billie, Ricky Martin, Manic Street Preachers, Macy Gray. I'd run around with a small camera, ready to interview anyone, totally not star-struck. Well, maybe a little. I wanted to make sure I was prepared for each interview and had something interesting to ask each of these mega stars and not make a total fool of myself too. If you don't do it, there's a queue of kids waiting to get in for the opportunity, remember? The queue was usually made up of kids whose family or family friends already work in the industry. They are usually from Surrey and usually not that keen to make cups of tea.

Twenty-year-old me had bags of energy and youthful confidence. I didn't care about fitting in or what other people thought. My first ever office Christmas party, the most glamorous event in the calendar, I was utterly clueless. I'd saved my pennies and made a special trip to Camden Market to get a new outfit. I haggled the price down to £50 (the market trader in me), which was a huge sum of money for cash-strapped me. I went dressed in a black kung fu suit, complete with Dr. Marten sandals and hair in pigtails, to the Christmas party. No, it wasn't fancy dress. I thought I looked the business. Plus, this outfit was perfect for the dancefloor. Did I feel embarrassed? Not one bit. I'm in awe of the girl who rocked up to that party wearing whatever the hell she wanted. The last thing on her mind was what people thought of her, only how she was going to maximise having a great time. Thinking back to that girl, I wonder when it started to change. When did I start to care what people thought, when did I start to worry about what to wear, when did I start to think again about what's to be expected, and become aware of my difference? Ironically, probably when I officially entered the world of TV and became a TV presenter.

After my time at the BBC was over, I had to go back to uni to finish my final year. On the day of my last ever exam, I got an email from Katie, the lovely producer I'd met, asking me if I was interested in coming to Manchester for an interview the very next day. I got a job as the researcher on a Channel 4 music show called *The Dog's Balearics*, coming from Ibiza every Friday night. Jammy git here was off to spend two months in Ibiza, my first summer out of uni, getting paid pennies, but getting paid – when you have nothing, a small amount is a fortune.

If I was bemused by the social lives of my flatmates at uni, nothing had prepared me for San Antonio, Ibiza, in the year 2000. Club 18–30 holidays, British kids popped up on pills and cheap booze, falling down stairs, throwing up in plant pots and humping in the corner of clubs. It was total carnage, a perfect situation for late-night TV. My job was to work in the office in our villa in the morning, interview DJs in plush villas in the afternoon, then film the chaos of the clubs through the night. These clubs didn't really get going until 4am. It was a wild and wonderful and utterly exhausting two months of my life.

My next job was working for a great TV company that specialised in music TV, called Free at Last. It was set up by a group of brilliant outsiders, who championed outsiders. These are the people that gave me my first break, Barry and Katie (same lovely Katie). It was Barry who one day said to me, 'We should put you on TV.' It was Barry's partner David who directed my first ever presenting job. It was this company that, without me knowing, had cut a showreel of me that they took to commissioner Sham Sandhu at Channel 5, who happened to be looking for a new presenter for a weekly live TV show. Sham thought I had something special and gave me the job. I don't think it's a coincidence that a Punjabi man spotted my talent. I don't think it's a coincidence that it was gay men who empowered me and gave me my first opportunities. People who are 'othered' see others. I presented Party in The Park, the MTV European Music Awards and a few other live music events Channel 5 put on next, all thanks to Sham. He kickstarted my career and I'll always be grateful to the people who supported me and gave me my first break.

I was now officially trying to a forge a career as a TV presenter. I wasn't self-conscious in front of the camera, I didn't take myself too seriously, I loved writing my own scripts, didn't mind early starts and was happy to work long hours. I was never short on something to say and crucially, I adored talking to people and made them feel at ease. It was a job that needed self-motivation and discipline because you only get out of it what you put in, AND to top it all off, it paid. Plus, I was good at it. I thought, I'll give this a go and see how far I can go. Which was as far as possible. Why the heck not? No false modesty here. I'm reclaiming ambition for women. I was, and always have been, ambitious and, in my mind, there are no limits to what I can achieve. There, I've said it. I used to keep this to myself because society has made me believe that ambition and drive are acceptable, admired even, for men only. I say let's actively encourage it, let's instil in our children that success is something for everyone, if that's what you want. We need our children to grow up in a landscape of equality and with a belief in equality that starts with something as simple as the belief that they can do whatever they want, regardless of gender. Then let's work on making sure the system is open to this idea, too. Therein lies the problem.

Once my year at Channel 5 ended, however, and I was out in the world of jobbing presenter, things got a little more complex. I was up for screen tests and would get to the final stages. The feedback was always 'she's a brilliant presenter' but:

'not sassy enough'

'a bit of a risk'

'so clever and funny but doesn't fit with what we are looking for'

And my absolute favourite, that has come up time and time again, 'Why you?'

Why me indeed. The only time this question doesn't come up is when I talk about anything to do with being brown, because somehow everyone gets that I've got that subject covered. I was even once asked in an interview if I saw myself as British. I took all these comments at face value. I thought I needed to change something about me to fit whatever it was those hiring were looking for. What was it that I could do to make sure I got the next job? I never wore my disappointments or my failures too heavily. I was pragmatic and positive, or maybe stupidly blind to what was really being said: 'We don't know what to do with a brown face.'

This may well have been the first time they were encountering an Asian woman, from Yorkshire at that, who was trying to explain to them that she wanted to be the next Oprah or Chris Evans. My thinking wasn't sophisticated enough to understand what was being played out. I never thought about my race and stupidly didn't think my ethnicity played any part in how other people perceived me. Particularly when it came to getting work as a presenter – I thought people just saw what I was capable of. I was ready to duck and weave and charm and graft and do whatever it took to make a career for myself. It was exciting. It wasn't easy but then I wasn't expecting it to be. But then you do get to realise it's not that hard for everyone, just harder for some.

* * *

Work is not a straightforward space to navigate. No one who looks like me holds the keys to power, so you are beholden to someone who basically doesn't get you. As well as doing your job, you feel you have to educate and explain who you are constantly. Battering the stereotypes constantly. Asian women are seen as meek and mild. We won't fight back, we'll do the job for free, be grateful for the scraps we are given. We're incapable of being leaders and if we speak out, we are angry and disruptive. Those in power think we are subservient and submissive. Off to have an arranged marriage then pop out a load of kids. This narrative doesn't just apply to Asian women but all women to varying degrees. Those in the workspace don't understand the depth of our complexity and brilliance. Or the fire that rages within us.

We begin to self-censor and keep our thoughts to ourselves and, in turn, don't show our true qualities and capabilities of being total badass boss babes. We hold our tongues to avoid conflict in the workspace because our gut tells us it won't end well for us, even if we are right. I've had a co-presenter throw ice cream in my face because he didn't like what I said. I'd made a very gentle, friendly joke at his expense. He thought he was being funny. Would he have done the same to a male colleague? I said nothing, just wiped it off my face and carried on, looking at the shocked faces of the people behind the camera. How telling that no one felt they could say anything to him.

I took the opportunities that came my way and made them work for me, which meant constantly having to prove myself. If I wanted to succeed and have any kind of career with longevity, I needed to be able to adapt. I'm adept at adapting. I've won a Royal Television Society Award for Best Presenter, have worked my ass of at every job I do, and yet I can still feel like an outsider. It's just what we misfits always have to put up with. I've had moments when I'm angry at the system, a system I have no control over, and all I can do is find the energy to soldier on. To keep pushing forwards so that I can continue to have a career and buy sourdough bread, but also change the landscape for the next generation. The system that works against me is helping to stoke the fire inside me.

Is it OK to talk about? How long before those in power think I'm ungrateful, or have a chip on my shoulder? Are these the conversations I should only be having behind closed doors with my black, Asian and trusted colleagues? Or should I speak out now? I still don't know. But what I do know is that it's time we were understood. What have I got to lose? A hard-fought career.[14] If I feel like this, as someone who has gained success, how must other women feel, with less of a platform and no authority? But adult Anita has made a decision. I don't want to feel like an outsider anymore. I want to own my space and recognise my power. I want to be grateful but not so much that it cripples me. I spent so long wanting

---

[14] Two days after writing this, I was asked to join *Woman's Hour* on Radio 4. What did I do to celebrate? I went for a long run listening to Kate Bush. I then called my brother and he cried with happiness for me. THE *Woman's Hour*. It is an honour and a privilege, and an important seat for me to be taking.

to please, trying to fit in, losing my mind over the lack of control I had over my life, that I'm just going to let go. I'm here, I'll work hard, I'll always do that. But I have also more than earned my right to be here, in any space, but especially in my profession.

You'll Never Feel 'English'

I don't have the same feelings about being 'English' as I do with being from Yorkshire. I'd never say I was English, as it's always been abundantly clear to me that English is not something I could ever claim to be, what with my skin not fitting the colour palette definition of white, cream or beige.

If I ever saw a St George's cross flying outside a pub it was a clear marker: do not step in. If you wanted any kind of confirmation about how I was made to feel about England, it's all tied up in the flag. Appropriated by racists/fascists/ the extreme right wing and football hooligans, 'It's ours not yours, so fack off back to where you came from', is what I can hear the flag shouting at me. The St George's cross could do with washing its mouth out with soap and water and then have a complete image revamp. Send it on a diversity training scheme, or simply to school instead.

If I was second generation Italian or Dutch, Polish or Norwegian, would I feel the same about being English? Well, no one would question my identity in quite the same way if I just blended in. I may feel shut out of being English, but I am British. Of course I am. Or am I British Asian, or British Indian? Which makes me wonder, when will I be seen as just being British? I think I'm the modern-day definition of being British. It's factually correct that my nationality is British. Born in Britain equals British. One for the forms, but even then, I'm in a sub-category of British Asian. See, always on the outside. On the periphery. I'm proud of being from my country. It's my home. And I am within my rights to tell you how I feel about it too.

I'm very comfortable here in the UK, it's what I know, even if some people try to other me, even if people who look like me were nowhere in the cultural landscape when I was growing up. Not films, TV, music, magazines. Thankfully I was able to see the universal in everything I consumed (I had no choice), even if it wasn't telling my specific story. (I hope you can do the same with this book.) It also means I internalised that white is the norm in every situation, which is severely problematic and detrimental to your mental health and self-esteem. I wished I was white for a long time as a young un, I just felt it would make life much easier. Nobody seemed to get what we were about or care to understand. We were just different, did things in a funny way, if we were thought of at all. I didn't realise that it was important to see myself reflected in popular culture, I just accepted that I wasn't. We all just accepted that we were on the periphery. The world in the telly belonged to someone else.

Which is probably why American TV always seemed more alluring – they at least had black people onscreen. (To be fair, we did have *Desmond's* and *The Real McCoy*, both superb TV shows.) America, as we know, is deeply racist and divided, but when it comes to representation in the creative arts, it's leaps and bounds ahead of the UK, which is why so many of our talent goes over there to find work. Not much space for black and Asian actors in period dramas, until *Bridgerton*. I watched and loved *The Cosby Show*, *The Fresh Prince of Bel-Air* and *Oprah*. The queen of daytime TV, my Queen. Oprah had a big part to play in me wanting a career in TV. I loved her style, her warmth, her openness, her generosity, her limitless empathy; I even loved her whooping demented American audience, but mainly I was so intrigued by her capacity to share her trauma and the pain of her childhood. I was fascinated by how she was able to shed her shame and, in doing so, made it easier for others to do the same. That is some kind of power. On the rare occasions we did catch a glimpse of someone Asian on British TV, our entire street would know about it: 'COME QUICK, APNA ON TV!'

We'd shout the house down, at the same time as every other Asian household in the country. All running into the front room to watch the Khans on *Family Fortunes* or Mr Singh drinking a pint in the Woolpack. We'd loyally gather around the telly, mesmerised by the novelty of seeing brown flesh on screen. Not seeing many brown faces on screen caused a major problem for me, a serious predicament, a life question I had no answer for: who on earth could I become on *Stars in Their Eyes*? 'Tonight, Matthew, I'm going to be . . .' No Asian popstars for me to transform into, no one in the UK knew about Nazia Hassan or Alisha Chinai. So, I decided I could be Sade. We were a similar shade and she always wore her hair tied back in a plait too.

I'd dream of being Kate Bush. If only I'd known Freddie Mercury was Indian back then. If only we'd *all* known. Not only did the world's greatest rock star have to hide his sexuality, he tragically felt he had to hide his ethnicity too. If only he felt the world could accept him as Farrokh Bulsara, a gay man of Indian Parsi descent. How far have we come 30 years later, I wonder. I also wonder how the heck we didn't guess he was Indian with that tash. I miss Freddie.

I may not feel English and I may have struggled to grasp my British identity, but I do feel like a citizen of the world. I can blend in most places. It helps to look culturally ambiguous and have a universal name like Anita. Brownness can be a global advantage, for a woman at least. I always have to wait at airports around the world as my husband is 'randomly' selected for checks. For me, a respectful, humble, open and interested attitude towards other cultures has got me a long way. A curiosity and ease with talking to strangers must have its origins on those cold days at Shipley market, watching and learning the charm offensive from the seasoned market traders. It's helped me not only when interviewing people all over the world but more generally when travelling. I'll make friends and collect people wherever I go. I even got a friendly reception in the most hostile place on earth: Immigration at LAX.

I made a series for the BBC in a refugee camp in Jordon. Zaatari is a makeshift home in the Jordanian desert for 80,000 Syrian refugees. Filming there was both depressing and uplifting. Depressing for the obvious reasons, as the people there had all had to leave their war-torn country and were now trapped in a refugee camp for the foreseeable future. I often think of the people I met, the young women with unfulfilled ambitions and hopes and dreams, their only choice in the camp to get married and start a family. The woman whose hand I held while she had a C-section in a tent. I went in 2016 and in all the time that's passed since then, they are still there, in the camp. The average time refugees spend in a camp is 17 years. There will be so many children born there who will know no other life. I was blown away, as I always am, by the human capacity to survive and thrive in the darkest situations and places on earth. Syrian people are some of the most generous and welcoming people I've met. Despite having nothing, every single family I met shared their food and always offered sweet mint tea – what a warm and beautiful aspect of Middle Eastern culture. Hands down, the tastiest falafel wraps I've ever had in my life were in that refugee camp. The people there were naturally all curious about where the team was from.

'England,' we'd say. Not much reaction, just deadpan faces. Definitely no smiles. But they looked at me and weren't having any of it.

'No, no, no! You. You Lebanese?'

Nice, I'll take Lebanese. 'Indian, but born in the UK.'

'Aaahh, Indian.' Faces instantly light up. Massive smiles and then they burst into song. Bollywood songs. 'Aaahhhaha ha kabhi kushi kabhie gham . . .'

They couldn't speak a word of Hindi but they knew all the actors, Shah Rukh Khan, Amir Khan, Katrina Kaif. They asked me if I ever wear sarees and bindis. Had I ever been to India? Did I watch Bollywood films? I was in. Here, in a refugee camp in Jordan, my Indianness was far more impressive and important than my Britishness.

My Indianness has worked in my favour a few times while travelling, too. It got me out of a few sticky situations while backpacking across East Africa in 2001, just after finishing university. I was hitchhiking and camping up through Zambia (my wonderful parents had allowed me at 21 to go for an adventure of a lifetime!) and making my way to a campsite I'd spotted on the map with the mark of a tent. It was a ten-hour journey to where tent marked the spot. On the bus journey, I was told to hand over my passport at a 'checkpoint' and then to hand over all my money if I wanted my passport back. Drats! I'd been suckered into a situation. I tried to argue and realised I was in the middle of nowhere and this could end quite badly for me. After an hour-long stand-off, I handed over the couple of hundred dollars I had in my wallet and a 20-pound note. But they didn't get the travellers' cheques stuffed in my socks. Travellers' cheques?! What bloody good are travellers' cheques 300 miles away from the nearest city anyway?

I just needed to get to the camp and thought there was bound to be someone who could help me out. Five hours, a smaller bus and the back of a truck later, I was trekking up to the gate of the camp. There are very high gates on this camp, I thought, that's very strange. A big blue sign outside too. Is this a popular backpacking spot? There weren't any other Westerners on the journey here, though. I was actually walking towards a UNHCR refugee camp for people fleeing the war in neighbouring Congo. (In 2021, 20 years later, I would be given the honour of becoming a UNHCR Goodwill Ambassador. But now was not the right time for me to enter the camp.) There certainly weren't any other backpackers. I was told there was a one-horse town a couple of miles away and the only shop was run by a man called Krishan. Krishan? Got to be Indian.

I got there and was exhausted so went straight for the killer line, no warm-up: 'Are you Indian? I'm Indian too. Can you help me?'

Krishan invited me in, with his little old Gujarati mother, to the back of the shop. I ate a fabulous Indian lunch and this lovely man changed my travellers' cheques, trusting that I would meet his brother in London to pay him what I owed when I got back. The diaspora connecting. He dropped me off at the most amazing waterfall to camp. This is how spotting someone who looks like you can add an extra dimension, a connection, and help you out in a tricky situation, even if they are Gujarati and you are Punjabi.

*   *   *

There was a lot that was different about me and Krishan based on the experiences of the countries we were born in, but also a lot of commonality. We shared the same references and understood what it meant to be brown and alien. Plus, we both knew what it meant to have an Asian mother.

I have a global network surrounding me and every time someone succeeds, it feels like a success for us all. This is why

Mindy Kaling, Lilly Singh, Priyanka Chopra and Kamala Harris are important for the global diaspora. While we sit and wait for South Asians to reach real positions of power in the media and creative arts over here, they are smashing it in the US. Lilly started as a YouTube star and now has her own show on NBC. Mindy's most recent show for Netflix, *Never Have I Ever*, has an Indian main protagonist. It was thrilling and emotional to watch, and I cried. Priyanka Chopra is the most famous Indian woman on earth right now – already a Bollywood megastar, she's now forging a path in Hollywood. A win for them is a win for us all. New ways of consuming entertainment, social media and online platforms have opened up the globe. We can now all find our tribes across the planet and see ourselves reflected somewhere. But our stories, all our stories, don't belong on the fringes. We want to see ourselves reflected in the mainstream. A true reflection of modern Britain. *My* Britain.

Travel Like Your Life Depends on It

My multi-layered identity, feeling like a global citizen and travelling with ease and bravery (with the odd wrong turn) all comes from belonging to two worlds. I have Britain and I have India.

My first experience of seeing India was from the front of a motorbike. The very front. Almost as though I was driving the thing. I was three. Mum held nine-month-old Kul on the back, and my seat was on the petrol tank, in front of Dad. Somewhere, also, was the baggage.

This was our first trip to India as a family and we had two weeks to do everything. By do everything, I mean visit relatives. Dad decided to buy a motorbike to get us around. My nan was terrified. How would this young man from the UK find his way around a foreign country? Dad pointed out there were milestones put in by the British, explaining how many miles to the next town. Indians have little faith in us 'Britishers', they think we're wet behind the ears. This was my first taste of how to tackle the motherland – not like a tourist, just go for it. Headfirst. Confidently. Treat it like your own. Neither of my parents are precious, nor do they talk to anyone in a patronising manner. They are life's adventurers. To be like them was my first travel lesson, which was to come in very handy when travelling the world making programmes 30-odd years later.

I have to tell you about India. I've never lived there and I feel more British than ever when I'm there, but it's also a place I feel so very at home. India taught me to be a citizen of the world. I've been visiting regularly since the age of three, to attend epic family weddings that go on for weeks, or backpacking to explore it on my own terms. I've made TV programmes about the place, I've had luxury high-end holidays there and I've been to meet up with friends for pure hedonistic, unadulterated fun. Young, modern Indians know how to party. I've lost count of how many times I've been but whenever I think about India, I want to be there, exploring more of it. It's an unquenchable thirst. I'm addicted to the place. All the clichés are true: food, smell, colour, every sense is stimulated and turned up to 11. It hits you as soon as the plane doors open. The distinct dense, warm, musky air of India. A combination of dust, incense, pickles and a mild undernote of sulphur.

My childhood trips were always to see relatives. There's no way you can enter Punjab without paying a visit to your extended family. The family politics of not seeing your family is something you do not want to have to deal with, so you've got to suck it up and know you will be drinking a lot of tea and making small talk with a lot of people you've never met before. It's enough to put some people off going.

It can be a major source of conflict for a lot of British Asians to have to visit family in India. We have been conditioned to take the next bit of food being offered to you, even if you will explode as a consequence. When you're in India you want to see the country and have experiences, you don't want to be trapped being force-fed another gulab jamun by your dad's third cousin. Taking people with you on adventures is also a common courtesy (and a good way around staying multiple hours at a relative's house). It's why my mum and dad's honeymoon, a daytrip to Blackpool, saw them take all my dad's little siblings and cousins with them, too.

India taught me and my brother so much about who we are. It was in India we understood our culture by seeing it being played out in context. It was here we saw being Indian in action, not just in Bollywood movies. It was in India we fully understood why our family in the UK did things differently. Why Granny dressed the way she did. It was in India we grasped that intense spirituality is just part and parcel of everyday life, not a 'lifestyle choice'. We learned that we are all connected to something much bigger than ourselves, not by religion, but because in the East understanding that we are part of the cosmos is a given. We were taught this in children's stories about wandering mystics and monkey gods and demon-slaying goddesses and gods in the form of cheeky children, who open their mouths to reveal the universe. Why wouldn't everything have a soul? Of course we are part of something much bigger than just this. We visited Hindu temples, Jain temples, Buddhist temples, all the temples, Muslim shrines and gurdwaras, and holy men and holy women and holy cows. And everyone meditates. It's just we've always called it praying. Simple paath, reciting holy text and mantras.

It was in India I learned to love Indian clothes. I understood how much effort, hard work and pride goes into hand weaving material and embroidery. That sarees are an heirloom to be treasured, not worn once and chucked away. My eyes would light up on seeing my aunts dress up in their finest silks, jewellery, eyeliner and bindis, and look more beautiful than any women I have ever seen. In India, strangers told me how lovely I looked in my Indian clothes. In India, I was told I was pretty.

We saw what it truly meant to be Punjabi, not some filtered down version based on the biased memories of relations who left many years earlier. We saw wedding traditions played out in the original way, before they had to adapt to semis in suburban Britain.

It was here that we realised how British we really were. How we freaked out at squat toilets! The first time I went, I refused to bend my knees – I was the motivation for the family to fit an English-style toilet. We were always clocked as 'foreign' without us even opening our mouths. It's the way you dress, your mannerisms, our gaping mouths and the permanent look of shock and awe that people from the UK have on their faces that gave us away.

When we visited when I was eight, my cousins had a live-in servant, a boy, Shankar, the same age as me. When you watch a child the same age as you cook your chapattis every night, it makes you realise a harsh truth about the unjust and unequal world we live in. You understand that freedom of choice is a luxury not afforded to many. According to my family, they were providing this boy with a good home and he was learning a skill. His money was paid to his elder brother every month. I'm not sure how much of it Shankar got. We'd insist Shankar sit and play with us of an evening, or at least sit and have his glass of milk with us before going to bed – we loved him.

India taught us that personal space is a privilege, especially if your entire life is played out on the side of the road. Even then you can be invisible to people walking right by you. India taught us that being treated with respect is a privilege not extended to those deemed beneath you, and that there is a caste system that brands people at birth. India taught us to question ingrained cruel systems of oppression. It was here that we learned the meaning of poverty, true abject poverty, of injustice and how cruel humanity can be. It was here we understood the delicate walk of life and we were taught to walk it with kindness and humility. To never think ourselves better because of our material wealth. To comprehend that it is by pure accident of birth that we are where we are. In India, I saw that just because I had a British education it did not make me in any way superior to any child I met in India, especially not the ones begging on the street. To treat them with disdain and disregard would be an act of cruelty and heartlessness and make me no better than colonialists. Humility before everything is a mantra my mother drilled into us. For better and for worse.

We know, from the umpteen programmes of posh white men heading out on Indian railways, that riding a train in India is an experience not to be missed. On the railways you will experience all of life and come face to face with the wealthiest people (before cheap airlines, most people travelled by train) and the poorest, Indian beggars, who are often kids. This was the first time my brother and I witnessed children begging, boarding the train from Delhi to Jalandhar, and we bawled our eyes out. Asking Mum to 'give them money', finding the pennies we had in our pockets. Their faces were dirty, their hair bleached light brown by the sun, wearing rags. They had no food, no home, no money, no voice. They were children just like us, but life had dealt them the shittiest card on the planet. So many people visit India and say 'they have nothing but they are so happy'. From my journeys to parts of the world where people really do have nothing, this is where you find the true strength of the human spirit. But, given the choice, don't you think they would swap with you in a heartbeat and have their basic needs met? It was here we learned we didn't have much to moan about.

It was in India where we also learned the meaning of love. Abundant love. The love you get from a massive extended Indian family. We experienced life and the human condition in a whole new way. It was in India I also saw my mum in full flow. In all her radiance, on her patch. Mum is a firecracker at the best of times but in India she flourishes. I saw her exuberance and fun-loving personality. The playful dynamic she has with her family. Unlike back in Bradford, Mum got all the jokes. Here, she knew how to talk to everyone, and she really did talk to everyone. Mum was loved and respected and not patronised. Here, she was happy. In the UK, she was constantly saying 'hai hai, no no,' and worrying about our every step. Here, Mum wanted us to experience it all. To see it all. She wanted to feed us every ounce of the world she grew up in.

My mother's family doted on us and called us 'vilayati'. Vilayati means foreign in Urdu but in Punjabi it's used as a term for the British. It's where 'Blighty' comes from. Vs and Bs are mixed up in Punjabi, as are Vs and Ws. Window becomes vindow and then bindow. So, Vilayati, Bilayti, Blighty. See? That was us, the kids from Blighty. Sometimes they might call us the 'gore', which means white folk, when we were doing something particularly British, like complaining about the toilets, or behaving like we owned the place, or taking pictures of everything we found quaint that was just their day-to-day. We provided hours of entertainment for our Indian relatives. Their cute little British Indian cousins, the first of their kind, Indian with a British twist, or British with an Indian twist, depending on your perspective.

We weren't just loved within the four walls of our village home, we were loved by the entire village. A village in Punjab is an extended family. We could wander the cobbled streets and in and out of people's homes as we wished. We'd get offered a glass of hot fresh buffalo milk sweetened with jaggery or a freshly made samosa. Everyone wanted to meet the 'vilayti bache', the British Kids. They'd giggle at us speaking Punjabi with our English accents. They loved seeing our peculiar British habits, like asking for food. In

Punjab, when it comes to food, you don't need to ask, especially not the grandchildren of the home – if you want an apple, you just take the apple. They adored that we said please and thank you every two minutes.

My young uncles enjoyed exposing our sheltered eyes to new experiences. We were given a lesson in how to slaughter a chicken, and it's true, a chicken will run around without a head before dropping dead. The sadistic sods loved watching the terror in our soft, young British eyes. We still ate the chicken curry.

Naniji's house was a decent size, a single-storey L shape, with four rooms, a kitchen, a large covered veranda in front of the rooms and a big walled courtyard in the front, or vehra, with beautiful potted plants and a guava tree. That tree has fed the sweetest guavas to five generations of my family. There was also a grain store for the wheat. This was taken to the village mill to turn into atta, or flour. We had a borehole and hand pump for water in the yard. Every home in India has a flat roof that you can climb onto, the koththa, a roof terrace if you like. From up on the koththa you could see the entire village and into other people's verhas. You could see all the hand-formed drying cowpat cakes, paathis, stuck to the walls, to be used as fuel to cook on. Even though there was an indoor kitchen with a small single gas hob, most of the cooking was done outdoors on an open fire, fuelled by the very sustainable source of cowpats. Somehow, everything cooked in this way was absolutely the best thing you've ever tasted.

Beyond the village, all that you could see were fields and fields of various crops, like wheat, sugarcane or corn. Every village had a small shop selling essentials such as sugar, and loose leaf tea, and raw tamarind, either sweet or salty, that we'd stick to our hands and lick slowly, screwing up our faces at the sharp, tangy taste. One day we fancied something that tasted of home, so we asked for sausages and chips for lunch. Someone was sent on the mission to source sausages. Success! They were hunted down at the army barracks not far away. I ate delicious flavours from every state as my nan was a very good cook and didn't just stick to Punjabi food. We had Bengali fish curry, South Indian idli and dosa and delicious street foods from every corner of the sub-continent. It's one of the joys of my aunts getting together, planning the daily menu of what to cook, planning like an army plans an assault: the starters to lure us in, blast us with the mains and completely finish us off with a hefty desert or three.

In India, I felt free. It's hard not to when you have people all around you ready to indulge whatever your desires are. India has a culture that loves children but, more than that, I felt a freeing of my spirit in India generally. I defiantly played with stray dogs in the mud while my mum panicked about me getting tanned in the Indian sun. My Indianness was put into context and I was allowed to let it out, to try and get my head around what it meant. I met my great grandmother, my dad's grandma. I remember the way she looked at me, with a sparkle in her eyes. Like she was magical. She sat my mum down on a charpoy in her courtyard and told her the family secrets. Every single one of her children had died in childhood, apart from my grandfather, her only surviving child. Her extended family pitied her as she only had one son. She didn't get on with my grandmother and prayed and prayed to the goddess Kali at her little shrine to provide her with a grandson, my dad. (She must have prayed really hard as my aunt was born too as an extra bonus.) She told my mum how precious me and Kuldeep were, because we are from a small line that made it. Our existence to her was a God-given miracle.

It was also in India where our cousins brought any of our hoity-toity British attitudes back down to earth by being way more confident, street smart and sassy than us. We had come from England, with its money and modernity, and our cousins would want to know stories about what it was like in the UK. Where everyone had a car and fridge-freezer and hot water and no poverty. I thought I was pretty cool, for about five minutes. They were more like little adults compared to the sheltered babies me and Kul seemed to be. Their English was superb and they were way smarter than us. The education system is rigorous in India. They didn't just study to learn in India, they studied to come top of the class. But what really gave my Indian cousins their edge was their street smarts. They knew how to handle themselves walking through the village, they'd talk to anyone and have fast, one-liner comebacks. OK, my cousins could outshine us at most things, but could they dance? Surely this was my trump card.

On our visit when I was eight, my masi was getting married. The night before the ceremony, the (gidha) was in full swing. Women were dancing for hours and I was watching in amazement and keen to get on the dancefloor myself. I had no idea how to dance gidha, and if I'd tried to join in,

I may well have got trampled: these women meant business. And then, finally, I got my moment to show them what I was made of. It was that point in the night when a cassette was put on for the younger ones who fancied a dance to some modern music. It was my lucky night – it was Boney M, the tune was 'Rasputin'. I knew this entire album, seeing as it was one of the few my folks had back home.

The music started. I was up. Stand back, you Indian lot, this is Western music, this was my moment to represent. I had a look of determination. Left together, right together, stepping from side to side while both arms pumped up and down, my hands in tight little fists. I'd seen cool people in the audience on *Top of the Pops* do this dance, or at least something like it. It was my interpretation of Madonna in the 'Holiday' video, just a stiffer, self-conscious, eight-year-old's version. I was fully concentrating on my left together, right together, enjoying my moment of glory, when I saw the crowd part to make way for my Indian cousins, who were coming to join me in the circle. Wait. What? They were coming in singing! Not only did they know the song, as Boney M were massive in India, they were amazing dancers. They moved their bodies in a way I'd never seen. A diet of Bollywood movies, Michael Jackson and just general badassery meant they were incredible, their hips doing one thing and their arms doing another, wafting and swaying in rhythm to the tune. I did the only thing I knew how to do: I picked up speed on the left together, right together and pumped my arms for all they were worth, but my cousins had out-cooled me once again.

While my friends were off having camping adventures in the South of France, I was trying to understand another land and its meaning in my life. A place where I felt both completely at home and totally alien. The older I got, the more confident I became at bringing my best mates, a select few, into my Indian world. The summer after my GCSEs, aged 16, I headed off to India for the first time without my parents. I went on a seven-week (seven-week!) holiday to stay with my masi in Delhi and I took Alison, my best mate at the time, with me.

Al got the full family experience as my family's novelty white person to parade around. We taught her basic Punjabi and slept on charpoys in the village. We travelled around north India and lost our minds in Delhi's Janpath Market, buying tie-dye clothes and beads for a fraction of what we'd pay in the UK. We hid from the monsoon when it first arrived, presuming all rain is cold, but quickly realised that monsoon rain is as warm as a bath and a welcome relief from the 40-degree dry heat of Delhi in August. We locked ourselves into a car to hide from giant flying monsoon insects. We stayed with family in Agra and visited the Taj Mahal with all my relatives. And we got sicker than we've ever been. We both got a serious case of dysentery, taking it in turns to poop out our organs in the bathroom we shared. This being India, everyone knew about our violent shitting. Everyone knows about your bowel movements in India. It's perfectly normal to be asked at a dinner party about your 'motions'.

* * *

What an absolute privilege it is to have been born into and to understand two worlds. I always took my relationship with India for granted, but now I recognise what an absolute gift it is to be able to step off a plane in another country, a country unlike anywhere else on earth, and instantly be able to switch into 'India mode'. Where I'm free in a way I'm not in my home, where I can blend in if I want to, stick out if I choose to, be a tourist or a local. And I'm privileged to have experienced an India of the past.

I took another trip round India, backpacking, doing the full temple tour of the south. I woke up at 4am to watch ancient rituals that haven't changed for thousands of years. I slept in ashrams, climbed holy mountains, yoga'd in Rishikesh, pooja'd in Haridwar, I even spent a week as the most confused person on a Tibetan Buddhism course in Dharamsala. This trip was with another inappropriate 'friend'. Travel broadens the mind, and having a broadened mind attracts people who are also broad-minded, or at the very least would like their mind broadened by you. This was better than being with someone who was more comfortable with me ignoring my Indianness.

Mumbai is one of my favourite places and one of the most fun cities on earth. You can have an awesome night out in bars and clubs playing great music and end up eating THE BEST kebab you've ever had at the end of the night. Bademiya's, I can taste you now. India has grown and changed and I've grown with it.

I have a global connection with the South Asian diaspora, particularly young, free-thinking women like me, who are challenging conventions, pushing boundaries and creating new stories and identities, redefining who young South Asian woman are around the world and how we are seen. I feel connected to something much bigger than me, something important. Something I have to stand up and be part of. I fully recognise that being a South Asian woman, no, just a woman, with a voice, with agency, gives me an advantage that so many women around the world do not have. So, I also recognise that it's time to make my voice heard, whether anyone agrees with me or not, when for a long time I've been slowly, slowly turning myself down. Losing my sense of self and my focus. It's time to tune back into who I am and turn the volume right up. My life has always been full of passion, now it has something much greater: purpose.

You Will Fall in Love and Be Loved

It was explained to me that if I didn't study, I'd be married off. Marriage was a threat, a terrifying threat.

No wonder Asian girls are so highly educated. We know, unlike the boys, nothing will be handed to us on a silver thaal, so we have to make something of ourselves. If studying means I can keep the preying beast of marriage at bay, I'll keep studying. For us, gaining an education means also gaining liberation. With an education comes social mobility, your earning capacity increases, but also your eyes are opened to the world and to your own potential. Often this means looking back and questioning the expectations and traditional values of your own family. We go through a transformation. Anyone who's bettered themselves can relate to this story. This can also cause issues when looking for partners, as Asian men have not always moved in the same direction.

SPOILER ALERT: I do get married to the dream Indian son-in-law and you will be invited to my massive Indian wedding. But, for the first time in my life, I will admit that standing in my wedding regalia at the doorway of the Gur-dwara, looking at the backs of the 450 guests invited to my own wedding and about 100 or so gate-crashers, what was honestly going through my mind was: 'What the hell am I doing here?'

My husband-to-be is sat in front of the holy book, wait-ing for me to walk down the carpeted aisle, to take my place cross-legged on the floor next to him, so we can begin our beautiful Sikh wedding ceremony. What happens at this point in the movies? Butterflies in your belly? Everyone turns to smile at once at the beautiful bride? A full-blown song and dance sequence for the happiest day of your life? Only, I'm freaking out. Do I need the loo? Don't I need the loo? Who are all these people? Why does the temple smell of paint? What am I doing here?

I'm looking out across the scene in front of me: serene, calm, quiet, and I am anything but. This was not how I'd planned life to be. I am 32 but I wasn't supposed to be get-ting married yet and, when I did get married, I wasn't going to have a big, elaborate, traditional Indian wedding. So how had I got here, a place I knew I didn't want to be, having my big bonanza traditional wedding?

I knew in that moment I was doing something I wasn't really prepared to do. I thought I was. I thought I'd made all the right decisions, made them just for me, but now, look-ing back, I can see I made these decisions for everyone apart from me. They were made to keep everyone happy. In turn, I thought that is what would make me happy. I then had an out-of-body experience and I watched myself get married.

I want to say that after years of feeling like the ugly duckling and making epic relationship mistakes, I eventually fell in love and lived happily ever after. Isn't that what everyone wants to hear? I've denied the reality to myself for a long time. It was actually my husband who said to tell you, the reader, the truth. To not pretend I was skipping around with white doves floating around me and a sitar playing sweet music. That I felt like I was making a mistake. Not because I hadn't met an incredible man (he's a gud 'un), just getting married seemed so final. It's what everyone else was doing as well, but did we even know each other? Did either of us really know what we were getting into, or were we just taking a punt and hoping for the best?

I want you to understand just how powerful my South Asian upbringing, with all its rules and regulations, really was. That no matter how successful and independent and high-achieving and free-thinking I thought I was, I was still under a huge amount of pressure. A pressure based on my ridiculous need to please and not let anyone down, which meant I did what was expected of me and not what I wanted. Maybe you have felt that pressure too and, maybe, knowing I've been through, it makes it a little more bearable?

* * *

I'd been living in London happily for seven years, carving out a career as a presenter. I'd managed to buy not just one but two flats in London, trying to be prudent, financially savvy and making plans for my own dependent future. Life was pretty goddamn good. I loved life in my little flat. I painted the walls whatever crazy colour I wanted (. . . white) and bought my first ever masonry drill from Argos. I really didn't have a clue what I was doing, but I built and put up my own wonky shelves and bought myself furniture for the first time. It was a learning curve and just the adventure I wanted. I was free. I went out when I wanted, which wasn't very often, because I enjoyed pottering around my house. I was peddling away at growing my presenting career and did I mention I was free?

I kept myself very, very busy, surprise surprise. As a freelance presenter, you have to have a high level of self-motivation and a ton of energy to constantly hustle. Thankfully, I am gifted with both and I see them as my superpowers. (Thanks, Mum and Dad, for never letting me have a lie-in.) You see, this is a strange profession to navigate, as there is no specific trajectory, no guaranteed promotion, no set pay rises, but pay reductions . . . It's completely subjective as an industry, which makes it even harder to crack when you look like none of the bosses. Add to that the general belief that British audiences want to see white faces and it was never going to be easy. So, you have to take the jobs when they come, even if it's not exactly where you want to be. You have to constantly remind people you exist, because you don't have the luxury of gigs just pinging into your inbox. When a couple of white TV presenters wanted to talk to me about how hard it has become recently to get work, I just thought, yeah, welcome to what the rest of us have known forever.

I wasn't moaning about it back then. I'm not a moaner. I was too busy having fun, going at it. I was up and down the country filming as a reporter for *The One Show*, I'd got a gig on *Watchdog*, I was even depping on 5 Live and, my favourite radio station, 6 Music. I'd made a beeline for the then boss at a BBC party and told him how much I love music and what a fan of the station I was, and he asked me to send him a showreel with a few musical choices. It worked! I depped for a while and it was joyful, until that boss moved on. Life was sweet and I was having a great time.

I spoke to Mum on the phone regularly. The conversations always, ALWAYS, went the same way:

'Aunty Pushpa's sister's husband's brother's daughter has had a baby.'

'Oh.'

'How did you get home tonight?'

'Tube and then walk.'

'Oh, be careful. I'm so scared of you walking home alone.'

'Mum, it's fine. I've lived here for years and I'm 30.'

'Yes, yes, 30 and single.'

Sigh. 'Yeah, but I'm happy.'

'No.'

'Yes.'

'Accha, but I won't be happy until you are settled.' And there it is, the sucker punch.

'Mum, I'm happy, I'm settled, I like being single, I don't want to get married.'

'I will never be happy until you are married. Only then my burden will be lifted.'

'I don't want to get married.'

'I know, what can I do with this girl?'

'Let me live my life?'

Every single time we spoke, 'I won't be happy until you're married'. That is the killer line. The one that gets you right in the solar plexus – and they know it. When all you have tried to do is make them happy. Your raison d'etre in so many ways, no matter how much you try and escape it, is to make Mum happy. It's the final and most effective control method, their suffering. In the pursuit of your own freedom and choices, you are still controlled by that innate drive, which means mothers can turn the screw whenever they want, consciously or subconsciously. All they can think about from the minute you are born is the day you will get married. Finally, they will be free of the daughter. I've spent and wasted so many hours of my life worrying about, panicking about, arguing about, the subject of marriage. Hours of my life I'll never get back. Asians are obsessed with getting wed, or rather getting people 'married off'. There's no consulting or interest in how YOU might feel about it. There's a life agenda and you have to fit it. Don't get me wrong, I wanted to meet someone too, but in my own time, in my own way, maybe with a bit of romance, with my own twist thrown in. Without the constant peck peck peck from Mum. It's not just them, it's the first thing your entire family want to ask you about when they see you.

Those conversations always went the same way too:

'Nitu.' (Nitu is what my family call me, it's my pet name. I'm Punjabi, of course I have a pet name.) 'It's time you got married.' Subtle.

It was a Friday night in 2008 and I was planning a lovely night in, disappearing into a YouTube musical journey, with a bowl of pasta. My brother wasn't having any of it. I'd made him move to London after he'd finished his degree in cybernetics and robotics and was back home moping around in his old bedroom. I had to get him out of Bradford. I asked my brother what his dream job would be, which company would he like to work for? He said Saatchi & Saatchi, so I suggested he write a personal letter to the MD, explaining who he was and why he'd love to work for them (as well applying to at least 80 other companies!). Guess bloody what? He got an interview with the MD of Saatchi & Saatchi and they created a ruddy job for him! Jamminess runs in the family. So now he was living in my spare room. 'Anita, you'll become a cat lady. Come ooooooon, let's go ooooout.' He may have started due to concern for his sister, but I think my brother was motivated by his own self-interest. I'd been invited to a warehouse party in Dalston that weekend, and in the mid 2000s, Hackney was a place only visited by those in search of the best music and underground parties. The gentrification wave hadn't quite fully taken over this corner of east London yet, it was still home to places that had such appealing labels as 'the murder mile'. We went, and as I climbed the concrete stairs of the warehouse, I was already happy. Industrial environments are a comfortable space for me to be in after a childhood growing up in factories.

I can hear a distant bwwwaaaaammm, bwwaaamm, bwwwaaammm of a baseline getting louder and louder. My space, my comfort zone – where strangers, for one night only, become your best friends. The air is thick and warm, even the walls are sweating. Everyone is happy. But hang on, this place is different to any club, pub, rave, festival, secret gig, any social gathering I've ever been to, because 80 per cent of the kids in this room are brown like me! It's like all the Asian misfits from around the UK have congregated in this room, for this one night. Beautiful Bengali girls from Birmingham, Gujarati kids galore, boys in make-up, boys who looked like Prince with double nose piercings. MY PEOPLE.

Muslims, Hindus, Buddhists, Jains, Sikhs, Christians, all those labels left with our parents. Here we were, kids with a shared love of music and a shared brown experience. Second generation misfits. The oddballs who felt out of place where they grew up, all represented. All these kids knew the pain and joys of growing up South Asian in Britain. There may be different twists and turns in each of our stories but there's an unsaid, unspoken bond between us. I met people who were creative and driven and trying to pursue their passions, all trying to make their mark, all hustling and battling a system not designed for them. In here, I found people who would lift me when I was down. Protect me if I messed up. Who would understand my hurt in an instant. They'd inspire me, support me and tell me terrible jokes. In here, it was us against them. In here, we were seen. In here, I met the man who was to become my husband.

How did I clock him? It was hard to miss him, seeing as there was a bright light shining out from inside him.

And, of course, he was well fit. We got chatting when I was about to leave but he insisted I stay as he was about to jump on the decks to play a set. Now he really had my attention! The first record he played was one of my absolute favourites, MJ Cole's 'Sincere'. There's no way I could leave now.

I called Mum to tell her I'd met someone.

'What's his name?'

'Bhupinder . . .'

'BHUPINDER! Indian!'

All my mum's Diwalis and Vaisakhis had come at once. 'Now get married, jaldi jaldi.'

It was the same message from all my aunts, as soon as they found out I was dating someone Indian. And not just Indian, but a Punjabi. This is precisely the reason no Asian kids ever reveal to their parents that they are in a relationship, whether they'd approve of it or not, because as soon as they know, they expect you to get married. For them it's the next logical step. The idea of long-term dating or, shock horror, moving in together, no no no no! That's something for the 'Western world'. For Asian parents, you meet and, if you're not put off immediately by any kind of terrible body odour, you wed.

A year later, we were getting married.

There was a specific moment that propelled our relationship along. Grief can do that. It was Christmas 2008, four blissful months into our relationship. Mum called with the devastating news that my favourite uncle, the tattoo-covered artist, my dad's little brother, had died. He was only 44. He was brilliant. The best human, the coolest uncle. I'd never lost a loved one, let alone the uncle who was the closest relation to me and Kul, who meant the world to us. I'd never experienced grief and, even now, I still find it very hard to talk about.

The lad drove Kul and me back up to Bradford on the same night we got the news. It was surreal walking into my mum and dad's home in Bradford at midnight. Everyone was in shock. Then the lad did something that came to him instinctively and I was amazed: he gave my dad a hug. Not an awkward back pat kind of hug, but a proper, meaningful, supportive, deeply thoughtful and moving hug. He held my dad. His capacity for vulnerability, sensitivity, compassion and kindness was something I'd never seen in a man and I was astounded. And, remarkably, my dad hugged him back. I'd never seen my dad hug like that before.

In that moment, I thought – yes. Two months later, on a snowy mountain in the Alps, he proposed. Did I cry? No, I just felt really awkward for most of it. I cringe at big romantic gestures! I love giving but I'm terrible at receiving and I hadn't yet made friends with my own vulnerability. So, marriage was always going to be an interesting exercise. We then snowboarded or rather, attempted to snowboard, down the mountain, towards the rest of our lives.

I didn't want a big Indian wedding in a hotel in Bradford, which is what pretty much everyone I knew usually went for. We had a couple of ideas for the type of wedding we wanted: Hackney Register Office with a tiny group of our closest family and friends, and a small party afterwards. Fat chance.

As me and the lad both came with a Punjabi mother, the wedding was pretty swiftly taken out of our hands, whether we liked it or not.

I didn't want a big Indian wedding in a hotel in Bradford.

We also had this wonderful idea of getting married in India, in my favourite state of Rajasthan. The state that has everything you expect India to have: palaces, ancient fortresses, elephants, camels, women draped in dreamy Rajasthani bandhani print, brightly coloured silk, dripping with chunky silver jewellery. It's as romantic as it gets, and I could handle this level of romance by visiting one of my favourite places in India at the same time. I'd always secretly imagined a parallel life as a free-spirited, horse-riding, sword-wielding warrior princess living in a palace in Rajasthan . . .

But I was marrying a British Indian who'd never set foot in India. The lad's family are East African migrants who landed in London in the sixties. His dad was born in Kenya and his mother in Uganda, their stories intertwined with Empire also. They'd lost their connection with India two generations earlier. So, getting married there would first mean acclimatisation for his entire family to a land of their ancestors, plus, and this was the main issue, although the guest list would be kept slim by only a few people making the trip from Britain, we'd both have to invite a ton of people we are related to in India, most of whom he had never met in his entire life. My mum's first cousins alone total 45, and that's not counting their children and grandchildren and great grandchildren. The politics of Indian families is a minefield. My Rajasthani dream was ditched.

Traditionally, Indian weddings take place where the bride is from. The groom's party make the schlep to literally go and get the girl.

I did not want a big Indian wedding in a hotel in Bradford.

The next most obvious choice was the place where my heart resides and I feel most at peace, in the beautiful open expanse of the Yorkshire countryside. I found the perfect place, a stunning manor house surrounded by the verdant rolling hills of the Yorkshire Dales. Peaceful, beautiful and classy. Completely different to the usual two hotels everyone in Bradford ends up getting married in because they're the only places big enough to deal with the enormous number of guests. This place was picture perfect AND it was big enough to have 250 people for a sit-down meal. Two hundred and fifty people, I hear you shriek! This, let me tell you, is a minuscule number for a Punjabi wedding.

When I was a kid, we'd attend weddings with over 1,000 people. They tended to be organised chaos in a uniquely Asian fashion. Chaos was something I wanted to avoid at my own wedding. Actually, there were quite a few things I wanted to avoid at my own wedding. Could we ditch the old tradition of giving and receiving gifts from every single member of my family and every single member of Bhupi's family? I absolutely didn't want my parents buying me a ton of gold and sarees as part of my wedding trousseau. Was it possible to swerve that one? How about we leave off the guest list all the extended family I hardly knew and would never see again in my life?

I had it all planned out. A simplified, classy, stress-free, streamlined, relatively intimate affair that would make a perfect day. *My* perfect day.

'OW MANY?' Dad blurted out when he heard 250. Then he just laughed. 'No, no, no. That's not nearly enough space. Where are we going to put the gate-crashers?'

It was explained to me why Indian weddings are done a certain way and why my parents would like to follow the traditions, but not before the situation escalated into a full-blown barney with my mother telling me what a rebellious daughter I was: 'I never asked my mother this many questions. Hai hai this kuri.' It's like Mum couldn't wait to get rid of me. The burden of the free-thinking, wilful, 32-year-old daughter was finally being lifted, and with an Indian man. I wasn't going to ruin it all at the last minute by doing away with all the traditions. They eventually explained that Punjabi weddings are a celebratory feast, a tradition left over from back in the day when we lived in villages (actually, really not that long ago, my dad was literally born in a barn) and the entire village would be invited as a way of connecting with your community. Most importantly, however, it was what my mum and dad wanted. And I couldn't shake that dutiful daughter thing, no matter how hard I tried.

I understood that my folks were part of a community in Bradford and they finally had the opportunity, after attending A LOT of weddings, to throw a big old party too. Marriage pressure aside, my parents had been pretty

amazing at encouraging me and allowing me to really follow my dreams. They'd brought me up to be wilful and
free-thinking, even if it did bite them on the arse at times.
I love them. The politics of Indian families is complex and,
if someone was missed off the list, my mother would never
have heard the end of it. My parents wanted the honour of
doing things the traditional way and even though I've spent
a lifetime fighting to carve my own independent place in the
world, they are my Achilles heel. Was this even really what
my parents wanted to do, or were they in turn also going
along with what was expected of them? Did they really
want to spend a fortune and go through the hell of organis-
ing a week-long shindig, feeling permanently stressed and
constantly managing difficult relations? This is community
control in action. It tightens its grip and no one knows if
they can actually just say no. What's everyone scared of?

Ultimately, I didn't want to upset my parents, it wasn't
worth the battle, and not for them to feel hurt by me demanding what I wanted. See how it gets under your skin? I wanted
my mum and dad to have their day. The day they'd always
dreamed of. The day they'd waited for all my life. I went
from the girl who was never getting married to the girl who
would have an intimate wedding to the girl who had, what I
call, 'My big fat Punjabi sweat fest'.

First, I had to schlep off to India with my mother and masi
for an episode we'll call *Carry On Wedding Shopping*. This
isn't uncommon for families with a connection to the motherland. The selection of wedding clothes in India is obviously
far greater than the UK, plus there was a lot more to buy

than just my wedding outfits: I get two wedding outfits, one for the religious ceremony, one for the reception. Outfits for every day of the week of ceremonies running up to the big day. There were all the outfits (21) for my wedding trousseau plus the jewellery. There were the clothes we give as gifts to my entire family, and to all my in-laws. Decorations for the house, all the bits and pieces required for the various ceremonies and, for some stupid reason, I thought it'd be a great idea to get invites and the matching sweet boxes I needed printed in Old Delhi. Most wedding invites are hand delivered with an accompanying box of sweets. I'd decided that I could at least have Yorkshire fudge in mine rather than the usual selection of barfi. We dashed around Delhi, Jalandhar and Patiala, frantic and fraught and of course we fought, but we also had a blast while we were there.

I mentioned my apprehension about getting married to my mum on this trip, but she wasn't having any of it. I needed to get on with what was happening, she said. I think she actually blanked me when I pressed. The wedding was organised in less than six months and the pressure was on from the beginning. I was already 32 and I wasn't getting any younger. Of course, they were all thinking about children too – everyone apart from me, that is. Thankfully this wasn't said to my face.

It was to be a week-long affair. The henna ceremony, the wedding bangles ceremony, the getting covered in turmeric ceremony (to beautify me before the big day). I loved all the pre-wedding rituals. Then a Sikh ceremony at the Gurdwara in Bradford followed by a reception big enough to hold 450, you heard right, 450, of my nearest and dearest! Yes, I was having a big Indian wedding in a hotel in Bradford.

Me and the lad were both the first in our families to get married. This was finally an opportunity for our families to do what they had always dreamt of doing. To be able to hold their heads up with pride at their children having a traditional Indian wedding. We decided as long as the two of us were there, we'd let them do what they wanted. And it was a hoot. My friends had an incredible time going from parties to ceremonies to rituals, to costume changes and chicken tikkas and seekh kebabs and aloo tikkis, to bhangra dancing and henna applying and curries and rice and chapattis and naans, borrowing sarees and being draped in silk, wearing all the bling they could get their hands on, and actual legitimate bindi wearing (not at a music festival). But my God, it came at a price. Punjabi weddings cost several arms and legs. They are like a mini festival.

The week of the wedding arrived, stressful, chaotic but joyful. Our house was crammed with relatives, doing what Indian relatives do best: eating and having conversations by shouting in each other's faces. There was dancing in one room, henna being applied in another, kids playing computer games, a permanent pan of chai on the go and a constant production line of food preparation for seven days straight. I tried to make sure I was present for most of it but there was so much going on, I really don't think it had sunk in. Plus, I had to make a dash back to London for two days during the week to present *Watchdog*. My favourite ceremony was the night before the wedding. A beautiful and intimate ritual of putting on my choora, my red wedding bangles. They are dipped in milk and then my maternal uncles and their wives put the bangles on me. I'd watched my aunt in India 25 years earlier have the skin scraped off her knuckles as the choora was too small, but thankfully, mine fit.

This was to be the calm before the storm. The day of the wedding, Bradford treated us to a torrential downpour. The rain came in so fast and at such an acute angle it was practically horizontal. Traditionally, the groom arrives on a white horse with the groom's party dancing behind him, but the weather was so God-awful the horse had to be cancelled at the last minute. Bhupi had to wade out into the deluge in his wedding regalia: turban, full-grown beard, sherwani and sehra (a sparkly curtain in front of his face), to see the bloke with the horse, who was pulled up right in front of the temple, waiting for his cash! What a hero (Bhupi, not the horse).

The guests made their way into the temple and took their seats on the floor, shoes off and heads covered. Bhupi took his seat in front of the holy book, awaiting his bride. For everyone watching, the ceremony was beautiful, Sikh weddings always are. It was serene and calm on the outside, but I was having an out-of-body experience for all of it. Not really understanding how this was happening in my life. I'm not sure my mum could watch. I think she had her eyes closed, praying throughout the ceremony. I don't remember Mum smiling. After a lifetime of pressure to get me married, on the actual day my mum was sad. Go figure!

Once the religious ceremony was over, we headed down into the temple basement to conduct the legal bit of the wedding. I had to jump over a hoover and slide between stacked-up tables. The 'uncle' registrar could barely speak English, so he got the names, birthdates and occupations all mixed up. My marriage certificate is covered in crossings out. Oh, the glamour!

All the non-Indian guests headed straight from the Gurdwara to the hotel reception, wondering where everyone else went. This is the moment all the wedding guests have a costume change. Weddings are an opportunity to display your finest outfits, so costume changes are essential. Bhupi took off the turban, shaved off his beard and changed into his sleek Ozwald Boateng suit, and looked like a different groom. The party was about to kick off but not until the newlyweds finally make their entrance, a full two hours after the wedding ceremony. This entrance was my touch and a first at an Indian wedding in Bradford: we came in dancing behind The Bollywood Brass Band. A 14-piece brass band with two booming Indian dhol players, blowing out Bollywood classics. I've never seen an Indian wedding party turn into a rave, with aunties and uncles and sarees and turbans bouncing all over the dancefloor. Finally, I relaxed. All of a sudden, I was having the time of my life.

* * *

In my family, people have married in all kinds of circumstances, to people from all over the world. We have plenty of people who 'married out'. English, Puerto Rican, Finnish and Persian, a cousin who eloped, a cousin who married a woman ten years older than them (who had a kid together and then got divorced). What's intriguing about all these examples is that they were all boys. The girls in our family have all had arranged marriages, until me. I was the first woman to pick who I wanted to marry. Did my family disown any of the boys? That's not how the system works, boys don't get disowned.

I have never regretted my marriage, only the way I was pushed towards it. At the time, I thought, maybe they're all right. Maybe it is high time I settled down. Whatever that means.

But I had a life to live, adventures to have, and nowhere in my own personal life agenda was there any mention of 'settling down'.

Change the world. Yes

Have adventures. Yes

Do something important. Yes

Get out of Bradford. Yes

Have a flash riverside apartment. Yes

Live life to the fullest. Yes

Get a tattoo. Yes

Understand Buddhism. Yes

Have a right laugh. Hell, yes

Set up a global charitable fund to educate young girls. Yes

Expand my mind. Yes

Visit Bhutan (I love mountains). Yes

Become a carefree eccentric. To come with old age

Settle down . . . Nope. That's nowhere on my list.

You may have deduced by now that my expectations of marriage were also pretty low. You can't blame me! The examples of marriage all around me weren't exactly selling the idea. They all seemed devoid of respect, romance or even the basic: love. I have a clear memory of seeing a couple holding hands when I was around five and I was so confused by the vision. Why would two people hold hands like that? Marriage to me just upheld the patriarchy. The boys got the much better deal. Women treated one way and men the other. Once an Asian woman is married, there's no getting away from expectations and now they come from your in-laws too. People who don't really know who you are. You are expected to adapt to this new family.

But I'd carved out my life and I treasured it and loved it. I was happy to just crack on.

Son-in-laws are treated like gods, just accepted, no matter how disastrous they may be. The only thing I understood about marriage was that it's a woman's job to make it work, at all costs, and if it doesn't work for whatever reason, it's the woman's fault. Marriage to me was women putting up with shit, for life, from everyone. I mean, who the hell would want to enter into a system like this willingly? Which is probably why parents start the marriage indoctrination mantra from birth. Brainwashing is the only way to get us down that aisle.

For the girl who had only ever craved freedom, I felt as though I was walking into a trap. Which is all very complicated and exposing to admit . . . as a married woman. But marriage has also been the only place that has truly helped me explore who I am. What the life I want is, what I will and won't accept. The older I get, the more I'm challenged, and the more I understand. But my checklist remains the same: I still want adventures and a tattoo and to live my life to the fullest. Now, I've got a partner along for the ride, one with a great record collection.

You Will Be Accepted

My job now sees me striding around the British country-side filming, milking goats and being chased by hungry cows. Going to places no Asian woman has gone before, on national telly. I find myself getting into conversations about neoprene-lined wellies and I'm on the constant hunt for stylish waterproof trousers. I can report they don't exist.

I definitely brought my own street swag to *Countryfile*. I wasn't going to change my style to country casual just because I was now in the bosom of pastoral Britain. At the beginning I used to rock up in box-fresh white trainers and the voice of God told me that wellies are the official attire to be worn in a field. I had a pair that I'd bought from a petrol station gathering dust and thought they'd do. What a fool. Wellies designed to splash around in puddles are not going to cut it on a 10-hour shoot day in a field in Scotland. The cold seeps in and your toes may have already dropped off but you are so numb to anything you wouldn't know. All those romantic notions of the countryside are out. It can be tough out there. I deploy thermals from September through to April. It's the only way to survive the great British outdoors.

The biggest trial was one of my early filming trips, right to the heart of rural Britain in Harewood House, just outside Leeds. I was pretty much in the deep crevice of the countryside at the GLA Game Fair. I've never seen so many guns, tweeds and red corduroy trousers, and there were flat caps a-plenty. I was terrified. This was the hardcore *Countryfile* audience, the ones who probably felt the programme had gone a little soft with it now being a popular factual show rather than solely a rural affairs programme. What the hell did this lot make of me on their favourite TV show? Once again, I was the only brown face there. Luckily my childhood conditioning meant I didn't feel self-conscious, I was hardened to being 'the only brown in the village'.

The show entered me into a clay pigeon shooting competition . . . as a total novice. Turns out I have a natural aptitude and I won the bloody competition! As I was walking up the main drag of the fair, a rather rotund, red-faced man, probably in his sixties, wearing bright yellow trousers and a tweed waistcoat walked past me then turned around to look directly at me. Oh God, here we go. This lot are not afraid to say what they really think. Straight-talking Yorkshire folk, remember? He looked as though he was about to tell me off. I stopped breathing for a second, preparing myself for the humiliation.

'You're doing alreet, lass, you're doing alreet.'

Then he turned around and carried on. This was the moment I knew I'd been officially accepted on *Countryfile*. It really didn't matter about anyone else's opinion now. No matter what nonsense I received on Twitter or what people might be saying behind my back, rural Yorkshire had my back! Or at least he did.

So, what was the reaction to me joining the *Countryfile* team from others?

'So, what is your countryside experience?'

'Did you know much about the British countryside before the show?'

'You'll never be Ellie Harrison.' Which came as a shock, because I always thought I was. Naturally, two women were pitted against each other.

'So, what is your field of expertise?' Erm, presenting.

'Have you always lived in this country?' I grew up in Bradford.

These are just a few of the things said to my face. I can't even begin to get into some of the nonsense I've received via Twitter. Luckily, I have a strong Twitter bullshit resistance forcefield. I try not to get sucked into it, most of the time, but sometimes a racist tweet will trigger me and I have to remind myself to not get into any argy-bargy with a numbskull. If I do respond to an insulting tweet, I'm usually backed up by an army of good folk. This gives me hope. Most people are sane, but to preserve the smidge of sanity I have left, I generally stay away from Twitter rucks as a rule. Ignore the idiots.

Presenting *Countryfile* is a gift. I got a call from the boss of BBC1 and she asked if I fancied doing a piece on it, just one item. It was never part of my plan, but then, as you know I take the opportunities as they come and any kind of plan for my career went out the window years before. I was sent to Cornwall to blow up 10 tonnes of dynamite in a china clay quarry, just in case people didn't notice me, and six years later, I'm still on the show.

A warm Sunday night hug of a show, the most popular factual show on national TV, no less. The *New York Times* once called it 'pastoral porn', fascinated by Britain's love for this rural programme and love for their countryside. It's a national institution and I find myself at the heart of it. I was once asked by a journo how important it was for Asian Britain that I was on a show like *Countryfile* and I replied that the Asian community are proud of me wherever I go. This is how I feel. I feel held by them and humbled by their support. I understand what I must represent for them, the importance of young girls watching a brown face like theirs seemingly at the heart of the establishment. It shows that it is possible to achieve your dreams. However, surely it's more important for the rest of Britain to see a brown woman striding around the British countryside and not self-destructing as soon as the air hits her? A brown and British woman, a Yorkshire lass taking ownership of the land. Having representation on screen isn't just for the benefit of people who look like me, it's for the enhancement of all of society.

When Noma Dumezweni, a black woman, was cast as Hermione Granger in the award-winning stage production of *Harry Potter*, people were outraged. The character couldn't possibly be black. They were prepared to believe in wizards and an invisibility cloak, but Hermione Granger, black? No way! Even little black and brown kids put white children at the heart of the stories they write, because they can't imagine people who look like them being their heroes. We need more colour-blind casting and we definitely need more authentically diverse stories and characters out there to be played. It's imperative that we start reflecting the society we are and who we want to be, and to not be afraid of upsetting a few narrow-minded, unimaginative troublemaking racists.

For a long time, I have had the thickest skin. Dinosaur thickness. I have also happily lived in a bubble of positivity. I've skipped around with my fingers in my ears, focusing on my own game, with my mum's mantra ringing in my ears: 'Be positive, be positive, be positive.' If I call Mum up with even a slight hint of a bad day, she won't want to hear anything about it and just sings her mantra down the phone. It does mean I've kept a lot of stuff bottled up. So, when anyone says something derogatory, or prejudice is staring me in the face, I choose to focus on something good and always see the positive. I believed, because it was instilled in me by my parents, that if I strove for excellence, I could achieve anything. But it's not quite so simple in the real world.

My advice to anyone wanting a career in the creative industries, particularly Asian kids, was always: you only need that one break. It's a numbers game. Nothing will come to you, nothing will land in your lap no matter how talented you are. You have to get out there and dazzle them with your skills, your mad-crazy brilliant skills. Don't worry about the negative, stay focused on your game.

* * *

Since turning 40, my attitude has changed.

If you have no connections, if you were not born with a sense of entitlement, if Daddy isn't the boss or your godfather isn't the king of the world, if you have no cash in the bank, if you have any level of melanin in your skin, it's going to be a lot tougher for you to get them breaks. First, every time you go for a job it feels like you are starting from scratch. There is no resting on any laurels. There is no big break, no overnight success. You will have to work hard, steadily and constantly. You will never really have the privilege of feeling like you've 'made it'. Even if you are one of the answers on *Pointless*. (Yes, I was.) And all of these challenges will make you stronger. They may piss the living hell out of you but overcoming them will give you superpowers. Secondly, if you have been turned down for 10 jobs even though you know you are really good at what you do, there is a problem. And, sometimes, no matter how skilled you are, those in charge won't always see it. They are blinkered to your badass-ery. There is a fundamental problem with the system.

Maybe I used to skip around with my fingers in my ears as my own self-preservation method? Knowing if I spent time looking and analysing and thinking about my place in my industry, it would not get me anywhere, because there was no space where I could begin to air my thoughts. I'd be seen as angry and bitter or chippy. I wish I'd opened my eyes sooner. I spent too long wanting to make people happy. To please. Allowing people to put me where they wanted me to be and believing I couldn't be anywhere else. I kept ploughing on, hustling hard. Mentally drained, but with no choice but to keep going. Because you still cling to the belief that, one day, you will get that break and be able to feel some kind of security, that you will not be defeated by the flipping glass ceiling. You will get what you deserve.

I wish I'd been braver sooner, but it can be a lonely business. Finally, people are talking about their own experiences. Powerful voices are calling the system out because enough is enough and we want to make a better, fairer and more equal society. Incredible, clever, creative, articulate, talented people are speaking their truth and in so doing are empowering people, myself included, to be able to free our little voices and finally release a bit of the pressure. See Michaela Coel and David Olusoga both giving landmark and powerful speeches at the Edinburgh TV Festival. Riz Ahmed in everything he does, with speeches in Parliament, his movies and music. Edward Enninful taking over as editor-in-chief of British *Vogue* and overnight changing the face of the magazine. Books like *Why I'm No Longer Talking to White People About Race* by Reni Eddo-Lodge, Afua Hirsch's *Brit(ish)*, Layla F. Saad's *Me and White Supremacy*, Nikesh Shukla and Chimene Suleyman's *The Good Immigrant*, Sathnam Sanghera's *Empireland*, Akala's brilliant *Natives*. Stormzy headlining Glastonbury 2019. Samira Ahmed taking her employer, the BBC, to tribunal over an equal pay dispute (and winning). Artist and filmmaker Steve McQueen. Just look at the momentum from the Black Lives Matter movement, which has had a ripple effect around the world.

So many others are fighting for a more equal space for all, trying to redress the balance, but I bet they'd all much rather just be getting on with their jobs. Not only do all these people have to be more than brilliant at what they do than everyone else, they also have to be politicised alongside their work, at the risk of pissing off the people that give them the work. The people who still may not understand that we all have a responsibility and a part to play in working towards a society that is equal for all. That's not going to be easy. It may make you bristle, but we should lean into what makes us feel uncomfortable and ask ourselves questions of how we can all make it better, no matter how hard it will be. And it will be hard.

I also know the answer to something everyone is looking for – where to find the talent. If you want to track down the next big thing, I'd say you could do a lot worse than head to Yorkshire. Your next best recruit is currently looking out of her suburban window, planning her escape. Go and find her.

In the meantime, we need to find a way to not let other people have that much control over our lives, careers and ambitions. If you feel your path is blocked in one direction, take another. If they don't see what you see, find someone who does. This is why we need people from all backgrounds in positions of power. Remember it's not you, it's the world around you that is still getting their head around you. You are creating space when it doesn't exist and it is going to be a struggle, it's going to push you and challenge you, but every time you are challenged, you grow, it adds to your armour. You have to stay positive and remember the long game. That what you do is so much bigger than you. It's a battle to change the landscape for everyone else. To change perceptions so the next generation of brilliant women and men may have to struggle a little less. Until everyone can recognise their unconscious bias, some of us have to keep punching people in the face. Metaphorically.

I spent too long wanting to please, second-guessing what's wanted, not being true to myself, having to navigate a space that was never for me. Taking opportunities where they came, even if it wasn't the exact plan I had for myself. Doing whatever I needed to do to carve out a space, a career. It is bloody exhausting. There will come a time when people of colour in the UK can just produce art rather than having to spend all our creative energy on explaining who we are and why we have a right to exist. I can't wait.

Your Anger is Legitimate

Most of the time, I am very happy and positive – I'm a TV presenter, of course I'm upbeat! Scratch the surface, though, and you'll see anger. Lots of it. I'm angry we can't feel compassion for people fleeing for their lives, from war and famine. I'm angry with our lack of humanity. I'm angry because we all buy into labels that seem to define us and hate others as a consequence. I'm angry because we are killing our planet, our wonder of a home. I'm angry that some people feel they have more of a right to it than others. I'm angry about borders and religion. I'm angry men make all the rules, including about women's bodies and our medical health. I'm angry because all of these things are out of my control.

I've always been angry. I thought I was angry because my dad was angry, and he was angry because his dad was angry. But I'm angry for so many reasons.

India was forcibly colonised and looted for Britain's financial benefit. The British first landed in India in 1608 but it was in 1757 when The East India Company essentially took charge and then the Crown took over in 1858.

Almost all Sikhs are Punjabi but not all Punjabis are Sikh. Punjab was the heartland of the Sikh Empire. The

Sikh religion is incredibly proud of its history of valour and defending the weak, and Sikh soldiers have a formidable reputation. Punjab was one of the last states in India to be annexed by the British. Punjab couldn't be touched while under the rule of Maharaja Ranjit Singh, a brilliant warrior and strategist who grew the Sikh Empire from the Khyber Pass in the West to Tibet in the East. It was a religiously diverse, secular state. But the Sikhs were known for their military prowess, even now Sikhs make up around 20 per cent of the Indian army and only 2 per cent of the Indian population and they would have defeated the British were it not for them being convinced to betray their own people. Over a million Indian soldiers enlisted for World War I, over two million for World War II.

Then in 1947, well over 300 years after first setting foot in India, Britain departed and left a deep bloody scar in the land in the process. The State of Punjab was severed in two, creating two independent states of India and Pakistan: East Pakistan and West Pakistan, which later became Bangladesh. This division saw the largest recorded migration in human history. Fifteen million people were displaced and one million people were killed. Including members of my family. All my family were affected.

Punjabis don't do anything by halves, including trauma. Alcoholism, male suicide, forced marriage, domestic violence, female infanticide, drug addiction . . . have I missed anything? Mental health, Obesity and Type 2 diabetes maybe. We have it all, in buckets.

Hidden away in every family are our dark secrets. But nobody discusses trauma, ever. And it shows – in the rates of alcoholism within the Punjabi community, the rates of suicide, the prevalence of domestic violence, we know there is a problem and yet we won't know the true extent of the problem because it's all hidden. Every Punjabi I know has experience of one or all of these. My aunt's husband took his own life, leaving behind my mum's sister and my cousins, his two teenage sons. My cousins are beautiful, tender and kind men, as was their dad. I don't know the full story of what happened but sons in Punjabi families can feel a great deal of pressure and there really is no space for anyone, particularly men, to talk about mental suffering. In my experience, they usually hit the bottle and/or are really, really angry. I lost this uncle to suicide and I then lost two others to alcohol abuse.

* * *

To truly understand our trauma, we must understand our history. My own family history was intertwined with England long before I was born. The British have been puppet masters of my family's fates for at least four generations. All of them serving the needs of the Empire, the needs of Great Britain.

My nan's father, my maternal great grandfather, was highly educated and got a job as a civil engineer on the railways in Burma. The British needed labour so employed the people they ruled over to serve the needs of the mothership, this tiny little green and pleasant land far, far away. The Indian experience in Burma is a piece of forgotten history. My nan and her 11 siblings were all born in Minbu in Burma, now Myanmar. From the conversations I had with my nan before she died, she had an idyllic childhood. They lived a comfortable middle-class existence. Separate from the wealthier, ruling white community, but in a nice house for her and her 11 siblings. Then, in 1942, when the Japanese invaded Burma, the Indians wanted to get out and back to the safety of their own land. The British organised a few boats and planes but nowhere near enough. Most escaped on foot, on a treacherous trek through the jungle, on 'The Road of Death'. Hardly anyone knows the story even though it was one of the most difficult mass evacuations in human history.

Families had to leave everything they had behind to get back to India. My nan told me this story when I was young, how my great grandmother had packed metal containers with water and rice for the children. Because they had a bit of money, they were able to get a cart and horse. My nan was 13 at the time and she remembers lighting fires at night in the jungle to keep tigers away. She told me about the dead bodies she saw lying on the side of the path; one woman dead, with a baby in her arms, still trying to suckle at her breast. It's harrowing and unbelievably tragic. Thousands didn't make it. Terrified and hungry, my nan and her siblings eventually made it into India, only to be faced with the horror of Partition five years later in 1947.

What a strange and surreal place Punjab must have been at the stroke of midnight on 14th August 1947. When Pakistan celebrated the birth of a nation and India their new freedom from colonial rule. When both flags were flown, as blood-soaked streets were being washed, as millions of people became refugees in their own country, were they cheering, were they flag waving? Partition was a plan of division that suited politicians and was a messy, hurried, slapdash exit. Britain drained India for nearly 300 years and then cut and run. There was no policing, no Partition management strategy, no soldiers left to ensure smooth transition. The thing was a God-awful mess, with the border not even finalised, with the gaping, seeping wound of Kashmir left to keep both nations at each other's throats for years to come. I can't believe that a nation as organised and strategic as Great Britain would have done such a shambolic job, had they cared a jot about India or its people.

All but one of my grandparents witnessed the Partition. The only one who didn't see it with his own eyes was my maternal grandad. He was away with the British Indian army and was scarred by it the most. While away, he lost all the family he had. His father, wife, son and daughter all killed in what became Pakistan. He was left totally alone until he remarried my nan, whose life had also been upturned by war and Empire.

I was lucky enough to film an episode of *Who Do You Think You Are?* and learn all about my grandfather Sant Singh, who my mother idolised. He was apparently the kindest, most thoughtful and generous man, with not an ounce of hate in his body, even though he certainly had a right to feel it. Filming the programme really did change my life and my connection with who I am and what it means to be from that region of India, the Punjab. It also made me begin questioning the history I knew, or rather didn't know, about Empire and colonialism. Why don't we talk about British history, warts and all? Why leave out the gory details?

Filming the programme also connected me to my grandfather who, as it turns out, was a total dude: forward-thinking, educating his daughters. He also wrote a memoir, his life story, in beautiful poetic English and Punjabi. The section I have is typed in English on a typewriter. I don't understand why it wasn't kept in a glass cage under lock and key as the family treasure it is. Apparently, it was in a storeroom for years in the village and got damaged by damp. He must have been writing it for his children and grandchildren, such an important historical document, this precious heirloom. I wonder what he'd make of his granddaughter reading it, or indeed telling his story on the BBC. He loved listening to the BBC World Service – he believed the BBC was the best news source in the world.

'Did you ever read it, Mum?'

'No, we never asked.'

'Why not?'

'We just knew not to ask and I wasn't really interested, I was too busy being a kid. We didn't ask as many questions as you.'

None of his children had ever read it. I suspect it's because my nan was quite strict, her husband was away with the army and she was at home, essentially a single parent. Mum and her brother were the two naughtiest and were often chased by Nan with a big stick. Sounds brutal, but

Mum laughs about it. Maybe they also knew that some things were not to be spoken about. I believe the pain of Partition was too much for anyone to speak about. It would take another generation before questions were asked. One of the most positive outcomes of those TV shows is that they sparked conversations in families who had never spoken about their past.

It's difficult to write about my paternal grandparents as there's only so much I know about them. Mysteries, the pair of them. They were both teenagers in 1947 when Partition took place, Grandad was 19 and Grandma around 15. They may have already been married. I did ask Grandma once if she had seen anything during that time. She didn't say much but what she said explains so much, almost too much to bear. 'Bodies lying everywhere,' is what she could recall, and then an image so savage I will never get it out of my head: 'Dead women with their breasts cut off.' Gran said it so matter of fact. Such gruesome, base level, animalistic violence towards women. But then, as I discovered much later, there was a huge amount of violence towards women during the Partition. They were raped, abducted, stripped naked, paraded down streets, they were branded, forced to convert, forced to marry, forced to kill themselves, murdered. My entire body is weighed down by that last sentence.

I feel the pain of all the women in my ancestry, of all the women I never met who had no choice in their life. Is this how trauma travels through generations? I feel a deep, burning, screaming rage. The same women who were the lynchpin of every family, who gave birth, nurtured, fed, grew, loved, worked, toiled, the most powerful force on earth reduced, shamed, humiliated, suppressed, owned, controlled. If you watch the episode you will see a change, a shift in the tone and direction of the programme. It goes from an historical journey of discovery to the moment when I become invested and connected to what happened and is still happening to the women in my past. I feel it like it's happening to me.

For the programme, I met an elderly Sikh gentleman in a small and peaceful Gurdwara, in Amritsar. I had no idea what he was about to tell me. Everything on the programme is kept secret so, as I was learning the story of Partition, the viewer could experience it along with me. He told me how he overheard his father, the eldest in the family, take the decision with the other men to behead all the women and girls in their own family, rather than risk them being abducted or murdered by Muslims. As a small child, he witnessed the women, one by one, his aunts, his sisters, cousins, pull their long, plaited hair to one side and, as he put it, 'bravely step forward reciting Sikh prayers' to receive their fate. The tears came from somewhere deep inside me, in the pit of my stomach. I couldn't control them. I couldn't believe what I was hearing. They each came forward 'courageously' to be beheaded. Did they really step forward with courage, or were they forced, kicking and screaming? Were they screaming for their lives, screaming at their fate, screaming at the barbarity, screaming at the world? When I've heard people talk about the women who decided to take their own lives by jumping in village wells, another common atrocity of Partition happening across Punjab, they say how they all went 'bravely' to their deaths. Is this a survival mechanism? To remember the women going willingly and fearlessly, that it was their choice to die, that there was no alternative? I wasn't there but I can see their faces and given the option, I think they would have wanted to live.

Something else I discovered while making not only my *Who Do You Think You Are?* episode, but later during the filming of my programme, *My Family, Partition and Me*, was how women were also abducted by all sides. Forcibly taken from their families, sometimes given away as a bargaining chip, to ensure the rest of the family was kept safe. If this had happened in the UK, there would be so many programmes and books and documentaries to discover all these stories, these hidden family secrets.

What is the meaning of a woman's life? The girl is a burden. Infanticide is criminalised in India but that doesn't stop it from happening. Once, when backpacking across India, I met a pregnant woman on a bus, travelling with her little daughter. We got chatting while I played with her little girl and she told me she was going to see a doctor in her hometown, who would tell her the sex of the child. If it was another girl, she would have it aborted. Not because any part of her wanted to do it, but because of the pressure being put on her by her in–laws to produce a son. My God, it's so exhausting and draining writing this, but write it I must.

After Partition, in 1949 the Indian government passed a law called the Abducted Persons (Recovery and Restoration) Bill, which gave the government the power to remove abducted women in India from their new homes and transport them to Pakistan. The government could use force against abducting families and it could also hold abducted women in camps, if needed. The official estimate of the number of abducted women was placed at 50,000 Muslim women in India and 33,000 Hindu and Sikh women in Pakistan. Until December 1949, the number of recoveries in both countries was 12,552 for India and 6,272 for Pakistan. The maximum number of recoveries were made from Punjab.

These women often did not want to go home as their families would not accept a 'fallen woman'. There were those who didn't want to return to the families who had traded their daughter's life for their own safety. There are thousands of women of my grandmother's generation who would have converted to Islam and remained in Pakistan, or converted to Hinduism or Sikhism and stayed in India. These stories are hidden deep within families. Maybe some know the truth, but so many will have kept their secret to themselves. If you know your granny converted, you also know your family abducted her and were complicit in the chaos and brutality. History is complex, history is devastating, history is vital to understand. Exploring my own family history, I never was able to learn categorically what happened to my Nanaji's first wife. Was she murdered? Did she jump in a well? Was she abducted? Is she still alive somewhere in Pakistan, with a family, *her* family?

My grandparents and others in their generation, who first came to the UK, brought with them the trauma of Partition etched into their souls. They never spoke of it. How do you? Where do you begin? There is no commemoration for the dead in India or Pakistan either.

When *Who Do You Think You Are?* came knocking, I was thrilled, but I really didn't know what light it could shed on my life and experiences. I believed that I was a product of my parents. That they were the only ones responsible for how I turned out. What a naïve fool I was! As a woman with ancestry in India, I feel inextricably connected to the place and to the women who came before me. I am them. They are me. The women India has lost fuel me and I owe it to the memory of all those forgotten and discarded, tossed into the dark well of history, whose names have never been spoken, whose memories are kept embedded in the hearts of the ones who knew them, but never mentioned – I won't let them be forgotten. My family, who I love dearly, never spoke of Nanaji's first wife. I never knew her name until 2015, when I discovered it was Pritam Kaur.

PRITAM KAUR

* * *

Often, when growing up, I'd hear family members talking about how grateful we need to feel for the opportunity of coming to the UK to make better lives for ourselves. I've started to learn that I don't need to be too grateful too much of the time. I've spent so long being told I should be grateful that it has made me feel servile. Being told to feel grateful makes me feel like I'm in a place I don't really belong. That I should recognise that I'm being given opportunities where others aren't and I should bow down in gratitude about it.

I've entered so many meeting rooms throughout my life laden with gratitude, like a nasty stench I can't get rid of. Living in this country, your place is to be grateful and never criticise or comment. Just keep your head down and get on with it. Work twice as hard but don't expect to get twice as far. My grandparents came here for economic reasons and my own parents wanted both social and economic status for their kids. So, we did what we should. We worked really bloody hard with no let up. We educated ourselves, learned everything. Figured out what we needed to do, how we needed to shapeshift to progress. I can move with effortless skill and charm between worlds, but I am not a gatekeeper.

I am angry, and I'm entitled to my anger. Young Anita, walk into those spaces like you own them, like you belong, like the rooms are yours. It won't come naturally, because those spaces alienate you, they isolate you. In those spaces you are visible and different and all that you want to do, all you believe you need to do, all you've been told you have to do, is try and blend in, to speak the language, to understand the cut of their jib. But blend you can't.

Really, all you want is to be seen. Seen for who you are. To have the space to express your true self. You will become sick of adapting to what you think is required of you. Changing to suit everyone else's needs. Making yourself small when you know you are big, bigger than them. Not saying what you think, second-guessing what they want you to say.

You will be told to be dutiful, to be calm, to be quiet, to be respectful, to be humble, to let things wash over you. Do yourself a favour: rip it all off. Strip it off and run for the hills. Let it out. And then empower yourself. Find your force. Turn down the noise in your head. Dismantle the oppression. Find your true self, your true voice. The world is not fair. The system stinks to the gods. But you can't live a half-life. You only have this one shot, let's make it the best life we can possibly have. Keep going. Even when you're tired. Find your allies and keep going.

Let it out, little girl. Be you. Rage Rage Rage. You are brilliant and they can't see that yet, maybe they'll never see, but don't hide away. Don't shrink, because it will mean they have done what they set out to do from the minute you were born. Rise Rise Rise.

Conclusion:
The Right Sort of Woman

When I was a child, in moments of introspection alone in my room, I'd write diaries. I'd feel ashamed of my writing and petrified someone would read my words, so I chucked most of them away. (I admit, I even went through a phase of writing spoken word poetry.) And I've never regretted it, until now that is. Now, in my forties, I'm trying to remember the girl who wrote. I'm giving her a hug (even though she'd try and squirm out of it), I'm listening to what she has to say and I'm encouraging her. I'm allowing her to be vulnerable. I'm explaining to her the importance of being kind to herself. I'm giving her the language of the 21st century. Language she has never heard. Empowerment, representation, vulnerability, compassion, self-love.

I'm telling younger me to keep writing and keep expressing, even if she's embarrassed or ashamed, even if, when she reads it back, she hates herself for sounding weak, for sounding as though she couldn't cope, when my mantra as a girl and beyond was always, 'I got this'. I wish you'd kept writing, young Anita; I wish you'd let the pen do the talking rather than that blade. From great pain can come great art. And that writing was good. It had meaning. At such a young age, there was an intense purpose to my words, but my old friends, shame and anger, came and took over. They dominated and took away my creativity, they hardened my tender spaces. I've always wanted to tell stories. We are no more than our stories; our stories are all that will matter. I love hearing and telling your stories and the more we tell and the more we listen, the more we learn about who we are.

I've told you a story that reflects my experience in a landscape that was always totally white. A story of trying to navigate and succeed in a career in an industry that, even after 20 years, I feel on the outside looking in. Trying to figure out how to dismantle some of my cultural conditioning to live the life I want, alongside the double whammy of not being seen by my own culture or wider society. But my experience has made me who I am. So, this is for my younger self, but it's also a reminder for me now. A look back to see how far I have come and how I got here. A reminder of *who I am.*

I'm done with living a half-life, and if this story can be an intervention in someone else's life at whatever age, then it is worth sharing my pain. It's bloody lonely carrying it around with you. It's been weighing me down for years and I didn't even notice. I've carried a lot of shame my entire life. It's crippling, debilitating, it crushes you and makes you small. The strangest thing for me is when you get to an age at which you are meant to have found your groove, I have

fear. I fear, I fear. And I hate it. I've spent a childhood trying to be brave, going forth regardless, being single-minded
in my drive and determination and, now all of a sudden, I
smell my fear. I stepped into writing this memoir at my most
fearful and confused, and I have had to dig deep to find my
courage to write these words. The bravest and most vulnerable me has emerged.

Writing this book, I wanted to empower you, the reader.
To stare down the shame. I've talked about everything,
bloody knickers and all, which would have been unthink-
able to little me. I've called out what I see. I've shared my
experience of being a brown woman in Britain. It's felt great
to put my anger onto the page. To use words to express my
pain. As the eldest daughter of a South Asian family, the
first to be born in a foreign land, all I know to do is do. I
can't relax. I don't have the privilege of just being me and
that being enough. I have to strive, I have to work, I have
to excel. I can't be average, or just sit back and let things
play out, no, not me. I've spent years, especially when starting out in my career in TV, adamant that I wasn't there
to represent anyone. How could I be? I was an individual
with my own experience of life, I'd never felt part of any
community, so why would I claim to represent one now? I
denied that I was any kind of role model, mainly because
I didn't feel like I'd done anything to warrant such a title.
I just wanted to make strides doing something I loved and
succeed, especially as there were so few like me doing the
job. Now, I feel completely differently. Now, I accept that I
represent, I proudly represent, and I take the role seriously.

If I don't acknowledge and talk about what it means to be a brown woman in Britain, then who will? I used to hate talking about my race, because I didn't want to be defined by it. I was always aware of the roll of the eyes from others if I were ever to bring it up, even in the most casual way. I could feel people bristle. But I have been defined by it in so many ways, whether I like it or not. So, I own it. I own my identity and I bask in its beautiful, sun-kissed glow. I will take the mantel, take a deep breath and tell you about my experience. Because I know I'm not alone and, if no one talks, nothing will change.

When I appeared on *Strictly Come Dancing* in 2015, I had no idea what the audience would think of me, seeing as I was no major celebrity, not a soap actress or a pop star, just a girl who was mistaken for every other brown girl on telly! Nothing prepares you for *Strictly*, apart from dance classes starting from the age of four. It's only having gone through it that I can see it's an interesting interplay of self-confidence and stereotypes. The public want to see someone grow in confidence over the weeks but remain humble. It's a difficult balance to achieve, especially if you're not a white man. Too much confidence is unappealing in a woman and viewers can see it as aggressive, while too much humility reinforces the stereotype of the servile and oppressed brown woman being given a chance to shine by white liberals. Considering it's a show about ballroom dancing, there's a lot going on under the surface.

My only plan from the start was to not look like I was trying to remember my steps and to enjoy myself. For those

90 seconds on that dancefloor, it was the only thing that really mattered – I danced as freely as I could to make people feel something, even if I did spend a lot of it being thrown around the dancefloor. I didn't question the insane moves I was being asked to do, I just got on with it and worked as hard as I possibly could to make sure I nailed each dance every week. It did feel as though I was having an out-of-body experience at times. What the heck was the little Indian lass, most comfortable in a pair of Dr. Martens or raving in a nightclub, doing gliding, shimmying and heel turning, often with her backside exposed, ON NATIONAL TV? This would never have happened even ten years earlier on British TV. I absolutely smashed it and, unbelievably, the wonderful British public voted for me every week and got me to the semi-final.

And then I was out. I won't lie to you, I still find myself wondering whether I would have got into the final if I didn't have a brown face. It's a question I often find myself asking about my work: How would it have played out if I was white? You would too if, every time someone looked at you, the first thing they thought was, 'They're Asian.'

So, this book serves as the lessons I wish I had known when I was younger, now I know there really is no such thing as the right sort of girl. There can't be. Such a person doesn't exist. Therefore, there can't be the right sort of woman, either. What a relief, which I'm thankful for as I head into my fourth decade, with more freedom and now more courage than I've ever had before. So, young Anita, here is my last letter to you, my last piece of advice I want to share:

Dear young Anita,

Take a deep breath, expand your chest, roll your shoulders down, ground your feet into the earth. Ready?

Life is always going to be full of failures and fuck-ups, and also moments of happiness and fun. This is how it's meant to be. Some moments will hurt. Other people will hurt you, you'll hurt yourself. The world is unfair and you will rage against the injustice. You will feel crushed at times, you'll crawl into a ball and feel so small. You'll fear the outside world. It will knock you sideways. It will try and squeeze the life out of you. Will you let it? Will you let anyone else define your existence?

The minute you were born, you announced your arrival by using your voice. Screaming your lungs off. We come out with a howl to the universe. That voice is in you, still, as it is in us all. All of the pain and shame that you experience will make you grow. Let it all sink in, let it sit in your belly, let it swoosh around and make you feel sick. Then digest it, have a good burp, whack on some red lippy and step out in the world to proudly own your space.

Break the rules, own your otherness. You are a proud outsider, a card-carrying misfit, an evangelical oddball. You are completely original and that's what makes you special. Forget about trying to belong and to fit in. Your magic comes from being uniquely you. Own all your identities: you are a Londoner, a raver, a global citizen, a loon! Put your fear to bed. You will feel as though some spaces aren't for you, but those are the very spaces that need you. You jazz them up, you are stopping them from going stale, you are doing those spaces a favour and, beyond all of that, you've more than earned your right to be there.

Did you know that you are pretty cool, you're independent, you work hard? You go on to do awesome things, you get an incredible job on the telly, you're self-made, don't answer to anyone, you still wear trainers and Dr. Martens, but can now also rock a pair of stilettos. And you have excellent taste in music.

You'll always feel you need to appease everyone around you – your family, men, colleagues, bosses. But do not stop speaking when you have so much to say, just because someone wants you to stay quiet. Recognise your power and who you are – then, and only then, will you meet someone worthy and someone who lets you be you.

You will make a ton of mistakes. But you'll always have power, so much magic power. You do own it and use it. You own every aspect of you: the great bits and the slightly dodgy bits. What's the alternative? Let the fear of never being the right sort of girl control you? Sod that. There is no right sort of girl, so just be you.

Do you remember that now is your time? That the pressure cooker has started to whistle? It's speak or explode?

So keep on speaking.

Love,
Anita

Bonus chapter:
Your Voice Will Be Heard

I'm writing this a year after *The Right Sort of Girl* has been released, and what a year it's been. 2021 is the year I became a published writer. I watched my story launch into the world. I was invited to speak at literary festivals, I fronted covers of magazines, generated pages of discussion in the media – all about my experience growing up in Britain today.

One of the most important and wonderful things to me has been receiving feedback – the stories, lives and matching memories of those that write to me. Readers have been kind enough to tell me how much this book means to them. It was one hell of an experience birthing it. I laughed, cried, cooked and conjured up so many delicious memories, especially for those of you who, like me, have never seen your story told. Too brown to be white, too white to be brown and constantly questioning the patriarchal nonsense you've been told is the norm. I see you and I thank you for sharing with me. I'm so blown away by how my story is resonating with so many. The conversations we're now having used to always be in secret, but it's time to regain our power. I set out to write this book to share a story that's often ignored and to blow the lid off things we've been told must never be spoken about. I wrote it so these very conversations could happen, so that people could feel seen and see themselves reflected back at them. Not all reactions to the book were positive, which of course is okay. I never expected everyone to love or even acknowledge what I shared or was trying to say. But I feel proud that I might have made a dent in the process of sharing brown women's stories, especially to the mainstream. Sometimes stories make us uncomfortable, and that's okay too.

One of the most amazing experiences I had over the past year was an evening hosted by the incredible Ravinder Bhogal to celebrate *The Right Sort of Girl*. I walked into a room full of kickass brown women, and it was an evening I'll never forget. We discussed everything: food, family, Partition, ancestors, the little issue of shame, inter-generational trauma, migration, identity, the patriarchy (spits). When there's a certain energy in a room, you don't need to mess around with surface conversations – and so we cried. We spoke truth from our hearts without fear. I wrote this book for exactly this reason, to be able to have these conversations out loud, which are long overdue. The sisterhood was strong that night, and it made me think of my dedication for this book: '*for daughters with secrets*'. I've waited my entire life to be seen as the right sort of girl, and that night I realised so fully that I was part of an incredible group of women – just the right sort. The sort who lift others up, who are brave, who speak the truth with me, who have worked hard and who straddle worlds and yet, sometimes, feel they belong in no world at all. We are forming a new planet and you are welcome to join us. There will be free samosas for all!

We were a group of daughters with secrets that night, but we shared them and that was important. Healing, almost. As I write this, in 2022, we mark the 75th year since Partition. My life gained more meaning six years ago when I discovered my family story filming *Who Do You Think You Are?* It made me see the importance and necessity of telling our stories, especially for those of us who have heritage beyond this island. Seventy-five years. 75. Since that line was drawn and millions of lives were destroyed, changed irrevocably, to better suit a colonial master and powerful men. Seventy-five years which hold everything, including the deaths of, and violence against, so many women.

This 'anniversary' has made me think back even more to the women in my past. My mother, her mother, my great-grandmother. I think of my dad's mum, but also my grandad's, my Nanaji's, first wife: Pritam Kaur. I say her name to honour her, and to remember her. That's what I'm taking into this year and the next, and the years that come after – remembering the women in my family, in our past, including the not so distant – that couldn't, or weren't allowed, a voice. I wrote this book in reverence to those who came before me and I pledge to carry on the work I feel I've only just started. The work of looking back as well as forward. It's mad to me that it was only 30 years after Partition began that I was born. Not even a lifetime, not even close.

It makes that magical evening with a group of women who looked like me, who felt my energy, who knew of our collective past, all the more special. Seventy-five years after India was torn in two by white male hands, brown hands joined together to celebrate *us*. Women with dreams, with big hearts, who hustle. Women who have had to keep their heads down, who have had to graft. Who have felt incredibly lonely. We lifted our heads up that night, and I had never seen so much power and beauty in one room. We are doing our ancestors proud.

We are writing our stories. And owning them. Look out for summer 2023, when my next writing project and first novel will be released into the world.

After 20 years of grafting, I finally feel like I'm at the beginning of something truly exciting. Roll on the next 20.

Rani's Dhal

This is my take on a simple and classic yellow dhal. Pour yourself a glass of something yummy, then put on some music. You will love how easy this is.

Ingredients:

200g split yellow mung beans
200g split red lentils
2 cloves of garlic, minced
1 medium onion, finely chopped
2-inch piece of ginger, grated or minced
3 green chillies, finely chopped
Half a tin of tomatoes (200g)
1 tsp cumin seeds
1 tsp salt
1 tsp turmeric
1 tsp garam masala
1 tbs butter
1 tbs oil
1 handful of chopped coriander

Rani's Dhal

Method:

1. Rinse the lentils, then cover them with twice the amount of water in a pan.
2. Add the salt and turmeric, bring to the boil and then simmer until the lentils are soft. If it gets too thick, add boiling water.
3. In the meantime, add the oil and butter to a frying pan and heat.
4. Add the cumin and fry for 30 seconds.
5. Add the finely diced onion and *slowly* brown for 20 minutes. Take your sweet time!
6. Blend, grate or finely chop the chilli and garlic and add to the onion. Fry for 5 minutes.
7. Add the grated ginger and stir fry for another 5 minutes, making sure nothing sticks – if it does, add a dash of water.
8. Add the garam masala and tomatoes and simmer until the oil separates from the onion and tomato. The tardka (curry base) must cook out.
9. Now mix the tardka you have just prepared with the dhal. Stir, then simmer for 10 minutes.
10. If the dhal is too thick, add a splash of boiling water. It should be the consistency of a thick soup.
11. Sprinkle coriander over the top, to garnish.

Eat with basmati rice, an onion salad, plain yoghurt and pickle of your choice. Enjoy!

Acknowledgements

I'd just like to thank a few people who are very important in my life and without whom this book would not have happened.

Firstly, thanks to you for choosing to spend time reading my words!

Mrs Bird, my English teacher, who made me feel like I had a gift for telling stories – I only went and wrote a book! Thank you for enjoying my naughtiness and encouraging my imagination.

Beth, Beth, beautiful Beth, my kind, patient editor, who basically talked me off a ledge every other week. I will miss sending you rambling messages. Thank you for your commitment to my book and your belief in my writing. High fives all round to the brilliant team at Bonnier: Perminder Mann, Madiya Altaf, Emily Rough, Nikki Mander, Clare Kelly, Jess Tackie, Ella Holden, Stuart Finglass, Mark Williams, Laura Makela. Top gang.

My powerhouse deal makers and ball breakers at Curtis Brown. My badass book agent, Cath Summerhayes, who basically told me I could do this. You rock. The force of nature and most incredible agent a woman can have, Meryl Hoffman – what a ride this is turning out to be!

Acknowledgements

Josh Byrne, Jess Molloy and Olu Abulude, for somehow keeping my life in check and on track.

Big up to team Dundas, my PR heavyweights. Max Dundas, thank you for getting me from day one. You are the best. Ross Clarence-Smith for your drive and all round wonderfulness, and Abi Etchells for always being positive and patient.

Team Glam – Oskar Pera, Sarah Jane Wai and Krishan Parmar, thank you for making me look shiny and boosting my confidence.

To all the people who have listened to me bang on about writing this book, or have wonderfully listened to me reading sections out to them, or have just made me believe I could do it. Thank you for being my trusted crew. Reva, Sangna, Nerm, Simon, Selina, Reju, Amy, Adrian, Ben, Yen, Henry, Camilla, Cinz, Rex, James, Hannah, Johnny. Alison, Rachel, Jo and Robyn, Geoff, Sinead, Aneel, my cosmic sister Krupa. Nikesh, Anoushka, Riz, Anita, Meera, Nisha, Gurinder, Mona, Suki D, Aisha G. The one and only Nikki Bedi, I adore you. Special shout out for Margi and Sweety, you lift my soul and make me brave.

My treasured WhatsApp groups that have kept me sane and anchored – the Ladies Curry Group, the Nasty Aunty Party and the Brown Mafia. You know who you are.

Special nod to a few other good eggs I've met along the way: Barry, Katie, David, V, Tommy Nagra, Sham Sadhu, Steve Pemberton who told me to vomit on the page. I vommed a plenty.

My beautiful extended family. Even the people I no longer speak to. I hope you are all happy.

And to the people I love the most in this world. Mum and Dad, thank you for giving me life and the fire in my belly. Thank you for encouraging me to speak my truth in this book, to hell with the consequences. Thank you for everything. My brother Kul, for his constant counsel and impassioned discussions, Shivani for helping put the world to rights and Vaneesha, our light – keep shining.

Rafi – the wonderful soul who came into our life with unconditional love, loyalty and a waggy tail.

Before anyone else, I want to thank my darling husband Bhupi, for living with a wife who never sits still, apart from when I wrote this, and for letting me get on with what I have to do.

Thank you to the Universe for always knowing what's what.